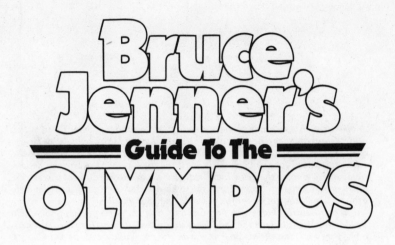

Bruce Jenner's Guide To The OLYMPICS

Bruce Jenner
with Marc Abraham

D1249131

Andrews and McMeel, Inc.
A Universal Press Syndicate Company
Kansas City • New York • Washington

A book like this requires the combined efforts of many people. Besides the athletes and coaches who gave of their time and shared their knowledge Bruce and I would especially like to thank Steve Rosenthal and George Wallach, who saw a need for the book and then brought together the various people necessary to execute the idea; Tom Drape, for his excellent editorial assistance and encouragement; Becky Turanski, who assisted Tom and was the hub around which the entire project turned. She kept us all up to date.

The copyediting chores were handled with a delicate and professional touch by Martha Masinton. In the shadow of an impossible deadline Lisa Michels and Mary McMenamin did a fine job on the production end, as did George Diggs the art director.

And a special thanks to Evelyn, who weathered the storm.

M.A.

Executive Producer: George Wallach

Library of Congress Cataloging in Publication Data

Jenner, Bruce, 1949–
    Bruce Jenner's Guide to the Olympics.

    Includes index.
    1. Olympic Games, Moscow, 1980.   I. Abraham, Marc,
1949–   joint author.   II. Title.   III. Title: Guide
to the Olympics.
GV722 1980.J46 1979   796.4'8   79-20578
ISBN 0-8362-6702-8
ISBN 0-8362-6700-1 pbk.

To millions of athletes around the world
in hopes they can fulfill their dreams.

Introduction

In April 1976, after months of studying the weather patterns of western Russia, a group of Soviet meteorologists determined that the sixteen days from 19 July through 3 August 1980 would provide the "most sunny days and most pleasant temperatures" for the staging of the summer games of the XXII Olympiad.

And so, on the afternoon of that, hopefully, sun-soaked July day, in the filled-to-capacity Lenin Stadium, the traditional opening ceremonies will begin. First will come the parade of athletes—over twelve thousand, the largest number of contestants to date. At the head of the procession, bearing their flag, will be the Greeks—the original founders of the games and always the first to march. Behind the Greeks, the rest of the nations will step in alphabetical order, except for the Russians, who, as hosts, will march last. After all of the teams have assembled in the center of the stadium, Lord Killanin, president of the International Olympic Committee, will face the president of the Soviet Union and announce, "I have the honor to invite the president of the Union of Soviet Socialist Republics to proclaim open the games of the XXII Olympiad of the Modern Era, initiated by the Baron Pierre de Coubertin in 1896."

Leonid Brezhnev will rise and say, "I declare open the Olympic games of Moscow, celebrating the XXII Olympiad of the Modern Era." What the Soviet president won't announce is that the 1980 Olympics will be the first ever staged in a communist country.

To a fanfare of trumpets, the Olympic flag, its five interlocking rings of blue, yellow, black, green, and red symbolizing the five continents, will be brought into the stadium. Representatives of the Montreal mayor, Jean Drapeau, will hand over a special embroidered satin flag to Vladimir Promyslov, the mayor of Moscow, for safekeeping until the next games.

The music of Soviet bands will fill the 103,000-seat, open-air arena. Hundreds of doves—flying symbols of peace—will be released. The excitement and tension will reach a crescendo, aided by a thunderous, three-cannon salute. And then all eyes will focus on the lone Russian distance runner entering the stadium, holding aloft a torch originally lit by the rays of the sun in Olympia, the site of the ancient games for a thousand years. The runner will circle the track, climb the seemingly endless stairs, and light the Olympic flame.

The diminutive man with the oversized, aristocratic nose and huge fire hazard of a moustache had calculatingly chosen to unveil his plan in the hallowed halls of the Sorbonne. Even before he addressed the men of the French Athletic Union, on that day in 1892, the Baron Pierre de Coubertin knew that his peers would find the proposal audacious: the reestablishment of the Olympic games. The purpose behind the games would be twofold—primarily, they would serve as a vehicle to promote peace; secondarily, they would embody the essence of competition.

"There are those you would call Utopians since they speak of the disappearance of war," he cried in his parakeet-pitched voice. "But there are others who believe in the diminution of the chances of war, and I don't see that as Utopian."

The Baron foresaw the games on a world scale. By bringing athletes from a myriad of countries together, having them share the same athletic fields, shelter, and eating halls, "the cause of peace would receive a new and forceful boost."

Though de Coubertin's plea had been passionate, it wasn't until two years later that he finally received the approval of the delegates from France, Russia, the United States, England, Belgium, Sweden, Spain, Greece, and Italy.

Unfortunately, while the Olympics have indeed brought together countries of vastly different ideologies, and while athletes from those countries have shared the same courses of cinder and snow, the cause of peace has not been greatly advanced by the modern games. Where the ancient Greeks demanded a halt to the wars between their various city-states so that all could freely attend the five-day festival at Olympia, the nations of the twentieth century have done the opposite, stopping the games so that they could wage their wars.

The Baron's Olympic corollary to peace was competition in its purest form—how much better for the young men of different nations to struggle against each other athletically, rather than militarily. And as a forum for competition the games have been very successful, perhaps too successful. Olympic competition, originally designed to test the skills of superior athletes, has expanded beyond the boundaries of the Baron's initial conception. Like a hardy weed, it has grown over the chalk stripes in the stadiums to engulf not only nations, as they vie for the right to host the games, but also television networks, as they square off for the rights to broadcast them. It is within the context of such competition that the story of the Moscow games, the XXII Olympiad, began.

A Ten-Year Campaign

By February of 1970 three cities, two in the Western Hemisphere, Montreal and Los Angeles, and one in the Eastern, Moscow, had submitted preliminary bids to host the 1976 summer games. It was the second time since holding the games in 1932 that Los Angeles had vied for them. Montreal and Moscow were bidding for the first time.

The Russians entered the competition late in 1969, not quite a year before the final decision would be made. The Los Angeles campaign was two years old by that time.

The California delegation, led by Mayor Sam Yorty, several politicians, and a prominent businessman, John Kilroy, had every reason to be confident. The Russian presentation had reportedly been awkward, and it was well-known that Montreal was having serious financial difficulties.

Despite their late start, the Russians pressed forward, courting the IOC with lavish cocktail parties and grand promises. Mayor Vladimir Promyslov indicated the city would spend $45 million on the games, including the construction of new hotels. A photographic album, *Moscow 76,* was distributed to members of the IOC and to foreign correspondents. Brochures and other forms of propaganda inundated the IOC delegates during the entire year.

The Canadians were led by Montreal's almost fanatical mayor, Jean Drapeau. The chief political architect of the 1967 World's Fair, Expo 67, Drapeau desperately wanted the 1976 games for his city. Montreal offered an enticing prospect—"a self-financing Olympics." The Canadians, by using devices such as a national lottery, would ensure that games would finish with a surplus (an Olympic euphemism for profit). And with the costs of the games exploding every four years in geometric progression, an Olympics that paid for itself and left the host city not only in the black, but also equipped with a significant new sports and housing complex, was not unappealing to the International Olympic Committee. However, as good as Drapeau's plans sounded, during the final presentation in Amsterdam, the IOC asked Montreal for a financial guarantee. Drapeau was not embarrassed by the request, and offered in an emotional speech, "the history of Montreal as our guarantee."

As the final IOC session in May approached, the three cities used every bit of chicanery and political influence they could muster, even resorting occasionally to strong-arm tactics. Despite Drapeau's efforts, Montreal's money problems seemed to keep that city mired in third place. In the Canadians' favor, though, was the fact that Montreal was a compromise selection between East and West, an easy way out for line-walking IOC members.

Los Angeles looked strong in the presentation area. Its twenty-one-minute film was polished and exciting. The city's communications capabilities (the television coverage would be prime time in Europe) were unmatched. The California delegation felt confident that they had the thirty-six first ballot votes necessary for victory. On the down side for Los Angeles was the recent political unrest in the United States; Kent State and Cambodia were making banner headlines in the nation's newspapers, and the Vietnam war was not helping U.S. prestige abroad.

Moscow offered excellent facilities, political stability, and controlled costs, but it was bucking a significant historical precedent; the games had never been held in a communist country. Implicit in the concern over holding any event behind the Iron Curtain was the fear that the games would not be totally accessible to the multitudes who would normally attend. Russia remained one of the most mysterious and unpredictable nations of the world. Ever since its initial participation in the 1952 games in Helsinki, when the Russian team disdained the Olympic Village and moved into a barbed wire-enclosed compound near the military base at Porkkala, Russia's Olympic motives had been suspect.

It was ironic that the Soviet Union, which embraces a political philosophy that ensures total government control, was now beginning to look like the ideal environment for the gigantic spectacle the Olympics had become. Yet those same politics were the basis for the fears among the aged IOC aristocrats that the Olympic torch, behind the walls of communism, would not burn with quite so pure a flame.

On 12 May 1970 the sixty-ninth congress of the International Olympic Committee opened in Amsterdam. Madame Klompe, the social and cultural minister of Holland, began the proceedings with a short speech. In it she reportedly asked that the games be returned to the small countries, in keeping with the true Olympic spirit. Avery Brundage, the IOC president, followed her to the podium and, according to John Kilroy, all but seconded the minister's proposal. Whether or not the two speeches swayed the delegates is difficult to know. On the first ballot the supposedly secret vote stood at Montreal, twenty-eight; Moscow, twenty-five; and Los Angeles, seventeen. On the second ballot all but one of Los Angeles's votes went to Montreal. It was the opinion of many observers, as well as a number of participants, that several IOC members, forced to make a pressure-cooker choice between the U.S. and Russia, opted for the neutral Canadian vote.

For the second time since 1932, Los Angeles had been denied. In their first foray into the political arena of the Olympic games, the Russians had been defeated. The drama of the XXI Olympiad would unfold in Montreal.

Two years after the XXI Olympiad was awarded to Montreal, the Munich games were held. The 1972 Olympics were mired in controversy from the beginning. The African nations, with 121 participating athletes, threatened a boycott if Rhodesia were allowed to compete. The IOC acquiesced. And although the Munich facilities were the most lavish and spectacular to date, the cost, $612 million, caused great concern among cities interested in hosting future games.

In an atmosphere tense with charges of politicization and doubts about the future of the games, the most tragic episode in Olympic history, the massacre of eleven Israeli athletes by Palestinian terrorists, occurred. Previous incidents of boycotting, drug abuse, invalid amateurism, and cheating had all violated the sanctity of the Olympic arena, but with the Israeli massacre the games were used for the most heinous purpose ever. On the morning of 6 September 1972, the games were halted for a memorial service that began with Beethoven's *Egmont* Overture played by the Munich Opera House Orchestra. The contests resumed in the afternoon.

Between the Munich and Montreal games, Los Angeles and Moscow prepared for a 1974 rematch to determine which would host the XXII Olympiad. This time it was generally conceded that Moscow occupied the front-runner's spot for the 1980 games. Barely breaking stride after their failure in 1970 to land the '76 Olympics, the Moscow delegation had been campaigning diligently for four years. Although theoretically no propaganda could be sent out until 1973, when the formal applications would be received by the IOC, the Russians had in the interim employed more subtle forms of political influence.

During the twentieth century, the Olympics have become a valuable medium for displaying and advertising the municipal wares of the host cities and, on a larger scale, the attributes and philosophies of the host countries. In many ways the Berlin games of 1936 served to camouflage the odious plans Hitler had for his Third Reich. The exciting '36 Olympics, the first to be televised (a closed-circuit broadcast to assembly halls throughout Germany), contributed to the feeling that all was right in Deutschland.

The 1956 Melbourne games showcased the charms of Australia to the rest of the world. The 1968 Mexico City Olympics helped to change Mexico's image from that of a country of sombreros and bullfights into one of a modern, progressive nation, ready to stand alongside the other great countries of the world. For the Russians the 1980 games would provide a massive, antiseptically clear picture window through which the rest of the world would view their country.

The Soviets have been quite explicit in stating the purposes they believe the Olympics can serve. On more than one occasion, the official newspaper, *Pravda,* has noted: "A successful trip by the sportsmen of the USSR is an excellent vehicle of propaganda. The success of our sportsmen helps in the work of our diplomats."

By the beginning of 1974, Moscow was ready to sweep aside

any competition to its bid to host the 1980 games—that is, if there was going to be any competition. At a press conference on 21 February 1974, Willie Daume, vice-president of the IOC, said, "Moscow will automatically be named host for the 1980 Olympic games if no other city submits a bid before March 31."

On 22 February, amidst cries that it was a sacrificial lamb with little chance of winning, Los Angeles entered the race. The United States government does not get directly involved in the Olympics; it considers the games a matter for the individual city and private citizens. Thus the Southern California city would be struggling alone against the political muscle of the Soviet Union.

American critics derided California's bid, charging that Los Angeles was just satisfying a need for competition in the IOC's prestigious hosting derby and that L.A. was actually dress-rehearsing for the 1984 games. But John MacFaden, vice-president of the Southern California Olympic Committee, disagreed: "We're going for it hammer and tongs," he said.

It was obvious that Moscow was several lengths ahead of Los Angeles in early 1974, even though neither city had begun its full-fledged propaganda barrage. After the candidatures of both cities had been formally accepted, the president of the IOC, Lord Killanin, made this pointed remark: "We must consider the matter of freedom of access to the city."

When pressed upon the subject of politics, Killanin dealt with the question head-on. "Politics could be a factor," he said. "We live in a political world and it would be ridiculous to think otherwise."

Killanin's forthright answer was in sharp contrast to the attitude of political detachment cultivated by his distinguished predecessor, Avery Brundage. Brundage, who had led the IOC for twenty years before stepping down in 1972, preferred the "ostrich" approach to the subject of politics— burying his head until the danger had passed.

The final word regarding the site for the XXII Olympiad would come in October. At that time the IOC would meet in

Vienna, where its members would listen to and watch presentations, be lightly blackmailed, slightly strong-armed, cajoled, bribed, and pleaded with until the time came for them to vote. In Austria, Moscow would be ready; hopefully, so would Los Angeles. The decision would then be left to the men of the world's most elite organization, the International Olympic Committee. Because of the power they wield, a closer look at these distinguished gentlemen is in order here.

The International Olympic Committee is a completely autocratic body, answerable to no authority but its own. Members are elected without regard to geographical representation, and there is no requirement that a vacancy in the membership be filled. The IOC sets all rules, policies, and eligibility requirements for the Olympics, and its activities are guided by three aims:

1. Ensuring the regular celebration of the games;
2. Making these games increasingly perfect, more and more worthy of their glorious past and in keeping with the high ideals that inspired those who revived them;
3. Encouraging or organizing all events and, in general, taking all steps likely to lead modern athletes along the right lines.

The IOC is certainly one of the world's wealthiest groups of individuals. And the blood that runs through its members' aristocratic veins is usually referred to as blue. Excepting those from the bloc of Iron Curtain countries, many of the men are titled. Included in the organization are the exiled King Constantine of Greece, the Prince of Liechtenstein, the Grand Duke of Luxembourg, the Marquess of Exeter, more than one sheik, a few rajahs, and the Lord Duke of Pavenham. The current president of the IOC is Lord Killanin, who succeeded Avery Brundage after the latter stepped down in 1972. Brundage's name is synonymous with the Olympic games in this century. He led the IOC for twenty years and was the embodiment of the Olympic spirit and ideal.

Much has been written about the self-made construction millionaire who was born in Detroit in 1887 — a large amount of it critical. Yet the inescapable conclusion is that the Olympic movement required just such a vital, dedicated man to lead it through its turbulent recent history. Brundage's fanaticism in the name of preserving amateurism was a right-wing rudder that rarely allowed the Olympics to stray off course. Nevertheless, many of his ideas were out of touch with the real world and its unavoidable imperfections.

To Brundage, the distinction between amateur and professional was perfectly clear. In a statement quoted by William O. Johnson in his excellent book *All That Glitters Is Not Gold* (New York: G.P. Putnam's Sons, 1972), he spelled it out: "The amateur does not rely on sports for his livelihood. The word is just what it implies—a lover, from the Latin word *amator.* An amateur engages in sport for the love of the game. Only love. The devotion of the true amateur athlete is the same devotion that makes an artist starve in his garret rather than commercialize his work. If a man has the ability to succeed in another field, he has no business taking part in professional athletics" (p. 84). The obsessed autocrat found in the games an exalted purpose, as embodied in a remark quoted by Johnson: "The Olympic Movement is a Twentieth Century religion. Here there is no injustice of caste, of race, of family or of wealth" (p. 24).

Many modern athletes disliked Brundage and believed his inflexible standards were so out-of-date that they were actually detrimental to the Olympics; rules that are impossible to follow end up being violated, and in the process they lose their significance and diminish the very ideals they are supposed to protect. Yet, as Johnson points out in *All That Glitters,* which was published before Brundage's death in 1973: "The Olympic establishment may never see an individual quite so strong again. Perhaps it shouldn't. Yet this stubborn, stiff-necked old millionaire has given much of himself and though he should have bent far more before the winds of change blowing in the world outside the Olympics, he rarely compromised his principles. One can admire the strength of his stance more than the substance of his views" (p. 101).

Fortunately, the man who succeeded Brundage has provided such strong and sound leadership that the fears of the

IOC and its supporters that after Brundage there would be chaos have never materialized. Lord Killanin was a vice-president of the Executive Committee under Brundage, and for a time in the early sixties was a favorite of the severe American. But on several key issues in the late sixties and early seventies they disagreed strongly, and it was privately reported that he was not Brundage's choice for the presidency.

Sir Michael Morris, the third Baron Killanin of Ganty Galway, is a wit and scholar. A former journalist, he is an even-tempered man with a sense of humor. By virtue of his Irish peerage he has a seat in the House of Lords, but has no vote or privileges. During his twenty years in the IOC over sixty new Olympic national committees have been formed. Lord Killanin combines confidence in the future with a realistic assessment of the struggles that lie ahead: "The future of the Olympic movement is, I believe, assured, although we shall always have our problems. Among these are the immense growth of the games; amateurism and eligibility; political interference; and the use of scientific advances in medicine."

Although he does acknowledge the difficulty of preserving the Olympic ideal, Killanin is not about to give up the fight to keep the games above politics. As he noted recently, "People waving flags cause more trouble. I'd love to see the flag waving and anthem playing go. But I have made no progress towards this."

These are the men and their leaders who, for the first ten months of 1974, would weigh the arguments and swing the vote in favor of either Los Angeles or Moscow.

Moscow and Los Angeles each had specific handicaps to overcome in their quest for the games. Working against Los Angeles was the feeling that the 1980 games ought not to be held on the same continent as the 1976 Olympics. Though many IOC members said that this would not affect the decision, it was known that certain delegates considered it a genuine concern. Los Angeles countered the problem with the example of ancient Greece, where the games had prospered for a thousand years.

Causing problems for Moscow was the bad publicity from the recent World Games. In 1973 the Russian capital had hosted the games, and there had been several unpleasant episodes concerning the Israeli team: there were reported incidents of the Soviets denying visas to Israeli journalists; Soviet Jews attempting to attend the games had been harassed; and during the competition itself, there was heckling of the Israeli athletes, with a few situations erupting into violence.

Also, several foreign teams had complained of the lack of interpreters and the prisonlike security that kept them confined too closely to quarters. Moscow parried these accusations by labeling the reporting of the World Games "inaccurate and sensationalist."

The pace of the two campaigns accelerated as the October IOC session neared. Circulars and magazines were distributed to anyone who had influence on the vote.

In 1964 Lord Killanin had introduced a rule which prohibited excessive entertaining of IOC members by the candidate cities. The rule was never adopted, and the practice continued. During 1974 invitations were sent to committee VIPs to visit both Los Angeles and Moscow at each city's expense.

The final stage of the competition was scheduled to take place in Vienna, at the IOC sessions on 21–23 October 1974.

John R. MacFaden is a gravelly voiced, forty-year veteran of the public relations business in California. He's been a member of the Southern California Olympic Committee since 1939. He was vice-president of the committee in 1974, and one of the men who represented Los Angeles in Vienna.

"I know a lot of people thought we weren't in with a chance," MacFaden said recently. "But I felt we had a good shot at it. We had an excellent presentation, it was very sophisticated, and I think better than the Russians'. Although they did have a lot more money than we had.

"You see, the Russians were a little upset with us when we came in and bid on the games. But we said, 'What the hell, it's a free world.' Then we put a fine presentation together and made the bid.

"Los Angeles actually should have won the games in 1970 in Amsterdam, but the Russians came in late and upset the apple cart.

"In 1974 the Moscow exhibit was very big and expensive. Ours was the opposite; tight and to the point. We had no money to speak of; I even paid my own way over there, as did a few others. We put the book together for $25,000 and the audio-visual for $4,500. The exhibit consisted of memorabilia of the 1932 games. It showed all the facilities then, and what we have now, and what we would construct.

"On October 23, we went to the Rathaus [the baroque city hall of the former Hapsburg capital] to give the final presentations. There was a drawing to see who went first, and we won. We definitely wanted to start off, because we had to set up our screens and projectors.

"The room was rather small. The IOC sat on the outside of a gothic U-shaped dais that was slightly elevated, and on the inside were the various sports people; archery to yachting. We had thirty minutes to make the presentation. I think our audio-visual took about twenty minutes. The mayor spoke for five minutes and the rest of us about five minutes, and then all of us fielded questions. When we got through they gave us a hell of a hand.

"I really felt very good about it, and thought we had a chance. After we left the room we held a press conference and explained what happened. But the European press was sure that the Russians had it wired. The Russians had worked pretty hard on the delegates. For instance, the man from Jamaica, who was brand-new, arrived late in Vienna, barely in time for the meeting. But as soon as he arrived, Alexandriov—the Russian IOC member—really cornered him. Of course, we were introduced, but we were pleasant and polite. There was no doubt, Moscow was in a strong position.

"That's not to say we didn't have a strong group behind us, too. The Asians, especially, and many of the Europeans didn't want the Russians. But the English writers couldn't believe we thought we had a chance.

"It just got down to the fact the Russians had reached everyone. They [the IOC] ask you not to pigeonhole members because they don't like that sort of treatment. On the other hand, if you neglect them, they don't like that either.

"It was a good week for us, all in all, and I thought we could win. But they did tell us to be sure and bid for the 1984 games, which we did of course, and won."

The next day the IOC members returned to the Rathaus to vote. After the results had been tabulated, Lord Killanin addressed both delegations and the press in the festival hall of the city hall. He was handed an envelope, he broke it open and announced Moscow the choice.

The usually staid Soviets were ecstatic. Members of the delegation jumped to their feet, let out great shouts, and bear-hugged each other. Mayor Bradley of Los Angeles elbowed his way to the front of the room and offered his congratulations to the exuberant Moscow mayor, Promyslov.

The Comte de Beaumont, the first vice-president of the IOC, stepped to the podium and spoke: "Everyone is happy the games are going to Moscow. It's good the ideal of the Olympic movement opens a new country."

Mayor Promyslov followed the Frenchman to the microphone to face the press. Obviously very pleased, the Mayor said, "We learned from our mistakes in 1970, and the world atmosphere has changed."

Although his English was suspect, his point was well made when he noted, "Politics was always not supposed to be in the Olympics. And we will try to hold peaceful, happy games." To a reporter's question about China, he replied, "China will be welcome; we hope the climate will improve by then."

Mayor Bradley told reporters later that he was very happy with Los Angeles's showing. According to his sources, the secret vote had been Moscow, thirty-nine, Los Angeles, twenty-two. The mayor said the twenty-two votes his city garnered should convince the critics, who had predicted a total of nine votes for Los Angeles, that the California bid was legitimate.

However, Bradley's exuberance at gathering twenty-two votes, slightly more than half of Moscow's total, was possibly quite revealing. It seemed to indicate that he had not expected such a strong showing, and, therefore, that he had never truly believed his city would be the choice.

On 24 October 1974 the IOC session came to a close. The games awarded in Vienna would commence six years later, but, in fact, the lighting of the Olympic flame in Lenin Stadium would be the culmination of ten years of effort on the part of the Soviet Union. History will be made in Moscow as the games, for the first time ever, unfold in a communist country.

The Battle of the Network Stars

With one round of Olympic competition over, the second began: Which American TV network would win broadcast rights for 1980? This time it wasn't Suzanne Somers of ABC's "Three's Company" against Adrienne Barbeau of CBS's "Maude" in the through-the-barrel, over-the-ramp, in-between-the-tires obstacle course. It wasn't Robert Conrad versus Gabe Kaplan in the softball throw. The prize money wasn't a paltry $25,000, and instead of endorsing the check, the winner would be signing it. This was NBC, CBS, and ABC in the "Showdown at the Moscow Corral" to see who would be bringing the 1980 Moscow games to America on the seventeen-inch home entertainment center. This was the real "Battle of the Network Stars."

To be completely accurate, the battle between the three networks to see who would be awarded the exclusive television rights to the 1980 games was just that, a single battle in the overall war between the networks, who were buying, and the Russian bureaucrats, who were selling. It was a long war, a three-year siege, with Nielsen points and prestige as booty. Each network had its chances to triumph, and each network blundered, then stumbled, but finally, as much by default and fortuitous timing as by design, NBC got the opportunity to spend $85 million.

Moments after Lord Killanin announced Moscow as the site of the 1980 Olympics, representatives from the three networks appeared at the front of the Vienna city hall to offer their congratulations to the Soviets. Nothing too formal, just a friendly "good luck and we'll be seeing you" from the best and brightest of Madison Avenue. During the next three years these icons of capitalism, who occupied bird's-nest offices overlooking Manhattan, would face off against the craftiest and most cunning politicians of the Soviet Union, tough

Russians who had survived the purges of Khrushchev, and, before him, Stalin, to rise to positions of power in the Soviet government.

ABC had owned the rights to six of the last eight Olympic games. NBC's Olympic experience was limited to the winter games in Sapporo, Japan, in 1972, while CBS had brought the games home via television in 1960 from Rome, shelling out a piddling $550,000 for the rights, a sum that, in retrospect, is very difficult to believe. But even in 1960, and certainly in 1980, televising the Olympic games had become a real crapshoot.

ABC paid $13.5 million for the Munich television rights in 1972; four years later in Montreal the network almost doubled that figure, spending $25 million. But ABC lost money with the German games, while it showed a slight profit with the Canadian Olympics. Of course, money is not the only gauge of Olympic broadcasting success. The prestige a network gains just by televising the games can certainly boost its overall image. ABC's excellent, professional reportage in Munich brought critical acclaim that more than offset the economic losses. On the other hand, NBC not only suffered financial losses with the Sapporo games, but there was some criticism of its broadcasting performance. Deciding whether or not to televise the Olympics is one of the most difficult decisions facing a network today.

Of the three networks, ABC seemed to occupy the strongest position. Under the shrewd and innovative leadership of Roone Arledge, head of sports programming, ABC had distinguished itself as the network of the Olympic games. Jim McKay, Bill Flemming, Frank Gifford, Dick Button, etc., had been the voices of the Olympics for most Americans. Unfortunately for Arledge and gang, neither NBC nor CBS was quite ready to concede the 1980 games. The quest for the TV rights would be an old-fashioned dogfight.

The offensive lineups for the networks shaped up this way: representing NBC, Carl Lindeman, vice-president for sports; from CBS, another vice-president in charge of sports, Robert Wussler; and for ABC, the veteran of the Olympic scrimmage pits, Roone Arledge. These weren't the only men involved, but they were, in a sense, the respective quarterbacks. Before the dollar-green dust would clear, no less a personage than William Paley, chairman of the board of CBS, would assist Wussler, while Robert Howard, president of NBC, would aid Lindeman. Arledge went it basically alone. Ironically, after all of the network heavyweights had huffed and puffed, flexed their dollar muscles, and traded on their reputations, it was a mysterious, thirty-eight-year-old West German impresario named Lothar Bock (about whom, more later) who turned out to be the pivotal man in the negotiations.

The two most prominent members of the Soviet negotiating team were Ignati Novikov, 70, the leader of the USSR Olympic Organizing Committee, and Sergei Lapin, 64, minister of the Soviet Committee for Television and Radio. While Novikov's rough manner betrayed his Ukraine peasant upbringing, Lapin, a former ambassador and head of Tass, the Soviet news agency, was as polished as his American counterparts.

The networks and the Russians spent most of 1974 and 1975 getting acquainted and tending to social amenities. Then in Montreal in 1976 the plot thickened. The Russians arrived in Montreal by air, but they chose to do business at sea. On the *Alexander Pushkin,* a Soviet ship moored in the St. Lawrence Seaway, the Russians threw their first soiree— an extravagant caviar and lobster affair. Later, after the party, Novikov and Lapin called the networks in, one by one.

It is common practice when negotiating to ask for more than you expect to receive. But no one at any of the networks was prepared for the opening figure Novikov and Lapin casually mentioned, $210 million. No one at any of the networks took the figure too seriously either, and privately the Russians were bandying about a number in the $70 million range. But for starters, the Soviets had shown that they were going to be tough, if not outrageous.

In the fall of 1976, following the Montreal games, the Soviets asked the networks for preliminary bids. NBC, now sure that it wanted the TV rights, came in at $70 million. CBS bid $71 million, and ABC, $73 million. All three bids seemed to confirm the rumored lower price. Then, in the next month and a half, CBS made its strongest offensive push, and that was when the name of Lothar Bock first surfaced.

Bock had served as a consultant on a 1976 CBS special about the Bolshoi Ballet, hosted by Mary Tyler Moore. But it wasn't until late 1976 that Bock actually began to assist the network in its efforts to land the Olympic games. Bock had been suggested to CBS by the documentary film maker, Bud Greenspan, who told the network Bock would be an excellent intermediary with the Russians—sort of a free agent in the TV bidding war.

Bock met with Wussler and Arthur Taylor, president of CBS, Inc. (CBS's parent company), and then signed on as a consultant. His arrangement with CBS turned out to be short-lived, but at the time he was their hole card, and an ace at that. Later Bock was described by CBS president John Schneider as "well connected with the Russians, that's why we employed him."

Information on Bock is now substantial, but during the very secret negotiations not much was known about him. Lothar Bock is a West German theatrical agent who lives in Munich. The basement of his suburban home serves as an office for himself and his nine employees. Six and a half years before the Olympic negotiations began, he was flat broke, bankrupted when he sponsored a tour of Soviet singers in West Germany during the Russian invasion of Czechoslovakia, a time when no one in Germany was particularly interested in patronizing Soviet arts. Evidently, the stoic manner Bock demonstrated in accepting his losses endeared him to the Russians. That was in 1968, and since then Bock has returned to his financial feet. A former business partner gives some insight into how: "Lothar never puts up his own cash for anything; he uses his ideas and other people's capital to make money." In 1975 his company, LBA, grossed over two million dollars; the result of an astute change of direction. Realizing that bringing Soviet acts— singers, dancers, theater—to Europe to tour was a risky business, Bock decided instead to videotape the programs and then license them to television. The formula has proved to be very successful. Bock's arrangement with the Soviet government, though, is a bit difficult to figure out. The Soviet Television and Radio Committee loans him on credit the production equipment and rehearsal halls for his taped specials, then recoups its outlay as the money comes back in. It is a cozy situation, but Bock maintains he is nothing more than a capitalist trying to make a buck, and not a camouflaged arm of the Russian propaganda machine.

In late October, after several trips between New York and Moscow, Wussler and Arthur Taylor, with Bock's assistance, had all but signed a contract with the USSR Olympic Committee awarding the rights to CBS. After briefing the other CBS people involved, Wussler was preparing to leave for an IOC meeting in Barcelona when he was given some shocking news: Paley had fired Arthur Taylor. According to Wussler, the sudden firing of Taylor scared and mystified the Russians, and consequently clouded the entire Olympic picture. For one thing, the Soviets have never really trusted any of the American television networks, primarily because of the many years of what they consider hostile reporting. That, in fact, is exactly why Lothar Bock's aid had been enlisted. For another, Taylor, along with Wussler, had assured the Russians that a deal was about to be struck. With the dismissal of such a pro-Olympic, high-level executive, the Russians panicked. It was left to Bock to apply the glue and patch the shattered CBS-USSR arrangement back together. Bock decided that the best strategy would be to get Paley himself to make a journey to Moscow. Such a gesture would reaffirm CBS's desire to televise the games and assure the Russians that Taylor hadn't been axed for his support of the Olympics.

On 16 November, the *New York Times* reported that Paley and Wussler were in the Soviet Union negotiating for the television rights. The venerated Paley, godfather of American television, met with the crusty Novikov. The two men showed genuine respect for each other; Paley's reputation had obviously preceded him. After three days they parted with an understood agreement that CBS would be the network of the 1980 Olympics. But three days later, Wussler was thrown the second, roundhouse curve: a letter from the Soviets arrived, indicating the procedure CBS was to follow if the network was interested in submitting a final bid for the rights. For the second time CBS had been told it would have the games and for the second time its representatives had been misled. The seeds of mistrust were beginning to flower at the Columbia Broadcasting System.

On 15 December 1976, all three network entourages arrived in Moscow, not quite knowing what to expect. They didn't have to wait long for the next Soviet surprise package. Over and above the price for the TV rights, the Russians demanded another $50 million for facilities and equipment. More disconcerting to the networks than the money (since in the long run the total package would cost approximately the same) were the political ramifications of such an agreement. Providing the Russians with sophisticated communications equipment that they were obviously not capable of building themselves and then leaving the equipment behind was not a particularly palatable idea. Besides, the equipment issue was not the only sensitive contingency that had cropped up. Earlier, the Soviets had attached another and even more delicate string: in return for the right to broadcast the games, the winning network would be expected to produce some programming extolling the virtues of the Soviet Union. Of course, the networks were already aware that up until the final decision was made, any programming favorable to the USSR would work in their favor. At the same time, to be indirectly employed as a mouthpiece for Kremlin doctrine was a precarious proposition for any American communications company.

As early as 1974, ABC president Elton Rule had said, "We anticipate a long and fruitful exchange between ABC and the State Committee to enable the people of the United States and Russia to understand and know each other better through TV and radio." ABC's commitment to better Soviet-U.S. relations manifested itself in the network's morning show, "Good Morning America." ABC presented five shows, ten hours of programming, that originated in Moscow. Bill Beutel anchored the broadcasts, assisted by the English-speaking Soviet TV personality, Svetlana Stardomskaya. Although ABC declared the show an ambitious undertaking that would provide information and insight into the mysterious Soviet Union, it ended up looking more like a pleasant travelogue, stopping in all the tourist spots: Red Square, the Kremlin, the Sports Palace. Nothing disparaging to the USSR showed up, and the omnipresent police state was not mentioned.

Perhaps most upsetting to other American journalists was the fact that three Soviet officials, one of them a cultural minister, had actually inspected the finished product before it was aired. Ostensibly, they had had no say in what was broadcast; nevertheless, it seemed that a dangerous precedent had been set.

ABC wasn't the only network bringing Soviet culture to the U.S. In 1976 CBS had aired the Bolshoi special. The network did not deny that the program was part of an effort to woo the Russians.

Once all three networks were in Moscow, the Soviet plan was to hold an auction. Each network would submit a sealed bid, and then the highest bid and bidder would be announced. If they chose to remain in the running, the losers would have the opportunity to bump the highest bid by 5 percent. It was an outrageous and insulting procedure, and it angered the network representatives so much that Wussler immediately began sending out feelers as to the feasibility of pooled coverage, in which all three networks would assume partial responsibility. Such a plan would help to erode a good deal of the Soviet bargaining strength. The Russians, on the other hand, were confident that the greedy American capitalists would do and pay anything in their rabid fever to make money. After all, it was the revered Lenin who had once said, "The capitalists will sell the rope to hang themselves with." Only in this case the Soviets figured the Americans would go one better and "buy the rope." Roone Arledge explained the situation in the most graphic terms: "They want us to be like three scorpions fighting in a bottle. When it's all over, two will be dead and the winner exhausted."

So far, the Russians had been holding all of the cards and dealing from a position of strength; but, now Novikov and the Soviets made their first tactical error. They threw what has since become known as the "80-million-dollar cocktail party," and for the first time since their respective arrivals in Moscow, the representatives of the three networks were brought together in the same room. In the large dining hall of the Hotel Sovietskaya, Lindeman, Wussler, and Arledge unleashed their pent-up anger and railed against the coarse and crude treatment they had received. The Russians had made vague promises and reneged; they had made detailed agreements (Novikov with Paley) and then ignored them. The networks were fed up, and the three men discussed walking out of the negotiations. The Russians were stunned by the actions and indignation of the Americans. They suggested a conciliatory meeting the next day. On 15 December, Wussler, Arledge, and Robert Howard met with Novikov. The Russians' position and attitude remained the same, and so all three networks agreed to walk out of the negotiations. Novikov threatened, "If you walk away you will never be allowed on Soviet soil again." The threat did not deter them.

The next day, in similarly worded statements, all three networks announced suspension of individual negotiations: "We will now review with the Justice Department the desirability of assuming jointly the costs and risks of television coverage." It would be left to the Justice Department to decide if antitrust laws could be waived.

Assuming the networks would stand firm on their commitment to a pool, the Russians' bargaining power had certainly been reduced. In the meantime, there was no contact between the Soviets and Americans. However, it turned out that the irrepressible Bock was continuing to lobby on behalf of CBS. Arledge got wind of Bock's maneuvering and asked Wussler if he was aware of the situation. Wussler responded that he was not, but promised to send a communication to Bock instructing him to cease negotiating as a CBS representative.

The next move belonged to the Russians, and they responded with an announcement that a company called SATRA had been awarded the rights. SATRA is an international trading company that is involved with the USSR in the areas of Soviet-American films and commercial trucks and vehicles. SATRA spokesmen were tight-lipped about the agreement, although they did indicate they were representing other, undisclosed interests. SATRA was taking the Soviet agreement seriously, but network executives felt that the SATRA arrangement was a face-saving gesture by the Russians, who were getting very worried that no single American network would purchase the rights.

On 18 January, the Soviets declared that their letter of intent with SATRA was only tentative and that the doors were open to new proposals from the networks, without ultimatums. The ameliorative statement indicated a softer-nosed approach. At a press conference Novikov said, "We are sincerely interested in conceding the rights to a competent body that enjoys a good professional reputation." However, the networks were still peeved. Herb Schlosser of NBC declared, "I'm not sure we should carry the Olympics at any price."

Eight days after Novikov's conciliatory remarks, the most surprising development of the negotiations occurred. CBS, which had, with Bock's help, become the apparent front-runner, announced that it was dropping out of the talks. The network that had produced specials on the Bolshoi Ballet and Nadia Comaneci, instigated the idea of pooled coverage, and introduced Lothar Bock into the picture, was calling it quits. Wussler's official explanation: "It is a right and wise course for us to take, in view of the many imponderables surrounding the 1980 games."

High-level sources at CBS wondered if the network wasn't worried about negative public reaction to the high Russian price tag. But others felt that the uncertainty of the games themselves and the unreliability of the Russians had made it impossible for the network to trust the Soviets. Later Wussler elucidated: "We were being asked to put up tremendous sums of money for an event seventeen days long, three-and-a-half years away. It began to seem not worth all the time and trouble."

Wussler's point about huge sums of money in advance—

the Soviets wanted their first payments in $20- and $30-million installments—had always been a sore spot with the networks.

With CBS out, the pool concept collapsed. Lothar Bock almost did too, when he learned the news from Wussler. Bock attempted to revive the CBS bid. He failed, and asked to be released from his contract so that he might contact NBC. CBS agreed to the request. Apparently, Bock decided to go to NBC because ABC, believing that its Olympic experience put it in the catbird seat, had not been interested in using the German impresario.

Lindeman and NBC sized up Bock's importance differently. In what turned out to be a very astute business decision, Lindeman arranged a morning meeting on 26 January, at the Plaza. Certain that the Russians were nervous, and therefore itchy to end the television rights fiasco, Bock assured NBC that a deal could be made very quickly. Lindeman gave Bock the okay to act. Bock contacted Moscow and outlined the network's position. Then he flew to the Russian capital, which had been his home for the last ten months. A day later, Lindeman, Howard, and two other NBC executives left for Moscow.

The NBC entourage had hoped to consummate a deal before ABC even knew anything was in the offing. But Roone Arledge is not easily kept in the dark, and even though the Russians wired ABC not to come, Arledge showed up, hoping to make a successful eleventh-hour appeal. However, by the time he arrived, it was too late. NBC had moved too quickly, and the Russians were eager to end the long and convoluted negotiations. The 1980 Olympic television rights would go to NBC.

On 1 February 1977, NBC agreed to pay the highest amount in the history of televised coverage of the Olympic games for the exclusive rights to broadcast the Moscow games. Vladimir Koval, executive vice-president of the Soviet Olympic Committee, disclosed the terms: $35 million for the rights (approximately $12 million of that would go to the IOC) and $50 million for equipment. NBC, which had actually been the underdog network throughout the negotiations, ended up the winner because of a combination of factors: personality, timing, and the strategic last-minute addition of Lothar Bock to its tactical force. For his part in the drama, the modish Bock was paid $1 million by NBC, with the network also agreeing to purchase fifteen of his programs through 1981.

NBC executives were not overly concerned with the heavy price tag; they claimed that the rights would have cost the same had the games been held in London or Paris—the $85 million was a function of increased costs and inflation, not of shrewd Soviet bargaining. Regarding the payment schedule, the network worked out a reasonable arrangement with safeguards that assured that most of the money would be returned if for any reason the games were not held. Addressing the question of possible pro-Soviet programming on the network, NBC said that this was not ever considered in the negotiations and that NBC News would never be compromised.

The network later disclosed its plans for the Moscow games. NBC, which first offered Olympic coverage from London in 1948 in the form of a nightly fifteen-minute program called "Olympic Game Films," will broadcast 150 hours of actual sporting events—with 65 of those hours in prime time. The staff in Moscow will number 650 people, and at least some coverage will emanate from each of the twenty-seven different venues. Soviet technicians will man the video from each venue, supplemented by NBC crews at fourteen competition sites. Forty-three cameras, forty-seven videotape machines, and six slow-motion units will be used to bring the games home, and coverage will include interesting cultural aspects of the city as well as related Olympic activities. The Olympic Radio and Television Center (ORTC), located four miles from Central Lenin Stadium, will serve as communications central. In the U.S. the last NBC sign-off each night will come at 1:30 A.M. EDT, which is 8:30 A.M. in Moscow, just about the time the next day's competition begins. The production effort—the largest and most extensive ever mounted by a single network—will be equaled in scope only by the cost of the undertaking.

So ends the story of the most expensive and bizarre bidding war in the history of the Olympic games. However, it should be mentioned that in keeping with the Keystone Kops manner which characterized the negotiations, twice during the final signing ceremony Ignati Novikov referred to NBC as ABC. Apparently, after all was said and done, one American television network looked pretty much the same as another.

Back in the USSR

In a 1939 radio broadcast Winston Churchill described Russia as "a riddle wrapped in a mystery inside an enigma." Forty years later the same thing could still be said about the Soviet Union. While in recent years the Soviets have displayed a more relaxed attitude toward tourists in their country and emigration policies have been redefined, most Americans are still uneducated about the USSR. Even Europeans, next-door neighbors to the Soviets, are in the dark about the vast expanse that was the world's first socialist state and that dominates not one, but two continents.

Of course, the Russians have not made it particularly easy to keep abreast of the social, economic, or political status of their country. For us in the West, most of what we know about the Soviet Union comes from its own press agency's news releases, and the accuracy of that information is often suspect. For instance, in the interest of national security, Soviet cartographers must actually alter the location of rivers, cities, and villages on the maps they produce. Certainly this type of bizarre preoccupation with secrecy has contributed to America's ignorance about the Soviet Union. Consequently, the European-Asian country that actually lies closest to the United States—fifty-six miles from Siberia to Alaska—is in many ways more mysterious to the average U.S. citizen than the most primitive regions in Africa.

Russia is the world's largest continuous political domain. Three times the size of the U.S., it occupies over 8,200,000 square miles—one-sixth of the globe. It contains fifteen different republics, and at the heart of those republics, in north central Russia, built, like Rome and Lisbon, atop seven small hills, lies its capital, Moscow. "Moskva" is the most populous city in the country. It is the cultural and industrial center of Russia, and the seat of power. All of these factors would seem a guarantee that the city would be alive and exciting. Yet Moscow is often maligned by visiting Europeans and Americans, who label it drab and closed. On the other hand, journalists who have spent considerable time there write convincingly of the city's underlying level of intensity. Throughout the latter half of this century many Russian citizens, most notably Soviet Jews, have clamored for their freedom, for a chance to leave Moscow. But I found the sentiments of most Russians closer to those of the poet Alexander Pushkin, who wrote, "Moscow: those syllables can start/A tumult in the Russian heart." In fact, so many Soviet citizens wish to live in the city that government permission is required before one can become a Muscovite. Then again, government permission is required before one can leave Moscow.

As the fourth largest city in the world, and as the capital of the powerful Soviet Union, Moscow possesses an international significance that cannot be denied. Beginning on 19 July 1980, that international significance will greatly increase, as the attention of the world focuses on the host city of the XXII Olympiad. The Soviet press agency, Novosti, estimates that 2 billion people will watch the Olympic competition, four times the half-billion that viewed some part of the 1968 Mexico City games. In 1980, 170 million of those viewers will be Americans, and for most of us it will be the first extensive look into the capital of the country which confounded Churchill and founded communism.

What you can expect to see is a sprawling city, built, like Los Angeles, out instead of up, and covering 127 square miles. From my visits to the capital both as an athlete and a journalist, I would have to say that I also feel there is a certain drabness to the city. Most of the buildings have identical facades and grey is the overworked color scheme. That's not to say there aren't a few interesting buildings. But there's no denying that the edifices that catch your eye definitely show Western influences. The Intourist Hotel, for instance, is a twenty-story structure with a glass and steel exterior that would fit rather comfortably into downtown Manhattan or Los Angeles's Century City. Oddly enough, the posters for the upcoming games which adorned the Intourist lobby were actually in English.

Moscow is built on such a huge scale that one feels swamped by its spaciousness. Despite the roominess, however, the streets are not overwhelming in their cordiality; Moscow's citizenry keeps its distance, except for the kids, who are absolutely crazy for anything from the West. Friends of mine were offered $100 for their jeans and $150 for their jackets as they walked along the street.

I found that a two-week stint in Moscow was just about the right length vacation. By the end of the second week I would find myself singing a song that was a switch on the great Beatles tune, only my version ended with "Back in the U.S., back in the U.S., back in the U.S.A."

The design of Moscow, like that of Paris, resembles a massive wheel, with boulevards extending out from the Kremlin, which is the hub of the city. The Kremlin was originally an island (the word means "citadel"). The boulevards that stretch out from it like the spokes of a wheel eventually cross two broad circular roadways that form inner and outer rings to the city. The inner ring is the Garden Ring, the outer is the Moscow Circular Motorway. Despite the roominess of the streets there are very few cars on the road. In fact, I was told that there are fewer than 100,000 privately owned automobiles in Moscow. Gasoline is a much less valued commodity in the USSR than in the U.S., and the absence of gasoline stations attests to that fact. Russians travel around their city by public transportation. Their metro is quick, clean, and cheap.

The modern layout of Moscow is a result of the Master Reconstruction Plan initiated in the 1930s. Up until the Master Plan was put into operation the city had experienced centuries of haphazard growth. The inner city, which had always consisted of luxurious mansions and government offices, was encircled by a periphery of primitive wooden structures. In 1920 Moscow was a decaying city, still devastated by the effects of the 1917 Revolution. Its population was one million, half of what it had been only five years earlier. Most of the streets were narrow and winding. There were nine thousand buildings of brick and stone, compared to sixty-five thousand dilapidated wooden houses. It was not until 1930, thirteen years after the Revolution, that a master plan was developed for the city. Now, sixty years after the Revolution, Moscow has replaced its muddy streets and barren vacant lots with wide, clean boulevards, numerous parks and greens, and, if not a skyscraper skyline, at least a modern one.

One of the reasons for Moscow's disorganized growth is that it wasn't always the capital of the country. First mentioned in A.D. 1147, Moscow was only a small village at the time, the principal cities being Kiev and Novogorod. Nevertheless, in the thirteenth century it became the capital. For the next 450 years Moscow alternately prospered and burned down. During much of that time Moscow was looked upon as a symbol of deliverance from the Tatar-Mongol domination of Russia. It came to be known as "the unifier of Russia's land." Then in 1713 Tsar Peter the Great proclaimed Russia an empire, himself the emperor, and St. Petersburg, a beautiful city he had founded on the Gulf of Finland, the new capital. St. Petersburg became an important European manufacturing city. It outgrew Moscow in population, commerce, and cultural significance. But most Russians outside of St. Petersburg continued to look upon Moscow as the heart of Russia. As evidence of this, the Russian Orthodox Church retained all of its important shrines in Moscow. And the coronation ceremonies for the emperors continued to be held in the Cathedral of the Assumption in Moscow. Also, from a geographic standpoint it was much closer to the provincial cities of Russia.

By the beginning of the twentieth century Moscow's population had doubled, and by the start of the first revolution it had doubled again. However, St. Petersburg remained the capital and the residence of the tsar, as well as the home of the ministries and the foreign embassies. Then came the First World War and the two revolutions, and the status of both cities changed drastically. In February 1917 the tsar was overthrown. By the summer of 1917 the Germans had captured Riga in Latvia, 300 miles from St. Petersburg, and the German navy had stepped up activity in the Baltic. St. Petersburg (Petrograd) was being threatened by invasion. The provisional government raised the question of temporary evacuation, but before it could act, the great October Socialist Revolution that forever altered the face of Russia swept it aside. The new Bolshevik government, led by Lenin, proposed a peace treaty to the kaiser. The proposal was ignored. The former tsarist troops now left to defend the city were disintegrating. In February 1918, the towns of Dvinsk and Pskov, which were dangerously close to Petrograd, fell to the Germans. Basing his decision on political, economic, and strategic considerations, Lenin proposed not just evacuating, but returning the capital to Moscow. In the late evening of 10 March 1918, a special train left Petrograd for Moscow. Today the same journey from Petrograd (now called Leningrad) takes 8½ hours on the Red Arrow Express. Then it took a day and a half.

The Council of People's Commissars, the official new title of the first cabinet, moved into a large, vacant courthouse in the conveniently located Kremlin. Lenin himself took a room in the National Hotel.

In the summer of 1918 the fourth all-Russian congress of soviets passed a resolution declaring the move to Moscow temporary. The first Soviet constitution actually omitted mention of any city as the Soviet capital. In fact, it took four years, putting the date at December 1922, before Moscow was officially confirmed as the capital of the USSR.

Now, sixty years after its inclusion in the text of the new Soviet constitution as capital, Moscow becomes the capital of international sports as it hosts the 1980 Olympic games. It is fitting that Moscow is the focal point of athletic competition in the first year of the new decade. It is the most prominent city in the world's most sports-minded country. The opportunity to participate in athletics is ensured by Russian law. Article 41 of the Soviet consitution "guarantees its citizens the right to leisure, a right ensured by the development on a mass scale of sport, physical culture, camping and tourism." For the Russian citizen, athletics is just about the only diversion from a very regimented life-style.

During my visits to Moscow I found that much of our American culture was either unknown or uninteresting to the people. But when it came to sports they were informed and eager to talk. Although I often went unnoticed on the streets, once the people heard my name they enthusiastically began speaking of the Olympic games.

The priority that Russians place on athletics is reflected in the remarkable abundance of sports facilities in their country. There are 1.4 million athletes in Moscow alone who participate in sporting competitions. Russia has 3,200 stadiums, 40,000 sports grounds, and 66,000 gymnasiums. There are 250,000 coaches who have diplomas and degrees and 23 institutes devoted to higher physical culture. For every 30,000–50,000 people, a city planner must provide a stadium, swimming pool, and shooting range.

Athletics are an essential part of the Russian way of life, and Soviet citizens believe that athletic superiority is a reflection of the supremacy of their economic and political system. For the Russians, the 1980 Olympic games will be not only a celebration of sport and peace, but a coming-out party for their capital city, and in the gold medals their athletes win, an affirmation of the communist way of life.

Facts and Figures for the Moscow Games

Over 12,000 athletes from 130 countries will be taking part in the 1980 games. Compare those numbers to the 9,000 athletes from 113 countries who competed in Montreal. Of course, in Montreal two dozen countries, most of them African nations, and their unfortunate athletes walked out before the games began. It was another graphic example of how the stench of politics has come to permeate the Olympic arena. The Soviets have declared the 1980 games "an Olympics for all." Let's hope that it works out that way.

Also in Moscow for the games will be 3,500 members of the various international sports federations. The city has invited 850 special guests of honor. There will be approximately 3,500 umpires, referees, and judges. The Novosti Press Agency anticipates 7,400 members of the media, while the Central Council of Tourism expects 200,000 to 300,000 foreign tourists and 300,000 visitors from other socialist countries.

Competition Sites and Facilities

The Olympic Village

Every host city since 1952 has built or designated a separate Olympic village for the athletes. Moscow has carried on the tradition. Situated on Michurinsky Avenue, ten minutes from Lenin Stadium and fifteen minutes from most other venues, is the new 260-acre Olympic village. The village will house 12,700 people in eighteen one-block–long buildings. The structures are sixteen stories high. When I visited Moscow in January 1978, the village was still under construction and slightly behind schedule. But there were no worries on the part of the Soviet officials about whether the complex would be ready in time. The strikes that played havoc with Montreal builders and turned the 1976 games into a multi-billion-dollar fiasco will not show up in Moscow. Soviet labor unions don't strike. In fact, many of the workers spend their off-time volunteering their services to the state. That doesn't seem like a very relaxing way to spend Sunday afternoon, but it does guarantee excellent facilities for the games.

The village appears to be a no-frill complex, although there will be a concert hall, movie theaters, and a discotheque, in addition to the standard restaurants, hospital, and training facilities. The no-frills concept is not new; the Montreal village was also built that way. Besides, it doesn't really matter because for the athletes it's not the movies and discos that are the sources of entertainment, it's the opportunity for a bunch of jocks from all over the world to get together and talk.

After the games conclude the government has specified that the village "will be handed over to the Muscovites," with 15,000 moving into the apartments.

Central Lenin Stadium

There are twenty-seven venues where the 1980 competition will take place. The total seating capacity of all twenty-seven is 428,000, of which 103,000 seats belong to the centerpiece of the XXII Olympiad, Central Lenin Stadium. Personally, I like Lenin Stadium. It's old and interesting, and in a way reminds me of Yankee Stadium. Not so much in how it looks, but how it feels. There is a lot of history in its concrete walls, and certainly a lot of great athletic feats have been performed there.

The stadium was built in 1956. It is located in the southwest portion of Moscow in the Luzhniki section, between the inner Garden ring and the Circular Motorway. The Moscow River oxbows to the southwest of the stadium, forming a semicircle around the Luzhniki (it means "meadows") Park. The stadium has been renovated for the games by one of the three general contractors responsible for the entire Olympic construction. By 1980 the stadium will feature a new boosted lighting plant, which is sorely needed. Most of Russia suffers from poor lighting. You can visit great museums, like the Tretyakov, and barely be able to see the paintings. The stadium will also have new matrix scoreboards that measure 250 square meters each. They are equipped to show instant replays and other television programs.

Scheduled for Lenin Stadium are the opening and closing ceremonies, the soccer finals, and all track and field events.

The Sports Palace, Small Arena, and Druzhba Gym

With a seating capacity of 12,000, the Sports Palace is the largest of the three other facilities located in Luzhniki Park. It will be the site of the 1980 judo competition. When I first visited the Sports Palace I was a bit taken aback. It was so uninteresting from an architectural point of view; just your basic brown box. But when I went inside and looked around I had to shake off a slight chill and the goosebumps. You couldn't help but think of all the great Russian gymnasts, the Korbuts and the Tourischevas, who had competed there.

The 1980 gymnastics competition, however, is scheduled for the new multi-purpose gym.

The Small Arena acquired its name almost twenty years ago. But since its conversion to a gymnasium, which raised the seating capacity to 9,000, the name is no longer accurate. The arena is now the third largest indoor facility in Moscow.

The Druzhba Multi-Purpose Gym is a new building that sits northeast of Lenin Stadium, beyond the Luzhniki Bridge and across the Moskva River. Competition in eleven sports, including gymnastics, fencing, wrestling, and volleyball will take place in this venue.

The Olympic Sports Complex

The first thing you notice about the Olympic Sports Complex is that it is the most modern-looking structure in Moscow. Located on Peace Avenue in the Prospekt Mira section, it is certainly the architectural showpiece of the games. The complex is the largest indoor arena in Europe. Built specifically for the 1980 Olympics, the facility features 33,000 square feet of floor space—room enough for a full-scale soccer pitch. There is, overall, seating for 35,000 spectators, including stands for viewing the swimming competition that will accommodate 13,500. The walls inside the complex are movable, and can be rearranged in minutes to divide the building into two separate facilities. The boxing, basketball, and swimming are scheduled for the sports complex. After the games, figure skating, speed skating, and even track and field competitions will be held in the structure.

The Dynamo Sports Palace

Another new arena, one of eleven constructed for the 1980 games, is the Dynamo Sports Palace. This hexagonal, two-story structure with a viewing balcony seats 5,000 spectators. It will be the site of the Olympic handball competition.

Dynamo Stadium in Minsk

Named for the famous Dynamo Soccer Club, the stadium is one of the oldest in Russia. Situated amidst the homes of

Minsk's working-class families, the stadium will be the site of the soccer and field hockey tournaments. For the finals the soccer tournament will move into Lenin Stadium. Dynamo has been completely renovated for the 1980 games. The facility is familiar to many American athletes, since on more than one occasion it has been the site of U.S.A.-USSR athletic meets. Next to the stadium are the smaller, rebuilt Tractor Stadium and twenty soccer pitches.

Krylatskoye Cycling Track

The new indoor cycling track at Krylatskoye may be the most unusual building used in the Olympics. The site of the pursuit and sprint competitions, the track is the first indoor facility of its type in Europe. The most distinguishing characteristic of the building is its unique roof, which, when viewed from the air, resembles a huge butterfly with its wings spread. The roof spans the entire 6,000-seat arena without a single support. The track itself is made of Siberian larch, a wood chosen for its hardness and the fact that it is knot-free, a necessary quality in a cycle track floor.

Krylatskoye Circuit Track

The 13.6-km cycling track is the site of the team road race and the individual circuit race. The course traverses the village of Tatarova and the hills that surround it. It closely follows the natural terrain of the area. The track is suitable for races up to 180 km long. The final leg of the circuit is the motorway that connects the rowing canal with the indoor cycle track.

Moscow Rowing Canal at Krylatskoye

The rowing canal, a spectacular new still-water facility, is the other half of the sports complex at Krylatskoye in the Moscow River valley. Also located at Krylatskoye are the Olympic archery fields.

Dynamo Shooting Range

The shooting tournament (pistol, rifle, and skeet) will take place at the Dynamo range in the town of Mytishchi on the outskirts of Moscow. The seating capacity is approximately 3,000.

Bitsa Equestrian Center

South of Moscow in the oak, birch, and maple forests of Bitsa is the Olympic equestrian facility. All equestrian events will be held there. The main Bitsa competition structure is a stadium that seats 12,000. The size of the stands attests to the international appeal of the sport. The team obstacle race is scheduled for the main stadium. Located next to the main arena is the 1,800-meter circular steeplechase track. The Bitsa complex includes a covered riding hall, with seating for 2,000, that will be used in case of inclement weather. Other special features at Bitsa are: stables with constant warm air circulation; lighting similar to actual daylight; and warm shower stalls for the horses.

Bitsa has its own press center, as well as a shooting range and a swimming pool where the pentathletes will train. A new hotel housing 150, a café, a bar, a cafeteria, and a veterinary office have recently been completed.

Olympic Sailing Center

The Olympic yachting competition will take place at Tallinn in the Estonian Soviet Socialist Republic, on the Gulf of Finland. I spent a week there in 1975 in a U.S.–USSR–West German meet. It's a great little town of very old and historic buildings that have survived thousands of years of wars. The people of Tallinn are the most open and friendly people I encountered in the Soviet Union. For one thing they are adamant about not being called Russians. They are Estonians and they make that clear. Estonia didn't actually become a part of the USSR until after World War II. Through the years Estonia has produced some terrific athletes and the folks of Tallinn are very quick to tell you about their Olympic champions. The athletes participating in the Olympic regatta will have a marvelous time there.

A new, twenty-seven-story hotel has been built especially to accommodate fans for the games. Also, the Tallinn Experimental Sports Vessels Shipyards have manufactured 450 sailing hulls for the competition.

Travel and Tourist Information

From an athletic standpoint Moscow will have no trouble hosting the Olympics. It is the city's ability to handle the great influx of tourists the games bring with them that is causing consternation among foreigners and realistic Muscovites. The athletes in Moscow will certainly have it better than the average spectator. After arriving in Russia they will be virtually sequestered in the village, fed and bedded and generally cared for. The tourists, on the other hand, will have to fend for themselves in a city that moves at a reasonably swift pace.

In 1976 Moscow had available 50,000 beds in existing hotels. Three thousand of these belong to the massive Rossiya Hotel, with its elegant concert hall and ten miles of corridors. An interesting feature of the Rossiya is the presence of four desk clerks at each of the four main entrances. Each clerk speaks a different language: English, Russian, French, and German. Since 1976, 27,000 additional beds have been added, a large number of them, 10,000, coming with the construction of the new Izmailov hotel complex.

For the 24,000 Americans expected in Moscow some time during the games, 8,000 beds per night have been allotted. Almost every American in Russia during the games will be traveling in some sort of package tour. The tours last a minimum of two weeks, of which only five or six days will be spent at the games. The rest of the time will be spent in Kiev, Minsk, Odessa, and Leningrad. The cost for the tours will be approximately $1,550 per person, but there will be no guarantees concerning the type of accommodations or the number of tickets to the Olympic events. The tour directors emphasize that the accommodations will be first-class; I emphasize that that means first-class Soviet style. Not that the rooms aren't clean, just that they're a little on the Spartan side.

Europeans and Americans who are accustomed to receiving excellent service are in for a severe culture shock in Moscow. The service industry in Russia is not one of the country's sparkling national treasures. Most waiters are under the impression that good service was supposed to have disappeared with the tsars. And considering that many of the waiters, clerks, waitresses, and bartenders manning the cafés and hotels will be new and inexperienced, the situation could not look more bleak. According to the Soviet Olympic Organizing Committee, six hundred restaurants, cafés, and dining halls have been renovated for 1980.

Eating out is a major event in Moscow, so tourists can figure on spending three to four hours minimum to accomplish the task, even in their own hotels. If you're a prospective Olympic spectator, I suggest taking along a jar of honey and some peanut butter, something to munch on, because by the end of the games you'll kill for a late-night snack. Most of the hotels are loaded with bars; the Intourist has nine more bars than restaurants. The Soviets do take their drinking seriously.

American journalists like Geoffrey Bocca who have spent quite a bit of time in the USSR report that long faces, slow service, and shortchanging are constant problems. Bocca also warns that tourists may be given their change in hard-to-negotiate currencies.

Moscow taxi drivers, who are often off-duty diplomatic chauffeurs, have been known to take advantage of tourists by dropping them off for dinner and then, unbeknownst to the diners, remaining at the location with the meter running until they return from dinner several hours later.

On the positive side, the Soviet government has trained 5,000 taxi drivers to converse in English, French, Spanish, and German to accommodate the foreigners.

In America we take a lot of things for granted, one of them being the efficiency of our phone systems. After a week in Moscow, Ma Bell, for all her mistakes and rate hikes, doesn't look so bad. Placing a call from Moscow to the U.S. will take a minimum of forty-five minutes, and cynical journalists argue that forty-eight hours is more like the average.

It's not my intention to paint a depressing picture of Moscow, only a realistic one. There are surely things about the capital of Russia that the first-time visitor will find upsetting, but a trip to Moscow is unquestionably a unique and enlightening experience. It is a city of magnificent museums and cultural activities, and if the schism between its luxurious cultural facilities and its limited consumer services seems unreasonably large, perhaps that is a reflection of the country's political philosophy rather than a sign of its inability to enter the twentieth century.

Olympic Post Office

The preparations for hosting the Olympic games involve much more than readying the athletic and housing facilities. For instance, in order to properly handle the voluminous amounts of extra mail both coming in and going out of the country, the Soviets have built an Olympic post office, located a few minutes from the village. The Soviets expect the new post office to process 50,000 letters and parcels a day.

For philatelists, the Postal Department has issued forty-three Olympic commemorative stamps and six stamp sheets.

Tickets for the Games

To give some idea of the value of the tickets to Olympic events, consider the case of the unfortunate ticket-scalper in Montreal in 1976. He was arrested for scalping, taken to jail, and then tried in a Montreal court. The judge found him guilty, but before the bailiff could escort him back to the pokey, he was surrounded by his attorneys, all of them attempting to purchase his tickets. Ticket scalping is also illegal in the Soviet Union, but it will certainly take place during the games. In 1979, concert tickets for Elton John sold for $250.00 on the black market in Moscow.

Ticket quotas for the Moscow games were determined by Olympiad 80, the organizing committee, which took into consideration the popularity of each sport in the various countries, the participation of each country in the specific events, the size of the national teams, and each country's tradition of tourist contacts. Foreign guests received one-third of the 1.7 million tickets. Moscow citizens received 35 percent. Russian citizens from regions outside Moscow received 20 percent, and 15 percent went to friends of the Olympic Organizing Committee.

The allotment for the United States is 201,520 total tickets. Here is the distribution:

EVENT	TICKETS
Opening Ceremony	2,860
Track and Field	60,000
Rowing	5,000
Basketball	10,000
Boxing	15,000
Canoeing	5,000
Cycling, Track	700
Cycling, Road	200
Fencing	3,000
Soccer (football)	40,000
Gymnastics	4,700
Weight Lifting	2,400
Handball	3,600
Field Hockey	6,000
Judo	5,400
Wrestling Freestyle	2,200
Wrestling Greco-Roman	2,200
Swimming, Diving, Water Polo	10,000
Modern Pentathlon	2,300
Equestrian	10,700
Shooting	700
Archery	600
Volleyball	4,800
Sailing	800
Closing Ceremony	3,160
	201,520

Sailing will be in Tallinn; Soccer (football) quarter-finals and semi-finals will be in Minsk, Kiev and Leningrad; Soccer (football) finals will be in Moscow. All other Olympic events will be in Moscow.

The 1980 ticket prices range from $4.00 to a high of $37.50 for the opening and closing ceremonies. The top ticket price in Montreal was $42.00. Each sports facility has its own individual ticket. The tickets are postcard-sized, and imprinted with a picture of the stadium, the name of the sport, the seating information, and rules for spectators in Russian, French, and English.

American Olympic Prospects

Themistocles, the great Athenian commander whose brilliant naval strategy saved Greece from the Persians, was once asked whether he would rather be Achilles, the Greek hero, or Homer, the writer who chronicled the feats of Achilles. Themistocles replied, "Which would you rather be—a conqueror in the Olympic games, or the crier who proclaims the conqueror?"

Themistocles' revealing answer—a rephrased question of his own—left no doubt as to who he would rather be. If the same question were put to me, I would have to agree with Themistocles. In Moscow in 1980 I will be a crier who proclaims the games. Sitting in the broadcast booth, connected by earphones to electronic voices and by TV monitors to electronic images, I will attempt along with my colleagues to bring the Olympics home to America. But in my heart I'll wish I was down on the artificial track of Central Lenin Stadium, feeling the adrenalin flooding my veins. It is not that I don't look forward to my job as a television commentator, because I do. In one way it will be just as difficult a challenge as actually competing. To do a good job requires extensive homework; you must develop a rapport with the athletes, and, perhaps hardest of all, you must learn when to talk and when to be silent and simply allow the action to speak for itself.

I hope that as an Olympic track and field sportscaster I can be informative without being obtrusive. It is very important to me that the commentators not take the spotlight away from the athletes: they are the stars, not the facilities, not the TV people, and, most important, not the countries. However difficult it is for people to understand or accept the notion, the games are for the individuals; they are not meant to be used as political weapons in an ideological war.

When you watch a specific event in the competition, do not think of it as Russia winning, or Italy losing, or Kenya upsetting Hungary. Enjoy it for what it is, a display of the skills of two or ten or however many marvelously conditioned athletes. I realize, of course, that fans, newspapers, and television commentators are still going to add up the point totals and medal counts and calculate that the Soviet Union has more medals than East Germany or that West Germany has more golds than England; I know that broadcasters will report a swimming race and say the U.S. has won another gold. But that is wrong. An athlete has won the medal, not a country. The games of Greece began as festivals for the athletes, and we should always try to be faithful to that concept.

The method of selecting Olympic competitors is different in each country. The United States has one of the most unique, and surely one of the most equitable, procedures for deciding which of its athletes will participate in the Olympics. The U.S. is the only country in the world whose selection process—the Olympic Trials—is based solely upon head-to-head competition.

Only athletes who have previously performed up to certain USOC standards are invited to the trials. Once at the trials, all of the eligible athletes compete against each other in their respective events, with the fittest and fastest surviving. It is a simple and direct process. An American athlete may go to the trials as the world record holder in a particular event, but if he or she doesn't qualify at the trials, someone else will make the magic trip to the village. I suppose that there are legitimate objections that could be raised as to the prudence of such a system, but certainly there are none about the fairness of it. In the United States every potential Olympic athlete gets his shot. Unfortunately, sometimes our best performers are not physically ready for the trials and are unable to qualify for the actual games; a runner may have the flu, for example, or a high jumper a slight sprain. Such misfortunes fall under the sad category of tough luck. Past performances can carry an athlete only as far as the trials; it is the effort there that opens the Olympic door.

In the 1976 trials the axe fell on two of our best track and field hopefuls. It hurt all of us to see it happening, but there wasn't anything anyone could do about it. Marty Liquori, the finest 5,000-meter man in the States, was injured in June and failed to qualify for Montreal. Steve Williams, 1976's most promising 100-meter sprinter—and the only man to have registered four 9.9 clockings—pulled a tendon and didn't make the team. He was also injured in 1972. When something like that happens, it is painful to the athlete and to the coaches, but it is a testimony to the fairness of the selection process.

On the other hand, you can be sure that possible charges of politics and a concern for fairness do not deter many of the other national sports federations from choosing for their Olympic teams the athletes they think will best represent their country. Vladimir Yaschenko of the USSR could come down with the the measles before the tune-up games for the 1980 Olympics, but when the high jump bar in Moscow is set at 7'7", you can bet he'll be there.

Since the makeup of the U.S. teams depends upon the results of the Olympic trials, it is impossible to know for sure beforehand which athletes will compete in which events. Of course, it's hard to imagine that Edwin Moses will not be the prime American threat in the 400-meter hurdles or Steve Scott a competitor in the mile. Tracy Caulkins should be a shoo-in to swim the individual medleys, and Kurt Thomas is surely destined to perform on the side horse. It doesn't take a crystal ball or a good bookie to figure on these athletes showing up in Russia, but you would have to be better than Jeane Dixon and Merlin the Magician to make predictions in some events—the 100 meters, for example. We have close to twenty 100-meter men—some young, some medium, and some old—capable of pulling the right trigger at almost any given time. Bear that in mind as we focus on the potential American stars of the 1980 Olympics.

Track and Field

For most of us, the first events that come to mind when we think of the summer Olympics are the track and field sports. Along with swimming, track and field is the one area in which U.S. athletes have established a history of excellence.

For that reason, a poor showing in track and field by American athletes is a major disappointment to the fans. It must be realized, however, that a "poor" showing by the U.S. athletics squad is a relative notion. For instance, in Montreal American athletes won six gold, six silver, and seven bronze medals, and although no other country's athletes garnered as many medals, the Montreal "tally" was considered a sub-par performance by U.S. standards.

In the spring of 1979, just before the Muhammed Ali Indoor Games in Long Beach, John Walker, one of the world's great milers and the 1976 Olympic gold medalist in the 1500 meters, told the Los Angeles press that "America should not expect a 'gold rush' at the 1980 games." According to Walker, who had sat out the 1978 season because of two leg operations, "The Russians are gearing all their athletes towards the Moscow games as a matter of national pride. They are already so dominant, but I expect them to be even stronger in Moscow. Russia more than any other country will certainly see it as a great victory to win at home."

There is no way I can disagree with what John had to say. From everything I've seen in the way of pre-Olympic performances, the Russians are better prepared than ever before. Our 1980 track and field squad will also be stronger than the team we sent to Montreal, but I believe we'll be lucky to see our athletes match the six-gold-medal performance of Montreal. Not only the Russians, but most of the other nations of the world will be fielding stronger squads as well.

To obtain the most accurate information about how the American track and field squad shapes up, I talked with Jimmy Carnes, the head coach of the U.S. team. Carnes has been coaching track and field for twenty-three years, the last twelve at the University of Florida and before that at a small college in South Carolina. Discussing athletics with Coach Carnes is a pure delight. He is a no-nonsense guy, but he has a smooth, easygoing manner. When you ask Jimmy Carnes a question, he gives you a straightforward answer: it may not be very diplomatic, but it will surely be honest. And it comes to you with a hint of grits and home fries, in a small-town Georgian accent that breaks through every few syllables.

The first question I asked Carnes was how he viewed his job as head track and field coach.

"I see my job as one of getting to know the total athlete a long time before the trials begin," said Carnes, "because by the time the trials are over, we'll have only nineteen days to get the squad to Moscow and ready to compete. By then I'll already want to know under what circumstances each of our athletes gives his best performance. I want them to be able to come to me with any problems, and I want to promote a team feeling as much as that is possible. After that, it's just a matter of making sure the athletes are comfortable and remain in peak condition."

I asked Coach Carnes how he would answer John Walker's assertion that the USSR would field the most talented team. With a slight hint of indignation in his voice he replied: "We fully intend that the U.S. men's track and field squad will be the most dominant team in 1980. I anticipate strong competition from the USSR and East Germany. Kenya will certainly be tough in the distance races—over 3,000 meters. And some countries specialize in certain other events. The Central American countries produce excellent sprinters. We expect Trinidad and Jamaica to again be tough in the 100 and 200 meters. Mexico has excellent race walkers. The Poles have terrific pole vaulters. So we anticipate a tremendous level of competition, but our athletes should perform the best."

John Walker talked about a home-field advantage. We know that it exists in many other sports, particularly basketball, where the crowd can truly make a difference. Personally I believe that the Russians will be very keyed up in their own country—possibly too keyed up. Coach Carnes looks at the problem differently.

"Certainly one of the hardest things to do is travel across the world and compete in a strange environment," he noted. "The food, the climate, it's all different. That, of course, is where experience pays off—where the athlete who has competed in the Olympics before can make the adjustment because he knows what to expect. We plan to take our boys into Moscow at the very last minute, to be there as short a time as possible. We'll stay outside the city until the last moment, then take the team in, process them into the village, and be ready for the competition the next day.

"Now as far as the home-field advantage goes, that's not much of a problem. One 400-meter track is pretty much the same as another, and our athletes will be ready."

Coach Carnes speaks in a soft drawl, but his measured words provide excellent insight.

When you look at the track and field "dope sheet" for the games, starting with the sprints and working through the decathlon, Carnes's remarks about the strength of the U.S. squad begin to make sense.

The sprints are generally a very pleasant topic for U.S. coaches to discuss, since U.S. teams have always had tremendous depth in this area. This year is no exception. There are twenty men who are fast enough over the shorter distances to make the U.S. team. And on a given day almost any one of them could win a 100-meter race.

"Certainly Clancy Edwards has to be considered a prime contestant for the gold," said Carnes. "Clancy is a proven competitor." The former USC sprinter was the 1978 NCAA and AAU champion in the 100 and 200 meters. His 10.07 in the NCAA 100 was the fastest time in the world. However, Clancy had a mediocre season in Europe in the transition period between college graduation and going it on his own, probably a result of fatigue after a long campaign. In 1979 Clancy failed to qualify for the AAUs after finishing sixth in the star-studded Pepsi Invitational 100 meters in May. But he still remains a top American threat.

Steve Williams is a veteran U.S. sprinter, a twenty-five-year-old hard-luck athlete who was kept out of both the 1972 and the 1976 Olympics by leg injuries. He has been one of the top five sprinters in the world for the past six years. Like Edwards, Williams has never been known as a fast starter, but he has always been a strong finisher.

Steve Riddick finished fourth in the 1979 AAUs. At twenty-nine, he is the oldest of the 100-meter men. Harvey Glance, out of Auburn, finished second in the 1979 AAUs; as a college freshman, he had made the 1976 Olympic squad and finished fourth in Montreal. These names are well known to track and field enthusiasts and others who read the sports pages. But who was the young athlete who blew away the competition in the 1979 AAUs? It was as though he was personally out to prove that Coach Carnes was correct when he said, "Anybody could win it." James Sanford ran a 10.02 at the AAU meet to defeat Glance and a slew of other world-class sprinters, including LaMonte King, who was third, followed by Riddick. A USC sophomore who didn't even concentrate on the 100 and 200 meters until this year, young Sanford came out of the starting blocks and into the limelight for the first time in the 1979 USC-UCLA dual meet. The soft spoken Pasadena, California, native nursed a groin injury all through the last half of '78 and into '79. He still considers himself a quarter-miler, but all of that may change by the trials.

Another "babe in wolf's clothing" is Jerome Deal, from the University of Texas–El Paso, who nipped Sanford in the 1979 NCAAs. Two other college-age stars are Mel Lattany of Georgia and James Mallard of the University of Alabama. You begin to see what Coach Carnes means when he says the U.S. is thigh-deep in top-notch sprinters. And we haven't even mentioned the most publicized American sprinter in recent years, Houston McTear, who won the 1979 Pepsi Invitational over a spectacular international field that included top-ranked Silvio Leonard of Cuba.

McTear is an unusual man whose story sounds a bit like a modern-day revision of the Pygmalion myth. He is probably the most unlikely young athlete in this country to have emerged into national prominence. The twenty-two-year-old grew up in a shack within smelling distance of the sawmill that his father sweated in twelve hours a day. Nine brothers and sisters lived in a squat shanty in the Florida Panhandle. To this day Houston has never run a race for a university, nor does he possess a high school diploma, though he did compete as a high school student. Instead, he has the equivalent of a third-grade education and the ability to run like a panther, which is what he resembles when he streaks out of the blocks with what is acknowledged to be the fastest start in the world.

After reading a newspaper account of McTear's plight, Phil Fairchild, a Pasadena millionaire, plucked the youngster out of the suffocating Florida poverty and brought him to California, three thousand miles away from the Panhandle and a million miles away from his roots.

The then nineteen-year-old Houston found himself under the tutelage of Harold Smith, a member of Muhammed Ali's massive entourage and president of the Ali Track Club. Smith became McTear's legal guardian. Fairchild eventually withdrew his financial support over a disagreement on how to handle the speedster. Smith went to Ali for help, and ever since then the fighter has been the sprinter's benefactor. It is a strange, somewhat stormy story with the quiet McTear in the eye of it. It would be impossible to deny that he's something of a pawn in the machinations of other people, but McTear is growing more confident each day—more his own man and more articulate—as he prepares for the 1980 games. Where at one time Smith accompanied him to all his interviews, Houston now talks to reporters on his own. He has improved his schooling to a ninth-grade level, and his wife, Janette, has recently given birth to a little boy, Isaac. The Olympic gold still looms as his goal, but the goateed McTear has already realized his dream—he's made it out of the Florida Panhandle.

In the 200 meters, *Track and Field* magazine rated Clancy Edwards as the number one sprinter in 1978. His 20.03 was the fastest time of the season. "He's a super athlete with all the tools," says Coach Carnes. In the '79 Pepsi Invitational, Clancy ran down Silvio Leonard in the final 100 meters, but in the NCAAs, Clancy finished fourth behind Greg Foster, the towering hurdler from UCLA (more about Foster when we check out the 110 hurdles). Here again the U.S. depth is astounding. Dwayne Evans, the bronze medalist in Montreal, was not a factor in 1978, but pulled off something of an upset in the 1979 AAUs. Other 200 hopefuls are Sanford,

Riddick, Williams, Glance, William Snoddy of Oklahoma, and James Mallard.

After Montreal, it taxed the imagination to dream up a man who could beat Alberto Juantorena in the 400 meters. A Ferrari of a runner, whose raw speed seems to throw you back in the seat as you watch him, Alberto often looks unbeatable. But Carnes and a slew of American runners are a long way from conceding the event to "El Caballo." Juantorena came to the U.S. for the first time in May 1979. It was the first time a Cuban athlete had competed in this country since Castro's revolution, but Alberto was greeted rather rudely by Willie Smith, the ex-Auburn star. Smith, the third-ranked 1978 performer, held off Alberto in the stretch. Willie was out to prove that his 1980 challenge is legitimate. Smith is a tenacious competitor who doesn't like being overlooked by fans or the press. He also came back to cross the tape first in the 1979 AAU 400 meters with a time of 45.10. In the Pan-Am Games in July of '79, however, Juantorena and Smith were both passed in the stretch by Arizona State's Tony Darden, whose finishing kick left spectators gasping. Also in the picture is Billy Mullins of Southern California, who didn't lose a race in 1978 and whose 1980 plans definitely include Moscow in the summertime. Coach Carnes feels certain it will take a time of 44 seconds or less to win in 1980.

In the 800 meters, according to Carnes, "Our strongest competitor is James Robinson—and right behind him, I mean right behind, is the versatile 800-1500 man from Villanova, Don Paige." Robinson is the type of runner who gives coaches heart palpitations and the fans goose pimples. James just plain takes his time during the first part of the race. He sizes up his competition on the first lap, and waits until he heads for home before turning on the afterburners. His laid-back style has earned him the dubious nickname of "Silky Sullivan," the appellation of the famous, California-bred racehorse who used to come from twenty or thirty lengths off the pace and win with a rush at the wire. Robinson, like his namesake, is California bred. The Oakland native works at the University of California–Berkeley, where he also went to college. Robinson, who is as articulate as he is fast, loves coaching young runners, which he did at a junior college until Proposition 13, the taxpayers' revolution, cut out the funds for his job. After the 1980 games, James hopes to go back into it.

Robinson is lanky, heady, and tough and in 1978 and 1979 was the only man to show his backside to Juantorena in the 800. The two-time AAU champ has often said he feels he is overlooked by the press in favor of the Cuban. In fact, it wasn't until he upset Paige in the 1979 Brooks West meet with a 1:45.5 that the twenty-five-year-old received any ink.

When James is reminded that Silky Sullivan won the California Derby but finished twenty lengths back in the big one at Churchill Downs when he failed to find the passing gear, he laughs and dismisses the possibility of something like that happening to him. This "Silky Sullivan" isn't worried about finishing twenty lengths behind anybody.

On a muggy Illinois afternoon during the first week of June, Don Paige won the 1979 NCAA 1500 meters. That in itself wasn't a big surprise—after all, he was the favorite, and a victory in the 1500 was expected. But then, thirty-two minutes later, Paige came back to win the 800 meters in 1:46.2, the fastest time in the world in 1979 up to that point. Twenty years earlier another Villanova runner, Ron Delany, had accomplished the same feat, but Delany had to run in only one trial heat. Paige ran in five races in three days.

It would figure that the last two athletes to roll doubles in the 800 and 1500 meters would be Villanova track men. The small school outside Philadelphia churns out track stars like the New York Yankees do Hall-of-Famers. And the primary reason is Coach Jumbo Elliot. For forty-five years Elliot has been training "race horses" and producing more winners than Calumet Farm: Ron Delany, Marty Liquori, Dick Buerkle, Eamonn Coghlan, Mark Belger, Sydney Maree, and Don Paige.

Paige came to Villanova from Baldwinsville, New York, twelve miles outside of Syracuse. Young, immature, and anxious, he soon realized he had made the right decision when he put himself under Elliot's care. "Mr. Elliot has trained so many great runners and none of them have come out wrong. He knows what he's doing. He does the thinking and I do the running," says Paige.

Don isn't thinking of doubling in Moscow, but he is planning on being on the starting line when the gun fires for the 1500. Along with Steve Scott, Paige is one of the best U.S. hopes for a gold in the event. Paige is six feet tall, 150 pounds, and has a slight facial resemblance to Jim Ryun, the brilliant Kansas miler. He was redshirted his first two years at Villanova because of stress fractures in his legs. Sitting out his freshman year had an adverse psychological effect on the youngster. Coming out of high school, he was all geared up, ready to compete, but instead he was forced to become a spectator. It left too much time for questions that couldn't really be answered yet. But Don began the next year with a big victory in the Martin Luther King Games mile, defeating Eamonn Coghlan, Sydney Maree, and Nyambui.

To make sure he is injury free and in prime condition for the U.S. trials, Paige has cut back his 1979 racing commitments to a reasonable number. If he continues to improve at his present rate, he's sure to be one of the three U.S. competitors in the 1500.

Many people consider the "metric mile" (1500 meters) the premier event in track and field. One reason for this is that even the most inexperienced spectator has enough time during the actual running of the event to see the different strategies develop. The distinctive element of the 1500, the magical "four minute" mark, makes it easy to follow the pace, since each quarter-mile lap takes approximately a minute to complete.

The Olympic history of the 1500 is peppered with familiar names: Bannister, Snell, Keino, Walker. And to that list, Californian Steve Scott hopes to add his name.

After Don Paige's magnificent double in the NCAAs, the media attention naturally focused on the slim collegiate runner. During the two weeks before the AAUs one would have thought Paige was the only middle distance man in America. Then at the 1979 AAUs in Walnut, California, Paige came on to post a personal best of 3:37.4 in the 1500 meters. But

Steve Scott had crossed the finish line one second and five meters ahead of him. It was the first in what surely will be many great match-ups between the two runners.

It would certainly be understandable if Steve Scott's idols were Christian Barnard and Jonas Salk instead of some of the great milers in history. The 6'1", 160-pound twenty-three-year-old belongs to a family that could singlehandedly sway the vote at an AMA convention. His mother is a nurse; his sister Alicia is a respiratory therapist; his wife, Kim, is a nurse; and his father and his oldest brother, Kendall, are doctors.

The bright but low-key Scott became the first runner since Jim Ryun to win the AAU 1500 meters three years in a row. After the national championships, Scott's coach at UC-Irvine, Len Miller, decided to hang up his coach's whistle in order to enter the business world. But he stated at the time, "I will stick with Steve through to Moscow; he's number one with me above all else." Number one with Scott is a gold medal, and he seems to have a reasonable chance at one.

In the 5,000 and 10,000 meters and the 3,000-meter steeplechase the U.S. athletes look strong, but not overpowering. The American long distance men will be running into a headwind of world record holders, but Coach Carnes believes they are talented enough to be near the favorites at the finish.

Top threats in the steeplechase are Doug Brown, Henry Marsh, and George Malley. The world record (8:05.4) in the event with the water hazard belongs to Henry Rono of Kenya, a student at Washington State University. Brown, of Athletes West track club, has posted the fastest American time. His 8:19.3 was the sixth fastest in the world in 1978. Marsh, who attends Brigham Young, owns an 8:22.5, while another Athletes West competitor, George Malley, has run an 8:21.7.

In the 5,000 meters there is a name that is as euphonic as it is well known. It belongs to an articulate sometime–television commentator out of Villanova—another one of Jumbo Elliot's boys. You probably wouldn't want to go skydiving with Marty Liquori, or have him looking over your shoulder at the blackjack table. His luck, especially when it comes to the Olympics, just isn't that good. He missed the 1972 and

1976 games with leg injuries—which must have been all the more painful because he was the pre-games favorite. But Marty is back for another try at the elusive gold. As of 1978 he was ranked second in the world in the 5,000.

The tenacious Liquori will be thirty by the time the 1980 Olympics arrive. Not exactly a young lion, but not too old for a distance man. If Marty can remain healthy, he's still very capable of a medal-winning run. His 13:16 in 1978 proved that.

Rudy Chapa of Oregon is a legitimate 5,000 threat, as is Craig Virgin, formerly of Southern Illinois University, if he chooses to run in the shorter event. However, it appears more likely that Craig will concentrate on his best event, the 10,000 meters. Virgin has continued to show improvement every year, and in the 1979 AAUs he toppled Steve Prefontaine's 10,000 meters American mark of 27:43.6 with a 27:39.4 of his own. The ubiquitous Henry Rono's name appears at the top of the list in all three events. His three world records, in the 5,000 and 10,000 meters and the 3,000 meter steeplechase earned him the honor of *Track and Field*'s 1978 athlete of the year. However, Virgin's best time is not that far away from Rono's record 27:22.5 in the 10,000. Another runner to consider in the 10,000 is Frank Shorter. The thing to remember about the Olympics is that in one super effort an athlete can surprise everyone and bring home the gold.

The mile may still be the class event of track and the decathlon the test of the total individual, but I'm guessing that the Olympic marathon will trap as many people in front of the television as any event broadcast from the games. Coach Carnes summed up the reason for the popularity of the marathon when he said, "Just to think that a few years ago we had to beg people to get out and jog, and now I don't even know how many millions are running to keep fit." Well, according to a recent Gallup poll on the subject, 25 million Americans are jogging through parks, on the beach, and over sidewalks. And an amazing number of those armchair quarterbacks turned runners are competing in 10 km runs and marathons.

In the 1979 Boston Marathon, the eighty-third in the city's

history, over eight thousand qualified runners took to the Boston streets. Fifty-four of those eight thousand actually posted times that were below the Olympic trials qualifying standard. The man who led the chilly wave of humanity from suburban Hopkinton to Boston in forty-two-degree temperatures and wind-blown rain was Bill Rodgers. Rodgers, a thirty-one-year-old exschoolteacher who now owns a small chain of running goods stores, is the toast of Beantown. Rodgers averaged 4:56 per mile over the twenty-six miles and three infamous Newton hills (his 2:09:27 was the fifth fastest marathon ever run anywhere). Toshiko Seko of Japan, who upset Rodgers in the '79 Fukuoka, was second.

Rodgers sneaked into the marathon scene in 1975 with an unexpected and startling victory in the Boston Marathon. His time of 2:09:55 was a then American record. Boston is a city that loves its runners, but at the time of his victory Rodgers was so unknown that the *Boston Globe* misspelled his name. In 1976 Rodgers went to the Montreal games as a bona fide contender. He finished fortieth because of a foot injury he sustained just prior to the games. In 1978 he captured the prestigious Boston race for a second time.

Rodgers's 1979 marathon win before a delirious and partisan crowd, which actually behaved quite admirably considering the circumstances, was the 125-pound hometown hero's most spectacular. The only man to even keep Rodgers within sight was the determined Seko, but on Heartbreak Hill, the well-known cemetery for exhausted runners six miles from the finish, Rodgers committed Seko's chances to the asphalt. For the slim Bostonian there's only one thing missing now, a medal in the Olympics.

Rodgers's athletic history would provide inspiration for any athlete. He graduated from Wesleyan University in Connecticut in 1970. During his stint there he competed as a rather ordinary two-miler. After leaving school, he applied for conscientious-objector draft status, received it, and then spent the next two and a half years as an orderly in the Peter Brigham Hospital satisfying his alternate service requirement. After two years of smoking cigarettes, drinking beer, and changing bedpans, Rodgers had his motorcycle stolen. In his lowly economic state he had one form of transportation left. He started running the four miles to work and back. When Rodgers eventually lost his job, he spent his afternoon hours running . . . and running . . . and now, seven years and thousands of miles later, Bill Rodgers is the 1980 favorite in the Olympic marathon. As Coach Carnes says, "There is nothing greater in the world for an athlete than finding a spot where he can be successful."

Although Rodgers is the big name in American marathoning, there are other fine athletes with excellent chances for making it to Moscow. Jeff Wells is probably the number two long distance man in the states. Craig Virgin can do it in the marathon, as can Randy Thomas. Frank Shorter, the 1972 gold medalist, is also a potential contender.

In the 20 and 50 km race walks the U.S. does not have a single athlete rated in the top fifty in the world. But Coach Carnes and his staff hope that these unusual events, which are truly national sports in countries like Mexico, may attract American athletes of better quality in the future. To that end, we've sent a few of our race walkers to Mexico to train. At this time Neal Pyke and Todd Scully appear to be the best U.S. hopes in the 20 km. Pyke and Scully are, however, still about ten minutes off the better times of the current Mexican race walkers. In the 50 km, the three athletes with the best chances for making the Moscow squad are Marco Evonluk, Augie Hirt, and Tom Dooley.

Discussing events like the 20 km walk and the hammer throw with U.S. track and field coaches is a bit like asking politicians for their opinions on school busing and gas rationing. They just don't want to talk about them. But ask a politician about tax reform or a U.S. coach about the hurdles and just see if you can shut either of them up. The hurdles have always been outstanding events for U.S. athletes. Of the fifty-four gold medals awarded in the modern games in hurdling, U.S. trackmen have captured forty.

This year the U.S. has two athletes who are the class of their respective hurdling events—Renaldo Nehemiah in the 110 hurdles and Edwin Moses in the 400 intermediate hurdles. Moses is a remarkable athlete. Not only is he the world record holder, but he has so dominated his event that one is hard-pressed to think of another legitimate contender for the Moscow gold. Moses has been the number one hurdler in the world ever since he screamed past his seven rivals in Montreal. In 1978 the man in the tinted glasses went undefeated and produced eight of the ten fastest times in the world.

In the past Moses has expressed disappointment with the amount of recognition he has received. However, in one respect, Moses' lack of public recognition is a function of his pure superiority in his event. Edwin is so talented that one does not really ever expect him to lose. A man so favored in an individual event does not always make sensational copy. Great newspaper stories are made by match-ups, showdowns, by Paige versus Scott or Wilkins versus Schmidt. Moses stands alone in the intermediate hurdles; his only real challenge, albeit the toughest, is how fast he can push himself.

In the other hurdles event, the 110 meters, it is precisely the intensity of the competition which has been responsible for bringing the event into the sports headlines. Throughout 1978 and 1979 the head-to-head competition between the two greatest 110 hurdlers of all time excited everyone in the track and field world. Greg Foster and Renaldo Nehemiah have lowered the world record just about every time they have faced each other. Recently, Nehemiah has emerged as the superior hurdler of the two, having not lost to Greg since June of 1978.

Renaldo set the world record in San Jose in May 1979—13.16, breaking Foster's American record of 13.22. In May 1979 at the Pepsi Invitational, facing Alejandro Casanas of Cuba, he posted a 13 flat. In June in the NCAAs he went 12.91, but it was ruled wind-aided. Not that he needed the wind—some trackside observers have sworn Renaldo has outraced it. In the Pepsi and NCAA meets Foster hit three hurdles. And in the collegiate championships he stumbled and pulled up. Nevertheless, Foster is a brilliant hurdler. He just happens to specialize in an event in which another remarkable athlete competes. The tremendous duels the two have staged are reminiscent of the Affirmed-Alydar match-ups. In many other years, the determined Alydar would have had horse racing's triple crown to himself, yet fate put the two three-year-old horses on the same tracks at the same time. However, it may be that the twenty-one-year-old Foster will turn the recent trend around and defeat his twenty-year-old nemesis in the Olympics. Whatever the outcome of their personal competition, it seems certain that both of them will be in Moscow. It's not unreasonable to assume that they will occupy two-thirds of the 110 hurdles victory stand.

Where Foster is a large man, 6'3", 190 pounds (some track observers say a bit too large for the 110s), Nehemiah is the perfect size at 6', 165. A business major at the University of Maryland, he is called by his coach, Frank Costello, "the shark"; it has to do with the way he stalks his prey. When Costello signed Nehemiah out of Scotch Plains, New Jersey, he predicted that Renaldo would become the greatest athlete ever to attend the school. Costello is beginning to look like a prophet.

Renaldo's family and friends call him "Skeets" because of the way he crawled around the apartment as a baby. Skeets's mother died when he was very young, and his father supported the family by working as a bookbinder. As a senior in high school, Skeets set the prep record for the 120-yard hurdles in 12.9. He also quarterbacked the football team well enough to earn a scholarship in the sport to the University of Alabama.

I don't often make unqualified predictions. It's too much like walking the gangplank—there's no going back—but I believe in Skeets and I expect him to win the gold medal in the 110 hurdles in 1980. Other excellent hurdlers are Dedy Cooper and Kerry Bethel of the Philadelphia Pioneer Club.

Coach Carnes smiles when he sizes up some of the field events, but when he speaks of others, the best he can manage is an optimistic half-grin. The pole vault is one that produces a full-watt smile. It has traditionally been a stronghold for American athletes. Out of the eighteen gold medals awarded since the inauguration of the modern games, U.S. pole vaulters have won sixteen of them. In 1978 four of the top ten vaulters in the world were American. With a bit of his tongue in his cheek, Coach Carnes drawled, "One of the reasons we've been so productive in the pole vault is because we've had the poles."

But of course we've also had the athletes to go with the equipment. There's Dave Roberts, for example, the world record holder at 18'8¼". Roberts was the U.S. gold hope in 1976 in Montreal, but in the rain and wind that blanketed Olympic Stadium, Roberts failed to reach the promise he had displayed in the trials. After the games, Dave enrolled in the University of Florida Medical School. He sat out 1978 and graduated a doctor in May 1979. Now he's back, and in 1979 he vaulted 17'6", his best vault in three years.

Track and Field magazine ranks Dan Ripley fifth in the world in the pole vault. The talented, intense twenty-six-year-old Californian has gone 18'5½" indoors. Ripley, like most world class athletes, has had his share of adversity. He was odds-on to make the 1976 Olympic team, but failed in the trials. He spent the next year teaching night classes while he nursed a pulled hamstring, one of the many injuries he's suffered. About the time the leg pull healed, Ripley and his wife were divorced, not exactly the right move for an athlete looking for that psychological edge. Ripley is concentrating now on making the trials and, as the old cliché puts it, taking things one vault at a time.

But the man who must be put on the top of the list of American pole vaulters is Mike Tully, out of UCLA. Not only has Tully been the best vaulter in the country over the past couple of years, but at 6'3", 195 pounds, the blonde twenty-three-year-old, who lives in Westwood, has been the recipient of TV acting offers from myriad casting directors. Those fellows go to sleep each night with dreams of guys like Tully dancing into their network television shows.

Mike, however, has put the propositions of the dream merchants on the back burner until he pockets the 1980 pole vault gold. His chances are better than most. He lives at eighteen feet. He also has the only world record that will probably never be a world record.

Last year in the Pacific Ten championship meet, Mike vaulted 18′8¾″, a quarter-inch past Roberts's world record. As he cleared the bar, Tully raised his hands in recognition of his feat. But the track officials, complying with the IAAF rule that states the bar must be measured both before and after the vault, accidentally knocked the bar down while measuring it, and when they reset the crossbar, it only measured 18′8″. Tully has since accepted the inevitable nonrecognition—probably because he doesn't really plan on letting 18′8½″or, for that matter, 18′8¾″ stand as a world record for very long. As he told Mal Florence of the *Los Angeles Times,* "If I keep on the same program I'm on now, I'll be jumping at record heights. I'm more or less training for nineteen feet."

Other American vaulters to watch for are Earl Bell, Bob Pullard, Steve Oravetz, and young Billy Olson of Abilene Christian.

In the Olympic history of the long jump only two other countries besides the U.S. have garnered the gold. At the 1980 games Arnie Robinson should be the favorite in the event. Ranked number one in the world in 1978, he is experienced, durable, consistent—and the 1976 Olympic champion.

The U.S. is loaded with talent in the long jump. There is James Lofton out of Stanford. Lofton has gone twenty-seven feet and must be considered a threat. Coach Carnes has very positive feelings about Larry Myricks, who made the 1976 squad and then broke a bone in the games. Other prospective long jumpers include Bob Calhoun, Tommy Haynes, Carl Williams, Randy Williams, and an amazingly versatile athlete, LaMonte King.

In the 1979 Pacific Coast Athletic Association championships, King had a day of performances as impressive in their scope as in their excellence. He won the 100 meters, the 200 meters, and the long jump, and anchored the winning 400- and 1600-meter relay teams. The twenty-year-old Sunrise, Arizona, high school product, who comes from a family of seven, could probably make the Olympic team in at least one of the sprints, but it's the long jump gold medal he's after.

The 1980 Olympic high jump competition will be conducted

without the entertaining presence of Dwight Stones. The flamboyant, outspoken athlete was, unfortunately, suspended by the AAU for his participation in the TV "Superstars" competition. Stones's disqualification leaves Franklin Jacobs of Fairleigh Dickinson College in New Jersey as the prime U.S. contender in the event. Despite Jacobs's prowess, it is unlikely he will be able to outjump world record holder Vladimir Yaschenko of the Soviet Union.

Jacobs became a high jumper after the track coach at his high school, Bill Shipp, saw him reverse dunk a basketball in a playground game. So what, you say, is there a basketballer around these days who can't stuff? Well, not many. But Jacobs isn't a basketball player. And besides he's only 5'8" tall.

Shipp pulled the high school senior over to the track and set up the crossbar at 5'9". It was the first time Jacobs had ever attempted to high jump, but he cleared the height. He was seventeen years old. In the five years since then Franklin has continued to raise the bar. He has cleared 7'7¼" indoors, almost two feet over his head. He won the 1979 AAU at 7'5", though he had to take the crown on fewer misses. Young Benn Fields of Seton Hall gave him all the competition he wanted. Another youthful prospect is Gail Olson.

In the triple jump the U.S. lacks the depth of the Soviet Union, although three men have what U.S. coaches feel are realistic chances for the gold medal. They are James Butts, Ron Livers, and Willie Banks. In the 1979 AAUs, Livers and Banks both jumped over fifty-seven feet, the first time two Americans have cleared the distance in the same meet. Livers copped the win. In 1978 Butts was ranked number two in the world by *Track and Field* magazine.

It has been tremendously satisfying for Coach Carnes to watch the development of world class triple jumpers in this country. The last American to win a gold medal in the event was Myer Prinstein in 1904, and up until a few years ago a competitive American triple jumper was a rarity. Since then, U.S. high schools and universities have added the event to their competitions, and that action has been richly rewarded.

For some reason the throwing events in this country have always attracted unusual and outspoken athletes—the real "characters" of track and field. The Olympic prospects this year are no exception, nor are they unknowns—or, for that matter, youngsters. The discus competition this past year has been particularly enjoyable to watch, and I'd have to say the primary reason is Al Oerter.

By 1968 Al Oerter had already established himself as one of the most remarkable men ever to compete in the Olympics. That year in Mexico City he threw the discus 212'6½" to set his third Olympic record and capture his fourth Olympic gold medal. As anyone who follows sports can recognize, that in itself was an almost inconceivable accomplishment. It is not unusual for athletes who compete professionally in such sports as baseball, football, basketball, or golf to begin their careers in their late teens and continue on into their thirties; the habit of playing regularly, the presence of trainers and teammates, and the monetary incentive help to keep players active for a long time. But the discus is a solitary discipline, an exercise in total self-motivation in which the athlete must gear himself up without the support of an organization and then, on a given day once every four years, call upon his talent and deliver to his full potential. Al Oerter won his first gold in Melbourne at the age of nineteen with a throw of 184' 10½". He was in Rome in 1960, and he won again. He came out of a Tokyo hospital in 1964, the cartilage ripped from his ribs, tape covering his side, to take his third gold medal. Four years later in Mexico City, he won another. And then he retired, the owner of four gold medals. But in 1977, like an oversized Don Quixote, the forty-year-old computer engineer emerged from middle-aged comfort and began throwing again. There was talk of its all being done for publicity, but anyone who knows Al Oerter, or realizes what it takes to get in world class shape, knows that publicity had nothing to do with it.

In 1979 Al threw the discus 217'10" and followed that a few months later with a 219'10" toss. At forty-two he surpassed his 1968 gold medal throw by seven feet. Al has never thrown the shot better, and as Mac Wilkins, the U.S. record holder, says, "I think it's great; I mean, how many people are going to throw it farther than that?" Not many.

Mac is a good friend and I believe, along with the U.S. coaches, that he is the best discus thrower in this country. Mac began 1979 by taking apart his proven technique, making some changes, and putting it back together again. In the 1979 Pepsi Invitational, it was obvious that Wilkins's new technique was a long way from being polished. He was consistently in the 205' and 210' range with all his throws, a good 20 feet off his former world record distance of 232'6". His friend and competitor, Wolfgang Schmidt of East Germany, toppled that record last year with a 233'5" throw of his own.

Mac is a prime example of what I said earlier about the throwers being the outspoken eccentrics of the sport. At a 1979 luncheon for track and field writers, Mac looked to the future: "I'll have to throw five feet better than the fellows from the communist countries to win in Moscow. The Olympics will be the ultimate forum for the Soviet Union to present its system as the best. They'll do anything possible to be successful."

What did Mac mean by "anything possible"? He continued: "They might just put a microwave gun to the discus and shoot it down. It will be a science fiction nightmare. I know, I've been there." Mac sounds like he's putting the press on, and to a certain extent I'm sure that he is. But he is sincere in his belief that the Russians would resort to technology to be successful. Whether these H. G. Wells fantasies come true or not will probably be a moot point, because there would be no way of proving that such interference had actually occurred. Regardless, it figures that 6'4", 256-pound big Mac would be the one to stand up and make the accusations out loud.

Wilkins has returned to form recently, posting a 231'10" at the 1979 AAUs. Right behind him is Ken Stadel, who had a 227'3" in the same meet.

In the shot put Al Feuerbach is ranked second in the world and is still our best hope, though he is a substantial distance behind Udo Beyer of East Germany. Dave Laut of UCLA has also been coming on lately. Laut is very strong and young and he could surprise a lot of people. His 1979 AAU toss of 69'3¼" was the sixth-best U.S. performance of all time. Colin Anderson is another potential Olympic contestant, as is former Texas highschool sensation Michael Carter.

As I mentioned earlier, the hammer throw is our weakest field event. According to Coach Carnes, "It's a shame, too, because we could sure win with all the talent we have, but it's just not an event that you develop stars in overnight." Emmet Berry of UTEP is our best bet, but his 230' range is 30 feet behind the West Germans and Russians.

In the javelin 6'3", 240-pound Bob Roggy out of Southern Illinois is, in the opinion of the coaches, a definite medal threat. Roggy has thrown the javelin for only five years. The kinesiology grad student has a 293' throw to his credit, somewhat short of the world record 310'4" set by Miklos Nemeth of Hungary in Montreal. In 1978 Roggy was rated sixth in the world. Other prospects include Bill Schmitt of the Tennessee Track Club, Rod Ewaliko, and Duncan Atwood.

The 1980 decathlon does not shape up as a great event for the U.S. athletes. The foreign competition, including Guido Kratschmer, the silver medalist who pushed me in Montreal, and Daley Thompson of Great Britain, looks very strong. Nevertheless, I believe that both Fred Dixon and Craig Brigham have the tools to make serious runs at the gold if they put it all together. Fred was ranked number one in the world in 1977, but a groin problem, a new child, and, I suppose, a loss of incentive made for an unimpressive and lightly competed 1978. When I spoke with him recently, though, he sounded very enthusiastic and his attitude seemed super. The question of his injury still remains; it has bothered him for a couple of years now, and that makes it tough to have a full recovery.

There is no doubt in my mind that Fred has more talent than I had. But I believe he needs to become a hungrier competitor, to want the decathlon victory so bad that he will stay on top of himself for the entire twenty hours (ten each day) of the competition. That's how I won in Montreal and set the world record. I did my homework; I was prepared; I knew myself, my capabilities, and what I had to do in each event to defeat my competitors.

Craig Brigham is also loaded with raw ability, and I am pleased with the aggressive attitude he has exhibited recently. One thing about Craig's training disturbs me, though; I think he has spent too much time with weight training and throwing the implements. In fact, I believe that's his biggest problem. He needs to concentrate more on running, not lifting, because the decathlon is primarily a running event. You should always count on the decathlon's coming down to the last event, the 1500 meters. Kratschmer and Thompson are both vulnerable there. Neither is a great 1500 man—I think they're both around 4:20–4:25. The guy who can go 4:10 can pick up sixty to seventy points in that event.

The athlete emerging as perhaps the most potent American decathlon threat in 1980 is 1979 AAU champ, Bob Coffman. Other American prospects are Mike Hill, Lee Palles, Roger George, and John Warkenton.

In the team relays, the U.S. teams are expected to win both the 4x100 and the 4x400. The men who make up those teams will come from the ranks of our Olympic sprinters.

Women first competed in track and field in the 1928 games in Amsterdam. Since then some of the most spectacular Olympic performances have been recorded by women. Babe Didrikson won gold medals in the javelin and hurdles and a silver in the high jump in 1932 in Los Angeles. Fanny Blankers-Koen of the Netherlands annihilated her competition in the 100 meters, the 200, and the hurdles at the 1948 London games. In 1960 Wilma Rudolph doubled in the 100 and 200 and anchored the U.S. relay team to a gold.

In the ancient Olympic games, women were not allowed even to attend, under penalty of death; in the 1980 Moscow games, they will compete in track and field, swimming, diving, archery, shooting, equestrian events, gymnastics, handball, rowing, canoeing, basketball, fencing, and field hockey. Women athletes have become an essential part of the spectacle; it is impossible to imagine the games continuing to thrive without their participation.

In Montreal in 1976 the U.S. women's track and field squad was victimized by an awesome team from East Germany. The athletes of the GDR won gold medals in nine of the fourteen events—a startling statistic for a country with only 17 million citizens. The U.S. women captured three medals, none of them gold.

These results were not simply a matter of luck. The East German athletes have excellent facilities and plenty of time for training. Their lives are, in effect, subsidized by the state, and they are free to concentrate their time and effort on upgrading their performances. As Branch Rickey, one-time owner of the Brooklyn Dodgers, put it, "Luck is the residue of design"; and that has never been more evident than in the overall design of the East German Democratic Republic to create an invincible track and field machine. Although I expect no less from the GDR athletes in 1980, I truly believe we can expect more from the women of the U.S. squad.

In the sprints we have some marvelous athletes. Evelyn Ashford of UCLA and Brenda Morehead and Chandra Cheeseborough of the Tennessee State "Tiger Belles" loom as the three likeliest candidates for Moscow berths. Ashford appears to be the best bet at this time. She is the fastest woman in the U.S. in the 100 meters, and her 10.97 semifinal effort in the 1979 AAUs makes her only the second woman in the world to travel the distance in under 11 seconds. At the AAU meet she also came back to win the finals in both the 100 and 200 meters. Her 22.07 in the 200 was the fastest ever posted by an American woman.

The 5'5", 115-pound Ashford arrived at UCLA as an un-polished but obviously talented runner. Under the influence of her coach, Pat Connolly, she has developed into the best woman sprinter in the country. Evelyn was married in 1978 and now supports herself by working in an athletic store in Westwood. Connolly has shielded her from the press and other distractions in what some observers have criticized as a Svengali-like manner. At Connolly's insistence, Evelyn does not grant interviews. In a move indicative of her determination, she dropped out of UCLA last year to concentrate on the 1980 games.

Chandra Cheeseborough and Brenda Morehead are also capable of winning medals in Moscow, especially Cheeseborough in the 200 meters.

Ashford occasionally runs the 400 meters, and rather quickly too, but Rosalyn Bryant and Pat Jackson of Prairie View appear to be the best U.S. hopes in that event. Other notables are Shari Howard, eighteen, a California high-schooler, Pam Jiles of Louisiana Southern, Arlise Emerson, and Jennie Gorham, a prep runner who recorded an impressive 53.58 after a foot injury.

The controversy over distance races for women continues, but as it stands now, the 1500 meters will be the longest event the women will run in Moscow. It is unfortunate that a lot of fine women distance runners will thus be excluded.

In the 1500 meters, a familiar name crops up, Francie Larrieu, the outspoken twenty-seven-year-old out of UCLA. Larrieu holds the fastest 1979 time, 4:06.6, which she posted in the AAU while besting the other two outstanding U.S. 1500 meter athletes, Jan Merrill, the current American record holder with a 4:02.6 clocked in Montreal in 1976, and Mary Decker. However, Decker, a senior at the University of Colorado, came back to defeat Larrieu in the 1979 Meet of Champions mile in June. Decker's 4:23.5 smashed Larrieu's American record by five seconds. It seems that Mary may be ready for bigger and better things in Russia.

In the 100-meter hurdles, Deby LaPlante of San Diego State is the front-runner. Currently the American record holder, LaPlante, who is coached by her husband, the track and field mentor at San Diego State, ran a 12.86 in the 1979 AAUs. But she had to use all her horsepower to turn back upset-minded, teen-age phenomenon Candy Young. Young is an eighteen-year-old sensation who comes from Beaver Falls, Pennsylvania, formerly in the limelight as the hometown of "Broadway Joe" Namath. LaPlante and Young are the only American women to have broken the 13-second barrier. Other prospects include Jane Frederick, Rhonda Brady, Brenda Calhoun, Linda Weekly, Mary Smith, and Stefanie Hightower.

In the high jump it appears that Louise Ritter of Texas Woman's University is the best in the country. She holds the American record of 6'3½". Pamela Girven of the University of Maryland is another excellent prospect, as is Pam Spencer of Cal. State–Northridge.

The U.S. squad has tremendous depth in the long jump. In a good field, the most highly regarded jumpers are Kathy McMillan of Tennessee State and Jodi Anderson.

Anderson is a fine all-around athlete who has put the shot forty feet and scored 4,475 points in the pentathlon. Jodi, twenty, believes she has a good shot at a world record in the long jump. In 1979 she stole a page from the European women's training program and turned to weight lifting. According to Jodi, the training change has definitely helped her to add distance.

McMillan was the silver medalist in Montreal and is an intense competitor. She bested Anderson in both the indoor and outdoor AAU championships.

An interesting story in the long jump is thirty-two-year-old Martha Watson, whose career, at least in terms of longevity, rivals Al Oerter's. Martha is a four-time Olympic long jumper who is not yet ready to give it all up. Though Martha has never won a medal in the games, she continues to jump— an example of someone who truly loves to compete. Although it's not easy for a woman in the U.S. to support herself and still find time to train, Martha has solved that problem, at least temporarily, by means of an arrangement with Caesar's Palace in Las Vegas. She works the noon to 8 P.M. shift dealing blackjack, which leaves the early morning for her workouts. Her employers have also agreed to give her the necessary time off for the trials and the games. Martha will certainly be a sentimental favorite in Moscow if she can come up with the right jump at the trials and put herself in the Olympics for the fifth time.

The women's throwing events, like the men's, seem to attract the most controversial athletes. Take the American record holder in the javelin, Kate Schmidt. Kate won $3,900 in the TV "Superstars" competition and fought the AAU for months to get them to allow her to keep it. She finally relinquished the prize money under the threat of expulsion, the fate bestowed upon high jumper Dwight Stones. Kate didn't compete in 1978 because of the uncertainty of her status, but she came back in the 1979 AAUs to best her opposition in the javelin by 20 feet. Schmidt is the only American woman in track and field to hold a world record—227'5".

Other Olympic hopefuls in the javelin are Cathy Sulinski of Cal. State–Hayward, Karin Smith, and Celeste Wilkinson.

The number one women's discus thrower in the U.S. is twenty-three-year-old Lorna Griffin. The 5'11", 170-pound American record holder from tiny Corvallis, Montana, is one of eight kids in an athletic family. Lorna originally started out with the shot put and didn't move to the discus until she went to college at Seattle Pacific. Lorna has already posted a 187'6" throw, and she figures to add some distance to that mark in Moscow. She credits Dr. Ken Foreman, the 1980 U.S. women's coach, with establishing a weight training program that has already produced excellent results for her. Lorna has publicly stated that she believes a 200-foot throw is within her capabilities. Former American record holder Lynne Winbigler of the Oregon Track Club and Rita Stalman Van Pedro of Arizona State also are promising prospects.

The finest American shot putter is Maren Seidler, and so dominant is she in her event in American competition that it is difficult to name another athlete who might test her. As of this writing, Maren has a very impressive 62'7¾" to her credit, and she is the only American woman to have reached the 60-foot mark. Other possible candidates include Ann Turbyne, who has a 54' toss, and Kathy Devine of Texas, who has gone 52'4½".

Jane Frederick holds the American record in the pentathlon with 4,704 points. Jane, like Kate Schmidt, had a squabble with the AAU about the $17,600 she won in the TV "Superstars" competition. Jane finally relented and returned the money, but as an amateur athlete in the U.S. used to living on chicken bones, she surrendered the sizable sum about as cheerfully as a hound dog gives up a T-bone steak. Now that the AAU is satisfied, the likable and attractive Frederick is back in the Olympic picture and promises to be our most potent threat.

As mentioned above, Jodi Anderson has registered some impressive numbers in the pentathlon, as has twenty-year-old Patsy Walker of UCLA. Patsy went to UCLA because she called up on the phone one day and asked if the school would be interested in giving her a scholarship. As it turned out, the girl who was supposed to get the last track scholarship had decided on another school, and Patsy wound up a Bruin. Walker has since made the coaches very happy they took her call. She has jumped 5'11" in the high jump, 19'10½" in the long jump, and thrown the shot 41'5". Patsy broke her foot in a 1979 meet, but she figures to be in top shape in time for the Olympics.

Swimming and Diving

"Our men's swimming team for Moscow will be every bit as strong as it was in Montreal. Now before the 1976 games I did say that we had a chance to win every event. And we almost did—we lost the 200 breaststroke, but we captured twelve out of thirteen possible events. I wouldn't say at this point that we have a chance to win every event in Moscow, but our team will be every bit as good as the one in Montreal."

That's the way George Haines, head coach of the U.S. Olympic swim team sizes up the American men's squad's chances in 1980. Haines is a relaxed native of Indiana who will be coaching in his sixth Olympic games. However, this is the first year the USOC has designated one man as the head coach, and the committee couldn't have made a more logical choice. As Haines puts it, "Aw, they needed an old guy that could keep everyone under control."

Before moving to the Foxcatchers' Club in Pennsylvania, Haines had been turning out champions on the West Coast. His previous four years had been at UCLA, and before that he coached twenty-four years at the Santa Clara Swim Club, where he was the mentor of Spitz and Schollander. The

USOC's decision to name one man as head coach seems to have been a good one. It was tried for the first time at the 1978 World Championship meet. At that meet the U.S. women reclaimed the honor of being the finest in the world. With the battering they had taken at the hands of the East Germans in 1976 fresh in their minds, the U.S. women swam to nine gold medals, while the East Germans won only one.

"In Montreal we had our best women's team in history; the East Germans just had better athletes," said Haines. "Also, our girls were a little intimidated. But this bunch is bulldog tough. If Tracy Caulkins and Cynthia Woodhead and the girl from Louisville, Mary Meagher, stay healthy, we're going to win our share of races.

"I'm not saying the East German women won't be strong," continued the U.S. coach, "and we expect the Russians to be very tough in their own backyard—men and women—but our girls will be ready and competitive."

Let's take a close look at how Coach Haines sizes up the men's and women's squads at this point.

In the men's 100-meter freestyle, 6'5" Jim Montgomery, the 1976 gold medalist, is one of the best U.S. prospects. Montgomery is doing his training in Texas with SMU coach George McMillan. Young Rowdy Gaines of Florida Aquatics and his teammate David McCagg are both potential gold medal threats. McCagg did have a bout with mononucleosis in late 1978, but he's been looking very solid lately. Haines sees a potential sweep in this event.

In the 200-meter freestyle, the same three swimmers should be there, plus Brian Goodell, should he choose to swim the event. The current Olympic record of 1:50.29, set in Montreal, is held by Bruce Furniss. Since Montreal, however, Bruce's life has undergone drastic change. In November 1978 doctors diagnosed in the twenty-two-year-old swimmer an hereditary form of arthritis, called ankylosis spondylitis, which attacks the spinal column. Essentially, the disease fuses the bones of the spine from the skull to the sacroiliac, although in most cases the chances are good that the disease will undergo remission rather than completely fuse the spine. While the disease was discovered in 1978, the doctors believe that Bruce had been afflicted by it as early as 1972 or 1973 — which means, of course, that he won the gold medal with an arthritic spine. As part of the treatment Furniss does stretching exercises in the middle of the night, takes hot baths — which relieve some of the pain — and swims. His doctors consider his swimming a form of therapy, but to Bruce it is a part of his training for the 1980 games. He is the first to admit that his chances for making the team are slim, but it is obvious that he believes he can still do it. If he does, it may just be a greater accomplishment than his gold medal.

In the 400 freestyle, Haines admits, "The Russian, Salnikov, is good; in fact, for the past four years he's trained at Mission Viejo. But Goodell had his best season last year. Brian is dedicated, he's the defending Olympic champion, and I like his chances in the 400. The same goes for the 1500. No one is better than he is in the distances.

"In the 100-meter backstroke I like Bob Jackson. Right now he's the best in the world in the event. If Clay Britt of Arizona stays healthy, he's also a real threat. There's been a lot said about Jesse Vassallo, but I'm not sure Jesse has the raw speed in the shorter event.

"Now in the 200-meter backstroke, I figure Jesse to be under two minutes. I don't think anyone will be able to stay with him. Also if Peter Rocca, the silver medalist in both the 100 and 200 in Montreal, continues to swim well, he'll be up there."

In the 200 backstroke in the 1979 Pan Am Games, Rocca posted a 2:00.98 to Vassallo's 2:02.07.

Coach Haines acknowledges that at this point Gerald Moerken of West Germany is the best in the world in the 100-meter breaststroke. "But we have some excellent young swimmers like Steve Lundquist of Jonesboro, Georgia, who became the first swimmer to break the two-minute barrier in the 200-yard breaststroke in the 1979 national AAU championships." The nineteen-year-old Lundquist is an easygoing, talkative athlete who has been swimming since he was eight. He won both the 100 and the 200 breaststroke in the 1979 Pan Am Games.

Along with Lundquist, there's Nick Nevid, and the old man

of the event, the 1976 100 meters gold medalist John Hencken. In Haines's opinion, "If John trains seriously, and those other younger fellows don't stay down under a minute, Hencken will give them fits."

Hencken graduated from Stanford and now works as an engineer with an electronics firm. He recently turned twenty-six, which in competitive swimming is the age for a retirement speech and gold watch. John is hoping to become the first swimmer to win gold medals in three consecutive Olympics. He has a reasonable chance.

In the butterfly, Joe Bottom, the silver medalist in Montreal, recorded some very fast times with very little training in 1979. Bottom, who works for IBM, decided in 1978 to give up swimming. But after he swam well in international meets in France and Holland, he decided to take one more shot at the Olympics. Craig Beardsley and Bob Placak are also excellent butterfly prospects. Beardsley won the gold medal in the 200 butterfly in the 1979 Pan Am Games with a 2:00.49 clocking, second fastest time in the world in 1979, and Placak took the 100 meters.

In both the 200 and 400 individual medleys, nineteen-year-old Vassallo of the Mission Viejo Nadadores will have to be reckoned with. Haines believes that Jesse is undoubtedly the finest 400 individual medley man in the world. And according to Mark Schubert, Vassallo's coach, his speed is getting better and better in the 200, which would indicate he's a top threat there also. The 5'8", 150-pound athlete was born in Ponce, Puerto Rico, and at one time tried to compete for his native country. However, the Puerto Rican Olympic Committee ruled that he would have to train for one year in Puerto Rico. Jesse felt that his swimming would suffer from the lack of competition and top-notch coaching, so he stayed with Schubert in California. The committee has since reversed itself on the ruling, but Jesse will compete for the U.S. in 1980.

The U.S., with so much strength in the individual events, will be favored in both men's relay events.

Turning to the women's squad, Coach Haines is equally optimistic. "You know," he said, "I don't think we've ever had two more dedicated girls than Tracy Caulkins and Cynthia

Woodhead. And neither one of them, or, for that matter, any of our girls, is the slightest bit intimidated by the East Germans."

Woodhead and Caulkins, along with fifteen-year-old Mary T. Meagher, Jill Sterkel, and Linda Jezek should spearhead a women's team that is out to reassert itself as the best in the world. Judging by the results of the 1978 World Championships and the 1979 Pan Am Games, they are on target.

Coach Haines doesn't discount the abilities of the East German women, even though they were almost swept in Berlin. But he does think that the German coaches are holding on to their older girls a little bit too long. At the World Championships it was his opinion that Barbara Krause didn't look nearly as strong or as dedicated as she had in previous years.

Haines believes that Cynthia ("Sippy") Woodhead could compete in, and conceivably win, the 100, 200, and 400 freestyle events, although he acknowledges that Tracey Wickham of Australia is an outstanding competitor in the longer freestyle distances. Woodhead, sixteen, a sophomore at Riverside Poly High, is an immensely talented swimmer; she set the world record in the 200 freestyle at the World Championships and won five gold medals in the 1979 Pan Am Games. Haines assumes that Sippy will swim in the 100, 200, and 400 meters.

Another youngster who figures to be a threat in the 200, 400, and 800 freestyles is seventeen-year-old Kim Linehan of Sarasota, Florida. The 5'1", 104-pound swimmer, whose mother calls her "Carbo Queen" because she loves junk foods and carbohydrates, has had multiple wins in several meets. In the 1979 *Seventeen* Magazine tuneup for the Pan Am Games, Kim was named the most outstanding woman swimmer in the meet after winning three individual events.

The breaststroke is our weakest event, partially because it has always been primarily a European stroke. Where young swimmers in the U.S. generally begin with the freestyle, the breaststroke is the first stroke of most European kids. The U.S. breaststroke lineup depends upon whether or not Tracy Caulkins chooses to compete in the event. If she were to concentrate on either the 100 or 200 breaststroke, she would surely be one of the favorites. Other strong breast-strokers are Patty Spees and Tami Paumier.

In the backstroke, the coaches don't think anyone in the world can touch Linda Jezek. Haines was blunt: "She owns the people in the event." Linda is the holder of every U.S. backstroke record, as well as the world record in the 200 meters, and she hasn't lost a race since 1976. A junior at Stanford University, she's been training under the eye of former Olympic gold medalist Claudia Kolb.

Coach Haines has been working with fifteen-year-old Libby Kinkead at Foxcatchers, and he believes she could be outstanding in the backstroke. Other prospects include Kim Carlisle of Cincinnati and Diane Gerard.

In the butterfly, the Americans will have to look out for Andrea Pollack of East Germany, but Tracy Caulkins at one time held the world record in the 200 meters and Jill Sterkel, nineteen, from Hacienda Heights, California, the national champion in the 100 meters, is also tough. But the big news in the fly is young Mary Meagher, from the Lakeside Club in Louisville, who is turning the swimming world upside down. In the 1979 Pan Am Games, Meagher, who at fourteen was the youngest swimmer on the squad, trimmed one second off the world mark held by Caulkins and Pollack for the 200-meter butterfly when she swam to a 2:09.77 victory over her teammate Karinne Miller. "If you picked her, I just don't think you could go wrong," said Haines. "I think she's unbelievable. In the second 100 of the 200 fly she just mowed everyone down, and in the 100 she came from 2 yards back in the last 15 yards to win in 1:01.6." Joan Pennington, a sophomore at the University of Tennessee, is another terrific prospect.

In the demanding 200- and 400-meter individual medleys, one name floats to the surface. During the past three years Tracy Caulkins's name has been synonymous with women's swimming. In the 1978 World Championships she won five gold medals. She was the 1978 Sullivan Award winner as the nation's finest amateur athlete. Not bad for a sixteen-year-old kid with braces on her teeth. Tracy, out of Nashville,

Tennessee, holds world records in the 200 and 400 individual medleys, and as Coach Haines says, "Nobody, and I mean nobody, can touch Tracy in those two events."

The lanky 5′8″, 111-pound swimmer, who stalks her competitors like a great white, yet speaks in a soft drawl, puts in five to six hours a day training, beginning at 5:30 A.M. That goes on eleven months a year, six days a week—and at 13,000 yards a day, by the end of a year Tracy has covered the distance from New York to Denver.

Tracy will only have to swim a total of a mile or so in Moscow. But she's planning on making it the fastest mile of her spectacular career.

In the men's diving the U.S. will most likely be represented by two outstanding competitors. Phil Boggs is the defending Olympic gold medalist in the springboard and the winner of three straight world championships. The only person to have mounted a serious challenge to Boggs's supremacy is his teammate Greg Louganis, who upset Phil in the Pan Am Games. Now a law student at the University of Michigan, Boggs, twenty-eight, is a former U.S. Air Force captain. Phil believes that the most important aspect of diving is concentration—which is consistent with what most great athletes feel about their individual sports. Jack Nicklaus says the same about golf, Rod Carew of hitting, and Chris Evert Lloyd when she analyzes her tennis prowess.

The 5′5″, 130-pound Boggs expects to encounter stiff opposition in Moscow from Louganis, as well as from the Soviets and the East Germans. Jim Kennedy is another top American prospect.

Louganis, a twenty-year-old junior at the University of Miami who trains at Mission Viejo, almost pulled off the upset of the 1976 Olympic diving competition when he came within a half-twist of defeating the remarkable Klaus Dibiasi of Italy on the platform. Louganis captured the gold in the 1979 Pan Am Games and said afterward, "I'm pretty pleased with the way I dove today—I guess I'm favored on the platform in Moscow. But the Russians have a good diver also. He's two years older than me, but I think I've matured quite a bit as a diver since 1976."

She's twenty years old, 5'6½" (actually a little tall for a diver), 115 pounds, and she's the finest women's springboard diver in the world. Born in Anniston, Alabama, but living now in Mission Viejo and training under Ron O'Brien, Jenni Chandler is a pure delight to watch sail off of a diving board. However, after she won the gold medal in Montreal, it appeared her diving career might be over. With the last slicing splash into the Canadian pool, everything Jenni had worked for and dreamt of had been achieved. To the seventeen-year-old, the future suddenly took on a menacing air. What was left to accomplish? For a year Chandler struggled with the devils in her head, finding them more difficult to bury than her diving competition. But now, three years later, she is ready once again to compete and win in Moscow. The desire is back and so is her championship form.

In 1979 Jenni suffered a lower back injury while performing her airborne acrobatics off the 10-meter platform. Her coach, Ron O'Brien, believes his willowy brunette charge is capable of winning a medal in the Moscow platform competition, but she probably will not compete in it.

After her competitive diving career is over, Jenni would like to teach art to children. But her time these days is so consumed with training that her progress through UC-Irvine has been slow. It is not a matter for concern. When this Olympic champion puts her mind to something, nothing stands in her way.

Gymnastics

Kurt Thomas was nineteen years old when he finished twenty-first all-around in gymnastics competition in Montreal in 1976. His name was known only to the true devotees of the sport. He had no real reputation.

The brilliant Nikolai Andrianov of the USSR went to Montreal with a name familiar to sports enthusiasts all over the world. He departed Canada with his already sizable reputation greatly enhanced and an astonishing six medals— four gold, a silver, and a bronze—around his muscled neck. A mere two years later, in the 1978 World Games, Kurt

Thomas captured a gold medal in the floor exercises, defeating an impressive field that included Andrianov. It was the first time in forty-six years that an American gymnast had placed first in international competition. It had taken two years for the 5'5", 128-pound Terre Haute, Indiana, native to explode out of obscurity and into the world spotlight. His name and handsome face are now recognized by most sports fans, and, more importantly, by the judges and his fellow competitors. Andrianov candidly admits he expects Thomas to provide his stiffest competition in Moscow.

Kurt has since graduated from Indiana State University and accepted a graduate assistantship at Arizona State in Tempe. His gold in the World Games floor exercises is his most impressive win to date, yet he considers the side horse his strongest event. It was on the horse, after all, that he developed the routine which bears his name—the Thomas Flair. The flair involves a variation on the double leg circle; in the routine double leg circle, the gymnast begins in a straight position with hands grasping the pommels, then, lifting the arms alternately, swings the legs, pressed closely together, back and forth over the horse under the arms. In Kurt's variation, the legs are opened wide.

Gymnastics, like several other Olympic sports—diving and judo, for example—is judged subjectively. It has always been apparent to informed spectators that the judges in such competitions often award higher scores to performers whose names and reputations they know. In some ways the Olympic gymnastics judging reminds me of the story they used to tell about Ted Williams. Williams, one of the greatest hitters in baseball history, was noted for having a keen eye when it came to deciding what pitches to swing at. Consequently, the umpires called more balls and fewer strikes on him than on less renowned batters, figuring that if Ted Williams didn't swing at a pitch it must be a ball. Now that Kurt Thomas is considered a world class performer, the judges no doubt will subconsciously give him more latitude when they score his routines.

Other outstanding male gymnasts include Bart Conner of the University of Oklahoma, who finished an impressive ninth in the World Games and who has beaten Thomas on more than one occasion; Jim Hartung of Nebraska; and a college freshman from Omaha, Phil Cahoy.

Kathy Johnson, a junior at Louisiana's Centenary College, is presently one of the finest all-around woman gymnasts in the country. Experienced and confident, Kathy has performed superbly in world class competition for the past three years and is a legitimate contender for a medal in the 1980 individual all-around competition. Kathy captured our national championships (USGF) by besting high school sensation Donna Turnbow. She also finished eighth in the World Games—after a performance that many thought should have received higher marks. Her 9.9 floor exercise routine was certainly one of the finest in the Strasbourg competition.

Right behind Kathy at the World Games, in ninth place all-around, was Rhonda Schwandt, the 1978 U.S. vaulting champ, who points to Cathy Rigby as her initial inspiration. But the 4'11", sixteen-year-old from Los Alamitos, California, calls Elena Mukhina of the Soviet Union her favorite gymnast. In early '79 Rhonda suffered a knee injury and underwent an operation for torn cartilage. But by the World Championship trials in late June, she had recovered sufficiently to take second behind Leslie Pyfer who may be the best American prospect for an all around medal.

Johnson's and Schwandt's eighth- and ninth-place finishes in the individual all-around contributed significantly to the exceptional fifth-place overall showing of the U.S. women. But it was 5'1", 94-pound Marcia Frederick who wooed and won over the World Games' crowd and judges. Frederick accomplished what no other female American gymnast had ever done: she won a gold medal in international competition. Frederick scored her victory, overcoming in the process a bad ankle, the judges' prejudice in favor of the Eastern Europeans, and Nadia Comaneci. Earlier in the year Marcia had scored a perfect 10 on the uneven bars at the U.S. national championships. At the time, her electrifying performance was hailed as "the most technically correct routine ever done." She came to Strasbourg, France, with the burden of that 10 resting on her slim shoulders. But her 9.95 on the uneven bars stood up to all comers, and even the Soviet sportswriters informed their readers that she had "deservedly won with a routine approaching perfection."

Marcia began her training at age ten under the tutelage of YMCA coach Leo Leger. When Leger realized that Marcia had surpassed his knowledge with her skill, he encouraged her to find a new coach, one who could take her further. Muriel Grossfeld, an intense, thirty-eight-year-old, three-time Olympian was that person.

With Grossfeld now since 1977 as a student in the Muriel Grossfeld School of Gymnastics in Milford, Connecticut, Marcia has blossomed into one of the most scintillating gymnasts in the world. Frederick puts in six hours a day, five days a week, yet the amazingly mature sixteen-year-old has said recently, "This is my life. All I want is to go as far as I can." How far that is exactly has yet to be determined, but according to Marcia, one gold medal is not quite far enough.

Another American hopeful is Tracie Talavera, thirteen, of Eugene, Oregon, who will reach the mandatory Olympic age of fourteen in the 1980 Olympic calendar year.

Archery

Since archery was reintroduced into the Olympic games in 1972, athletes from the U.S. have won every single gold medal in the men's and women's divisions. It seems a bit ironic that in a time when gold medals are counted like notches on a gunfighter's belt, to be used by countries as indicators of a superior political system, the U.S. has not publicized the sport more.

The U.S. archers in Moscow should again be dominant. Darrell Pace of Cincinnati, 1976 gold medalist, is certain to return. The twenty-two-year-old is the current world record holder at 300–90 meters distances.

LuAnn Ryon, the 1976 gold medalist in the women's division, seems likely to return to defend her crown. However, the 1978 national champion from Riverside, California, failed to qualify for the 1979 Pan Am Games and the World Championships, finishing a disappointing fifth.

Richard McKinney, manager of a family-owned archery shop in Muncie, Indiana, was the 1977 world and national champion and is Pace's closest rival. He captured a gold medal in the '79 Pan Am Games. Another prominent contender, Rodney Baston of Bossier City, Louisiana, won two golds in the games.

Judy Adams, a student from Phoenix, was the 1978 champion of America and bested Ryon in the Pan Am trials. Lynette Johnson of Cypress, California, is the favorite for the 1980 games based on her Pan Am and NSF victories.

Other legitimate prospects are Rich Bednar of Safford, Ohio, and Carol Strasburg of Huntington Beach, California.

The 1980 U.S. Olympic coach is Dwight Nyquist, a professor at Shoreline Community College in Seattle, Washington.

Basketball

With a growing number of underclassmen declaring themselves "hardship cases" and the best of the college seniors turning professional as soon as they graduate, the range of choice among U.S. men's amateur basketballers has become rather restricted. It is a rare college graduate these days who will delay signing his name to a multimillion-dollar, no-cut contract so that he may dunk, dribble, and shoot his way to glory for Uncle Sam. This situation makes it difficult to predict before the Olympic trials which athletes will compete for the U.S. men's basketball team in 1980.

Coach Dave Gavitt of Providence will no doubt field an excellent squad, for there will be no shortage of athletes who wish to play ball for the U.S. But he and his staff will not have their pick of the very finest young basketball players in the country. By the time Moscow rolls around, half of the men who might have played on the team will be toiling in training camps for their new professional meal tickets.

And as the U.S. team gets younger and younger, the foreign squads get older and more experienced in international competition. For that reason, expert analysts like the former Marquette coach, outspoken Al McGuire, have predicted the U.S. team will enter the Moscow games as an underdog in the sport for the first time in Olympic history.

As Al says, "The Russians and Yugoslavs are experienced, and they know international basketball. There's a big difference between international basketball and what we play here in the States. It's like the difference between hardball and softball—they're completely different games. Also, remember the Soviets are going to be playing with a home-court advantage and that's going to make it a lot tougher for us to win."

For the selection process, Gavitt will invite sixty to seventy players to the trials, and then the selection committee, headed by the 1976 Olympic coach, Dean Smith, will help Gavitt make his final choices for the twelve-man squad. Gavitt expects the team to practice six or seven weeks after the trials, then play a series of exhibition games against teams of NBA rookies. After that, he plans a whirlwind, two-week tour against the top European teams, and then it's on to Moscow.

One athlete who figures to make the squad is 7'4" Ralph Sampson of the University of Virginia. The Harrisonburg, Virginia, native was one of the most highly sought-after prep roundballers ever. Two of Sampson's teammates at UVA, 6'5" Jeff Lamp and Lee Raker, also have excellent chances for making the team. The Atlantic Coast Conference was well represented on the 1976 squad, and before he brought home the gold, UNC coach and '76 head Olympic coach Dean Smith received some criticism for stacking the team with four players from his own college crew. The ACC has some excellent prospects for the 1980 squad, with Mike Gminski and Eugene Banks from Duke and Mike O'Koren and Al Wood from UNC all strong contenders for berths on the team.

Other potential Olympians include Mike Woodson, 6'5" forward from Indiana, a star on Bobby Knight's winning Pan Am squad; Darnell Valentine, the highly talented guard from the University of Kansas; Sam Clancy of Pittsburgh; John Duren of Georgetown; and Steve Stipanovich of Missouri.

The U.S. women's basketball team, coached by Sue Gunter of Stephen F. Austin, is the current FIBA world champion, and the team's chances for a medal in Moscow are excellent.

The Russians, the 1976 gold medalists, are just too big and too strong, aside from the fact that they'll be playing in front of rabid home-country fans—a significant factor in basketball.

The top U.S. prospects are as follows: the very highly acclaimed Nancy Lieberman, 5'10", out of Old Dominion; Carol "the Blaze" Blazejowski, 5'10", out of Montclair State; Lynette Woodard of Kansas, 6', the two-time Kodak All-American who led the nation in scoring in 1978–79 with a 31-point average and was second in rebounding with a 14.3; Ann Meyers out of UCLA, another two-time All-American and the sister of Dave Meyers of the Milwaukee Bucks; Jill Rankin; and Tara Heiss.

Boxing

Unlike a swimmer or a sprinter, it is almost impossible to judge a boxer's progress until he steps in the ring. There are no practice times or scores that can be assessed. Only when the referee holds aloft the winner's hand is a man's talent confirmed. The unusual physical and psychological demands of boxing make it impractical for a boxer to compete as often as a track and field athlete. Also, while a long jumper might lose two or three meets in a row, he may just as easily come back to triumph in his next outing. Ring losses weigh more heavily on the fighter's mind. One or two losing decisions, or, worse, a KO, and the fighter's confidence quickly begins to disintegrate. A fighter without confidence is impotent. For these reasons boxing is a difficult sport to handicap. The makeup of the U.S. Olympic team will be as much a matter of timing and luck as of skill. Superstitious boxing coaches must pray to the god of fisticuffs for a team to peak at the right time—for their boxers to hit the games physically ready and hungry for victory.

In 1976 the U.S. boxers went to Montreal as unknowns; they departed in glory, needing footmen to carry the booty—five golds, a silver, and a bronze. A duplication of that success is unlikely.

Jackie Beard, the eighteen-year-old national champion at 119 pounds from Jackson, Tennessee, appears to be a genuine contender for the bantamweight gold. In the 1979 Pam Am Games, he took the gold in that event. Another bantamweight prospect is eighteen-year-old Kenneth Baysmore of Washington, D.C., while a solid middleweight boxer is Tony Ayala, seventeen, of San Antonio, the younger brother of two professional prizefighters.

Only one 1976 Olympian is returning, Davey Armstrong at 132 pounds. The rest of the '76 team have turned professional, which points up another problem the U.S. encounters on the way to fielding a competitive squad—the lure of the rich professional purses. Armstrong will have to eliminate John Bumphus and Melvin Paul. Jackson, if he doesn't turn professional, probably will face Jeff Stoudemire, a twenty-two-year-old Cleveland product, or Roosevelt Green.

Both light-flyweight Richard Sandoval and light-heavyweight Tony tucker look promising for 1980. Sandoval took a bronze in Belgrade in the 1978 World Championships.

In the heavyweight division no one has shown the potential to stop Teofilo Stevenson of Cuba. Tony Tubbs of the Muhammed Ali Boxing Club in Santa Monica did survive three rounds without succumbing to the bazooka right hand of the Cuban. But Tubbs is slow and ponderous, and he is not a classy enough boxer to outpoint the 1976 Olympic champion. Perhaps Jimmy Clark of Philadelphia will remain an amateur through Moscow, but that does not seem likely.

An interesting story in the heavyweight division is Marvis Frazier, nineteen-year-old son of former world heavyweight champion and 1964 Olympic gold medalist, "Smokin' Joe" Frazier. Marvis is quick and dedicated and actually closer in style to his father's nemesis, Ali, than to his father. Where Joe, a hulk of a man, short, broad, and powerful, fought at 207-210, Marvis, at 6'1", 192, is a lithe, lanky athlete who looks more like a high jumper than a boxer.

Joe Frazier is watching his son's career closely. He kept him out of the 1979 Pan Am Games, presumably to avoid contact with Stevenson. Apparently Joe felt that his son was not ready for the fight and that the encounter would have been detrimental to Marvis's Olympic hopes. If Marvis, the national Golden Gloves champion, makes it to Moscow, he will have a chance to make Olympic history. There has never been a father-son gold medal combination in the same event in the games (Imre and Miklos Nemeth of Hungary took golds in different events; Imre, the father, in the hammer in 1948, Miklos in the javelin in Montreal).

Canoeing

Under the guidance of former Hungarian and U.S. Olympic team member, Andy Toro, the 1980 U.S. canoe and kayak squad hopes to take significant strides towards its goal of several Olympic medals.

In the 1978 World Championships, the East German paddlers won seven golds, and the Hungarians captured four. The finest U.S. performances were recorded by the women's single (K-1) and double (K-2) kayaks. In the K-1 Leslie Klein paddled to a very respectable ninth place, then, less than an hour later, teamed with Olympian Ann Turner to post a seventh-place finish in the K-2.

Klein and Turner, along with Turner's brother Brent, a 1976 Olympian, and two-time Olympian Angus Morrison, share a small house in Hadley, Massachusetts, which serves as the "unofficial" U.S. canoe and kayak training site for 1980. The Turners' father, Howard, is the Olympic team manager.

Coach Toro calls nineteen-year-old Jackie Scribner of Alexandria, Virginia, the most talented young paddler in the country. Scribner should make the Moscow traveling squad, and two other prospects, Linda Dragon and Theresa DiMarino, also have a good chance at it.

The men's kayak pairs team of former Olympians Steve Kelly and Brent Turner claimed seventh place in the 10,000 meters in the 1978 World Games. Kelly and Turner have won the National Championship the past three years, but they should expect tough competition at the trials from brothers Bruce and Greg Barton of Michigan. Three-time Olympian Andy Weigand of the U.S. Air Force is a favorite in the canoe singles, and Terry White looks strong in the kayak singles.

Cycling

American cyclists have not won a medal in the Olympics since the 1904 games in St. Louis. In fact, George Mount's surprising sixth-place finish in the 1976 individual road race was the closest an American has come to placing since the 1920s.

Although no one at this time would realistically pick the U.S. racers to displace the plethora of East Germans, Russians, Italians, and Danes on the victory stands, there have been signs recently that the American cyclists are closer to being competitive internationally.

In the 1979 Pan Am Games, the U.S. 100 km road time trial team of Wayne Stetina of Indianapolis, George Mount of Berkeley, Tom Sain of Bisbee, Arizona, and Tom Doughty of Hobart, Indiana, pedaled to a gold medal, defeating a highly acclaimed Cuban squad and a very respectable Canadian foursome. As Ernie Seubert, chairman of the U.S. Olympic Cycling Committee, said, "It wasn't even so much the win that was impressive as it was the fact the boys beat the Cubans by three minutes and forty-four seconds and the Canadians by eight minutes. This in a sport where you usually find a group of countries within one minute of each other."

Seubert believes the U.S. is becoming more competitive because "we have a lot more depth than ever before. Not just one or two good riders. Our pyramid of riders is getting broader at the bottom. And as they say, the more good riders you develop, the more 'better' riders you get."

Seubert attributes the U.S.'s failure to develop outstanding international racers to three factors: lack of money; the size of the country; and, finally, lack of facilities.

"We only have about twelve velodromes [tracks] in the U.S. and that can't help but retard the development of good track racers," said Seubert. "Also, the U.S. is so large that our best riders don't get to compete against each other as often as they should. It's just too expensive to get them together. The new Olympic training facility in Colorado Springs has helped out a lot, the USOC has been very supportive lately, and the hiring of Eddie Borysewicz as national coach has aided the program tremendously. I'm sure that as we do more and more for our riders, our efforts will be rewarded with better Olympic results."

Other prospective Olympic team members are Andy Weaver, Ian Jones, Dale Stetina (brother of Wayne), and Steve Wood in team road racing.

In the sprints, the Barczewski brothers, Leigh and Les, are very strong, as is Jerry Ash. Leonard Nitz and Dave Grylls are likely representatives in the 4,000 individual pursuit. And in the team pursuit, Danny Van Haute, Gus Pipenhagen, and Roger Young should join Nitz and Grylls.

Other candidates for the 1980 squad include Scott Andrews, Mark Gorski, Bob Cook, Mark Pringle, and John Howard.

Equestrian Events

In April 1979, at the Volvo-World Cup Equestrian Competition in Goteborg, Sweden, seven U.S. riders finished in the top sixteen places. Of the seven Americans, six were amateurs, while the majority of the European riders were professionals. The strong showing by the U.S. riders, especially Katie Monahan's second-place finish, portends an outstanding Olympic games for the U.S. equestrian team.

The most acclaimed U.S. rider in Moscow, by virtue of his back-to-back world championships in the three-day event, should be Bruce Davidson, whose latest victory in the grueling three-day was accomplished aboard a horse of truly undistinguished lineage, Might Tango. Davidson, a twenty-nine-year-old Pennsylvanian who spends his leisure time fox-hunting, is a partner in his family's construction business. His wife, Carol, is an international competitor in the three-day, and they have a daughter, two, and a son, Buck, who is four.

Davidson is not the only American threat in the three-day. The 1976 individual gold medal winner, Tad Coffin, will be back to defend his title, as will Mike Plumb, the silver medalist in Montreal. The depth of U.S. talent—Davidson, Plumb, and Coffin—makes the American squad the pre-games favorite.

In stadium jumping, Michael Matz, who took third in the Grand Prix in the 1979 World Show Jumping competition in Aachen, West Germany, aboard Jet Run, should do very well. Others expected to place in the jumping are Katie Monahan, Dennis Murphy, and Conrad Homfield.

The Olympic dressage has always been the domain of the Austrians, West Germans, and Swiss. The U.S. has never been particularly strong in the event, one of the main reasons being the lack of top-caliber dressage horses in this country. In an effort to improve the quality of the horses, the U.S. team has imported foreign trainers like Mille Van Briggam from the Netherlands to work with both horses and riders. Moscow may be too soon to expect significant improvement in that event, but the general prospects for the U.S. in equestrian competition are excellent.

Fencing

It is unlikely that the U.S. fencers will take home any medals in the 1980 games. However, if there is one thing that's certain in sports, it is that nothing is certain. And there is always the chance that during one ordinary day of competition, an Olympic athlete might turn in an extraordinary performance.

In the fencing competition, the one area in which the U.S. may have a chance to place is the saber, where Peter Westbrook has demonstrated world class form. In the men's foil, Michael Marx, twenty-two, from Eugene, Oregon, is expected to compete, and other prospects include John Nonna, Ed Donofrio, and Greg Massialas.

It appears that young Timothy Glass, a Notre Dame graduate training in Houston, is currently the finest American épée fencer. He will probably join seasoned veterans Paul Pesthy, Edward Bozek, and Charles Shelley to represent the U.S. in Moscow.

Serious saber competitors besides Westbrook are Tom Losonczy, who recently graduated from the junior ranks, Phillip Reilly, and Edgar House.

Possibly the most exciting U.S. fencer is a young woman who at fourteen was voted the best potential fencer in the junior world championships (under twenty). Now eighteen, Jana Angelakis has fulfilled that promise. In the 1979 nationals in Colorado Springs, Jana excelled, taking first-place honors in the foil. Other women who figure to be strong in the foil are Gay D'Asaro, twenty-six, a graduate student at San Jose State, Nikki Franke, Ann Russell, and Debbie Waples.

Field Hockey, Handball, and Judo

Women's field hockey will be included in the Olympics for the first time in Moscow in 1980, and the U.S. squad has a very good chance to qualify for one of the six international berths.

The women of the American squad are an interesting and talented lot. Among the members is Nancy White, twenty-one, the daughter of Supreme Court justice Byron "Whizzer" White. Nancy is a human biology and economics major at Stanford University. Another accomplished young woman is the captain of the current squad, Julie Staver, twenty-six, a magna cum laude graduate of the University of Pennsylvania who is now a second-year veterinary student. Other team members are Karen Shelton, Charlen Morett, Anita Miller, Susan Marcellus, Beth Beglin, Gwen Cheeseman, Sheryl Johnson, and Onnie Killefer.

The U.S. men's field hockey squad has won only one medal in Olympic competition—a bronze in 1932. It appears unlikely that the U.S. men's team will qualify for a spot in the Moscow tournament.

Also somewhat dubious are the chances of the U.S. handball team. If the Americans do make it to the 1980 games, they will probably be led by two-time Olympian Rick Abrahamson and Tom Schneeberger.

Judo is one of several Olympic sports (others are rowing, canoeing, fencing, the modern pentathlon, handball, and cycling) that are treated like unwanted orphans in the U.S. For that reason, this country rarely fields a judo squad of bona fide Olympic contenders.

In 1980 America has five prospects, each of whom has a reasonable chance of winning a bronze medal. Four of the hopefuls are Californians: Tommy Martin of Stockton and Leo White of Monterey in the 189-pound-and-under category; Brett Barron of San Mateo, the current AAU titlist and 1978 Pan Am champion in the 172-pound (78 kg) class; Keith Nakasone of San Jose, the defending AAU champion in the 132-pound division; and James Martin of Wheeling, Illinois, in the 143-pound class.

There will be eight classifications in the 1980 competition, two more than in Montreal. The 1980 U.S. coach is Paul Maruyama.

Modern Pentathlon

U. S. athletes have made excellent progress in recent years in the modern pentathlon. Up until 1966, the only modern pentathlon training facility in the U.S. was located at Fort Sam Houston in San Antonio, and, logically, all of the competitors in the event came from the military. But in 1966 John DuPont, the senior vice-president of the U.S. Pentathlon Association and a member of the distinguished family that put chemistry into our lives, established a training facility on his Pennsylvania estate. Located on the 800 acres of grounds are a 50-meter Olympic swimming pool, 25-meter indoor shooting range, 100 horses, and many riding and running trails. All four of the men who competed in the 1978 World Championships trained on DuPont's estate.

Historically, the fencing and shooting segments have been the downfall of the American pentathletes, while the running and swimming events have been their forte. In 1976, Olympian Bob Nieman of the U.S. set a world record in the 300-meter swimming competition (3:13.6), but still finished twenty-sixth overall.

The most promising U.S. pentathlete for 1980 is John Fitz-gerald, who finished an impressive fifth in Montreal. Other potential contenders are Nieman, Michael Burley, and Neil Glenesk, who finished third in the 1978 World Modern Pentathlon Championships in Jönköping, Sweden, where the U.S. team finished fourth overall.

Rowing

From 1920 through 1956 the American coxed eights men's rowing teams won every gold medal. In 1960 the West German squad triumphed, but the U.S. men came back to defeat the Germans in 1964 in Tokyo. This was the last time the U.S. men won a gold medal in the sport, and the chances of their winning a medal in 1980 are again very slim. However, the U.S. women would appear to have several prospects with chances of winning medals. Among them are 1976 bronze medal winner, Carol Brown of Seattle and Joan Lind of Long Beach, 1976 silver medalist in the demanding single sculls.

Other likely members of the women's squad are Nancy Storrs and Hollis Hatton of Philadelphia, Cosema Crawford of Washington, D.C., Lisa Hanson of La Selva Beach, California, Anne Warner of Lexington, Maine, Elizabeth Hill, Anne Marden, Valerie Barber, Janet Harville, Susan Tuttle, and Anita de Frantz.

The U.S. men's quadruple sculls has a legitimate shot at a bronze if all the members stay healthy. The four potential rowers are all Harvard graduates; Al Shealy, Christopher Wood, Greg Stone, and Chris Allsop. Stone is also a potential Olympic single sculler, while Allsop and Wood could go in the double sculls.

America's best hopes in the coxed pairs event are two brothers, Fred and Mark Borchelt. Mark, twenty-eight, is a congressional administrative aide who is married and has three children. Fred, twenty-four, is single and works for the U.S. Patent Office. They row out of the Potomac Boat Club. Although the two brothers have been serious competitors for over eleven years, it wasn't until 1975 that they teamed up. Considering their relatively short period of time together in the pairs, their progress—sixth in the 1978 World Championships—has been exceptional. Fred, 6'5", 195 pounds, went to Montreal as a member of the U.S. coxed fours. The 6'3", 195-pound older Borchelt, Mark, was an alternate in the pairs. The determined siblings believe that an Olympic medal is within their abilities. And to that end they have worked three to four hours a day for the past four and a half years.

Shooting

Lanny Bassham, the 1976 gold medalist in the small-bore rifle three positions competition, will surely be the 1980 pre-games favorite in the small-bore rifle event. Bassham, thirty-three, is the reigning world champion at 50 meters and has been a member of every U.S. competition team for the last nine years.

Margaret Murdoch, the silver medalist in Montreal, should also be returning in the three-position small-bore (.22 caliber) rifle. In the English match, look for Murdoch, Tom Whitaker, and Bassham to fight it out, along with Lones Wigger, who won gold medals in Tokyo in 1964 and Munich in 1972.

Named as one of the top ten shooters of all time by the *International Shooting Sport* magazine, Lones Wigger, forty-two, has been a powerhouse in international shooting events for the last fifteen years, and in the 1979 Pan Am Games, he took four golds, two in individual and two in team events.

Dan Carlisle, a twenty-four-year-old manager of a gun club, is a double threat in the shotgun competition. He is a former Pan Am Games champion in the clay pigeon, as well as a member of the U.S. team which won the gold in the 1975 World Skeet Shooting Championships. In 1978 Dan won the clay pigeon championship and placed second in the skeet shooting competition.

Bill Clemmons, twenty-seven, a sergeant in the U.S. Army marksmanship unit holds the world record in the skeet competition with 199 points. Other skeet competitors are Matt Dryke and Jeff Sizemore.

William McMillan, fifty, is a member of the San Diego Sheriff's Department and is a likely U.S. prospect in the rapid-fire pistol competition. He has been a member of six Olympic squads and won the gold in Rome in 1960. Challenging him for one of the two berths will be Darius Young and Mel Makin.

Soccer

The U.S. soccer team's hopes for a 1980 Olympic berth were dashed by the foot of a young Mexican "pro footballer" on a dusty night in Giants Stadium. In the second game of a home-and-home qualifying series, the Mexican national squad goose-egged the Americans 2–0, after kicking a 4–0 shutout in the first game in Mexico City.

Walt Chyzowych, the fiery U.S. national soccer coach, was not pleased about the outcome, and he protested what he called "the rampant use of professional players by Mexico." But Chyzowych is also aggravated by the lack of support given amateur soccer in the States.

"We should drop the sport from our Olympic program if we're not going to build a world class team," he said after the elimination at the hands of Mexico. Once again, U.S. soccer fans will be without a "home team" to pull for in the Olympics.

Volleyball

At this point it seems unlikely that the U.S. men's volleyball team will qualify for the Moscow games. It is not unusual for the U.S. squad to have to sit out the games—the last time the U.S. men competed was in Mexico City in 1968. However, in hopes of fielding a competitive squad, the volleyball federation has had the men's team playing and training together in Dayton, Ohio, since 1977.

The most publicized, and possibly the finest, male player in the country is Paul Sunderland, a twenty-seven-year-old, 6'5" ex-basketball player from Loyola University in New Orleans. Sunderland is the only active U.S. player who is world class at the net. The four-year veteran of the national team lives in Malibu, California.

While the men's team may have its difficulties qualifying for the 1980 games, the U.S. women's squad is a cofavorite for the gold medal. According to the U.S. coach, former Israeli National Team coach, Arie Selinger, the women are in excellent shape to finish first in the B pool in Moscow. The B pool will consist of Korea, Japan, the U.S., and Bulgaria or Poland.

At the North American-Central American Championships, the women defeated Mexico, the Bahamas, Canada, the Dominican Republic, and Guatemala to qualify for an Olympic berth.

The present U.S. women's squad has trained and lived together in Colorado Springs since 1975. Selinger describes the team this way: "By definition we have our 'cannons,' the big hitters. They are Flo Hyman, Laurie Flachmeier, and Patty Dowdell. Then there are the 'machine guns,' our quick hitters, Rita Crockett, Debbie Landreth, Sue Woodstra, and Terry McCormack. Next would come our setters, what I call the 'triggers,' Debbi Green, Laurel Brassy. Our defensemen are Landreth, Janet Baier, and Terry Place, and our front-line blockers are Julie Bollersten and Caroline Becker."

Both Pat Dowdell of Houston and Flo Hyman of Inglewood, California, are considered to be among the twelve best volleyball players in the world. Dowdell, twenty-five, was named the MVP at the 1978 World Championships, as well as the MVP at the 1978 North American Championships. The 6'1" chemistry major at the University of Houston has been on a leave of absence from school and will return to her studies after the games.

Flo Hyman is considered by many to be the finest spiker in women's volleyball. The 6'5", twenty-five-year-old native of California also attended the University of Houston, where she majored in mathematics.

Water Polo

The U.S. water polo team failed to qualify for the 1976

Montreal games, but the chances of that's happening again in 1980 are slim. The U.S. team had a surprisingly strong second-place finish in the FINA World Cup and now looms as a potential gold medal threat in Moscow. The thirty-member national team is made up primarily of Californians, since that is the only state in which the sport is played at the high school level.

Weightlifting

Once upon a time, so the story goes, in the late 1940s and continuing through the 1950s, the strongest men in the world lived in the United States. And every four years those American strongmen assembled at the Olympics to see who among them could snatch and jerk the most tonnage above his head. During the Olympic games of the forties and fifties, the U.S. weightlifters staked their claim as the "world's strongest" and exposed all pretenders to their crowns. But now it has been twenty years since a weightlifting gold medal has left the Olympics in the powerful hands of a U.S. athlete. And, unfortunately, it appears that we will not see an American champion at the Moscow games.

In 1976, twenty-three-year-old Lee James of Gulfport, Mississippi, won a silver medal (the only U.S. medal) in the 90 kg (198 pound) class. James has since had knee surgery, however, and is not likely to travel to Russia.

Mark Cameron went to Montreal as one of the favorites in his division. Competing in the heavyweight category—110 kg (242 pounds)—Cameron finished a disappointing fifth and later suffered the embarrassment of being disqualified for using illegal steroids—common, if not prudent, practice among weightlifters. After the games the University of Maryland graduate student in biomechanics, found himself depressed and unmotivated. It appeared that he would not return to world class form. But Cameron decided to rededicate himself to reaching his full potential, a potential U.S. coaches believe is greater than any other lifter's in this country.

In 1977 Mark dropped down in weight class to 100 kg, but

after finishing fourth in the World Championships, he returned to the 242-pound class, finding the heavier weight more exciting to compete in. Cameron has not yet demonstrated the same dedication he showed prior to Montreal, but he took three golds in the 1979 Pan Am Games, and if he chooses to go after it full force, the Olympic gold medal is not beyond his reach.

Another U.S. Olympic hopeful is Phil Sanderson in the 132-pound featherweight division. The thirty-two-year-old parole officer from Billings, Montana, was second in the 1978 AAUs.

In the 220-pound category, a new division for the 1980 games, Kurt Setterburg of Masury, Ohio, deserves consideration, along with Guy Carlton of LaPlace, Illinois. Carlton twenty-six, took a respectable ninth in the world in 1978 and second in the 1979 Pan Am Games.

In the super-heavyweight category, 242-plus, Tom Stock may challenge the great Alexeiev, although not very seriously. And a newcomer to the scene is Steve Cameron, a former track star who has shown excellent progress.

Wrestling

National wrestling coach Stan Dzedzic believes the U.S. will again field a very powerful free-style wrestling squad for 1980. In Montreal U.S. wrestlers won six medals in the ten free-style weight classes. The highest finisher in Greco-Roman was Brad Rheingans, who took a fourth. He will again be the top Greco-Roman wrestler from this country.

You can expect the Peterson brothers, John and Ben, to be back on the mats in Moscow. The two brothers from Wisconsin have both earned Olympic gold and silver medals. John will face his stiffest competition at the trials in the nation's finest collegiate wrestler, Mark Lieberman, a graduate of perennial college wrestling power, Lehigh University.

Lieberman is a two-time NCAA champion in the 177-pound class, and the Pennsylvania native has not lost a college match since March 1977. In fact, Lieberman's only recent losses—two of them, the last in April 1978—came at the hands of Peterson. Lieberman acknowledges the defeats and admits they were one-sided, but he is not discouraged.

The son of a well-to-do advertising executive and the younger brother of another NCAA champion, Mike, Mark has a reputation as a grinder, a guy who will bulldog his way to a win. The question is: Can he bulldog his way past John Peterson?

Dzedzic also likes the chances of 1978 World Cup champion, Leroy Kemp in the 84 kg (163-pound) class and Jimmy Jackson, two-time World Cup champion in the unlimited class. The 350-pound Jackson has defeated the 1976 Olympic gold medalist, Soslan Andiev of the USSR, twice and took the gold at the 1979 Pan Am games with four consecutive pins.

In the 105-pound free-style, Bill Rosado looks promising, as do Jimmy Hines and Mike Farina in the 114-pound division. In the 57 kg (125 pounds), Randy Lewis should be the U.S. representative, and in the 62 kg (136 pounds), Jim Humphrey, 1979 NCAA champ, appears ready. Chuck Yagla is a threat in the 68 kg, as is 1976 silver medalist Russ Hellickson in the heavyweight class.

Yachting

The U.S. figures to send a very strong yachting squad to Tallinn in 1980. The American sailors are formidable in all six classes—Finn, Flying Dutchman, Star (which replaces Tempest), Soling, Tornado, and 470.

Obviously, the squad will be more potent in some classes than in others. According to Sam Merrick, director of the U.S. Olympic Yachting Committee: "We're particularly strong in the Soling and Star classes, but I feel we have legitimate gold medal threats in just about all six classes. Historically the U.S. has never been extremely deep in the Finn class, but this year there are five or six solid contenders. For instance, I don't think the Europeans can believe how good John Bertrand is. He did very well in Europe this past summer. He won Kiel Week in Germany, and yet Bertrand was defeated four out of four times by Carl Buchan in the 1979 Olympic Regatta."

Buchan is a twenty-three-year-old University of Washington student. The other top Finn prospects are Cam Lewis and Stewart Neff.

In the 470 class, David Ullman and Tom Linsky of Newport Beach have an excellent chance for a medal in the two-man 470. They are the current world champions in the class. Other potential pairs are Steve Benjamin and Neal Fowler, Skip Whyte and Fran Charles, Steve Cucchiaro and Charlotte Lewis, and David Kellogg and David Pritchard.

In the Tornado class—the two-man catamaran—Richard Lowfek and Jay Glaser of Costa Mesa had an excellent summer. Keith Notary and David Gamlin are another fine Tornado crew, as are Randy Smythe and John Hill.

In the Flying Dutchman, the largest centerboard boat, Augie Diaz and Mark Reynolds won Kiel Week in Germany. Reynolds skippered in the Pan Am Games, and his crew won six straight races and the gold medal. Steve Taylor and David Penfield, as well as the Bowers brothers, Gordy and Mark, are other excellent crews.

The Star and Soling classes shape up as the two strongest events for the American sailors. The Star is the smaller of the two keel boats. Tom Blackaller and Olympian Ed Bennett definitely are gold medal prospects there, and Willie Buchan and Doug Knight are another strong crew.

The crew of Robbie Haines, Ed Trevelyan, and Rod Davis should be the pre-Olympic favorites in the Soling class. In July 1979 they won the World Championship, in April they captured Kiel Week, and before that the U.S. Championship. Another fine Soling crew includes Buddy Melges, John Porter, and John Gluek.

The Druzhba Multi-Purpose Gym is known locally as the Crab. Competition in eleven sports, including gymnastics, fencing, wrestling, and volleyball, will take place here.

(Dmitri Kessel/Life Picture Service)

(Dmitri Kessel/Life Picture Service)

(Dmitri Kessel/Life Picture Service)

Bicycle racing will take place in the new Velodrome at Krylatskoye. The roof of this structure spans the entire 6,000-seat arena without a single support and, when viewed from the air, resembles a huge butterfly with its wings spread.

The Olympic Sports Complex, still under construction here, is certainly the architectural showpiece of the summer games. It is the most modern-looking structure in Moscow and the largest indoor arena in Europe.

The boxing, basketball, and swimming events are scheduled to be held in the sports complex. The inner walls can be moved and rearranged in just minutes to divide the building into two separate facilities.

Lenin Stadium has the "feel" of Yankee Stadium—there is a lot of history in its concrete walls. The opening and closing ceremonies, as well as the soccer finals and track and field events, will be held here.

The interior of the old Lenin Stadium is being renovated for the games. By 1980 the stadium will feature a new boosted lighting plant and new matrix scoreboards equipped to show instant replays and other television programs.

View of the harbor at Tallinn in the Estonian Soviet Socialist Republic, on the Gulf of Finland. The Olympic yachting competition will take place here.

(United Press International Photo)

Construction is underway in Tallinn on a building to accommodate the athletes and on a twenty-seven–story hotel to accommodate fans. (United Press International Photo)

(Dmitri Kessel/Life Picture Service)

The new 260-acre Olympic village will house 12,700 people in eighteen one-block-long buildings, each sixteen stories high.

The most luxurious hotel in Moscow is the Cosmos which was designed by French architects and will provide accommodations for 3,500 tourists.

New international traffic signs are on display in Moscow pointing the way to the various Olympic events.

Chief engineer of the Olympic village, V. Kostenko (right), presents his model for the Olympic village to Lord Michael Killanin, president of the International Olympic Committee (far left, with hand at chin), and other Olympic officials. (United Press International Photo)

The thirty-two–story Moscow Tourist House hostel contains enough rooms for 1,300 guests.

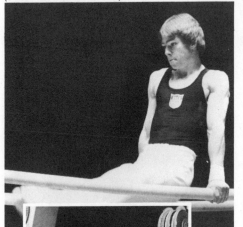

In the 1978 World Games Kurt Thomas captured a gold medal in the floor games and is now a serious contender for the gold in Moscow.

Mike Tully has been the best pole vaulter in the U.S. the past few years.

Heavyweight weightlifter Mark Cameron took three golds in the 1979 Pan Am Games.

The great weightlifter in the super-heavyweight category, Vasily Alexeiev, should capture the Olympic gold once again.

At the recent World Games, Marcia Frederick accomplished what no other female American gymnast had ever done: she won a gold medal in international competition.

Gymnast Leslie Pyfer is perhaps the best American prospect for an all-around medal.

The Russian women's basketball team, 1976 gold medalists, are just too big and strong for the other contending teams. Here 7'2" Iuliyaka Semenova holds the ball above the reach of U.S.A.'s Ann Meyers.

In the bantamweight competition of the 1979 Pan Am Games, Jackie Beard of the U.S. (right) was victorious over Mexican Dan Zaragoza (left). Beard is a genuine contender for the bantamweight gold in Montreal.

Two strong U.S. swimmers who hope to reassert the women's team as the best in the world are: Cynthia Woodhead in the freestyle (below), and Tracy Caulkins in the breaststroke, butterfly, freestyle, and individual medley (bottom).

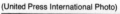

Jenni Chandler, 1976 gold-medal winner in springboard diving, hopes to return for another gold in Moscow.

Displaying his form in the Montreal springboard diving competition, Phil Boggs is the defending Olympic gold medalist and the winner of three straight world championships.

Richard Sandoval (right), shown here defeating Chile's Eduardo Burgos (left) at the Pan Am Games, looks promising in the Olympic light-flyweight competition.

With his victory in the 1979 Pan Am Games, diver Greg Louganis poses the most serious threat to the supremacy of teammate Phil Boggs.

Mary Meagher, U.S. butterfly hopeful.

In Montreal, Cuba's Teofilo Stevenson (left) easily defeated John Tate (right) of the U.S. in the heavyweight division. Stevenson should have little problem gaining his second gold medal in Moscow.

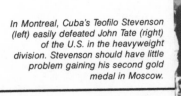

Named as one of the top ten shooters of all time by the *International Shooting Sport* magazine, Lones Wigger took four gold medals in the 1979 Pan Am Games. (National Rifle Association)

James Robinson (right) finishes ahead of Olympic champion Alberto Juantorena (left) in the 1979 Pan Am 800 meters. Robinson's laid-back style of running has earned him the dubious nickname of "Silky Sullivan."

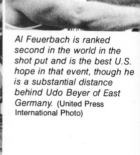

Al Feuerbach is ranked second in the world in the shot put and is the best U.S. hope in that event, though he is a substantial distance behind Udo Beyer of East Germany. (United Press International Photo)

Steve Scott hopes to add his name to the prestigious list of runners who have earned gold medals in the 1500-meter run.

Don Paige is one of the fastest 800- and 1500-meter runners in the world. In the 1979 NCAA competition he won both events in the same day. (United Press International Photo)

Olympic Events and Forecasts

Archery

The oldest sporting tournament in Great Britain is an archery contest—the Ancient Scorton Silver Arrow in Yorkshire. But in the days before champion archers won blue ribbons for their prowess, archery was a means of putting food on the table and putting enemy soldiers into graveyards. Archaeological surveys indicate that archery has over ten thousand years of history behind it. Buried in the rock and soil of every continent are stone arrowheads and sticks in the shape of bows. The Egyptians, Turks, Mongols, English, Japanese, and American Indians all used bows and arrows to conduct warfare. Through the years, most of England's monarchs issued edicts which made archery practice compulsory for their subjects. Ultimately, of course, bows and arrows gave way to firearms as weapons of war.

It is the shape of the drawn bow, the arc, that gives the sport its name. The design of the bow itself has undergone many modifications over the years, with such variations as the crossbow, the arbalest, and the Asiatic bow each adapted to suit specific tactical purposes. In modern times, the demands of tournament shooting have shaped the bow used by sportsmen.

The ancient hunting and target bows were a far cry from the sophisticated machinery that today's Olympic competitors operate. The ancient bows of North Africa, France, and Switzerland were usually made of yew, an elastic wood from an evergreen tree of Europe and Asia. The bows used by the archers in Moscow will be made of laminated wood and fiberglass, with built-in stabilizers to minimize the vibrations. They will have calibrated bow sights and the strings will be made of nylon. The accuracy the modern archer achieves with these instruments is phenomenal.

Archery was first introduced into the modern Olympic games in 1900 in Paris. It remained on the program through 1908, was dropped after London, and was reintroduced in Antwerp in 1920. However, that year the competitors all came from Belgium because several other countries boycotted the event. It seems that one of the competitions was "popinjay shooting," a contest in which the archers aimed at artificial birds sitting on a mast. For some reason, a number of countries objected to its inclusion. This was not the last time that a boycott would affect the Olympics.

It took fifty-two years for archery to again become an official Olympic sport. In Munich in 1972, John Williams and Doreen Wilbur of the U.S. won the gold medals over their Polish and Swedish rivals, and Williams set a new world record in the process, scoring a remarkable 1268 points out of a possible 1440.

In Montreal, four years later, the U.S. once again took both golds. Darrell Pace of Reading, Ohio, captured first place in the men's competition, and LuAnn Ryon of Riverside, California, copped the top prize for the women.

Rules

The international governing body of archery is the Fédération Internationale de Tir à l'Arc (FITA). The Moscow competition will comprise a double FITA round, shot over four days—30 July to 2 August 1980. An FITA round consists of a total of 144 arrows, with 36 arrows shot at each of four distances. The men shoot at 90 meters, 70 meters, 50 meters, and 30 meters. The women shoot at 70, 60, 50, and 30 meters.

The round archery target is made of straw ropes stretched together and covered with paper. There are five concentric rings on the face of the target: the center ring is gold, the next is red, then blue, black, and white. For the longer distances the target is 122 cm (50 inches) in diameter. It is 80 cm wide for the shorter distances. The bull's-eye is 9.6 inches in diameter and is worth ten points. The point value decreases as the distance from the center increases. Thus the red ring is worth eight points, the blue is worth six, black is worth four, and the white is worth two points.

Viewing Tips

Olympic archers must have incredible concentration, as well as the ability to control their bodies at the exact moment of arrow release. When drawing the bow, the contestant is pulling back the equivalent of forty-five to forty-eight pounds—and that weight must be held until the optimum time to release. Although medalists Williams and Pace are both very slender, their forearm, shoulder, wrist, and chest strength is considerable. Champion archers must develop those specific "archery muscles" if they are going to compete in international tourneys. They must also train diligently to build up their stamina and endurance. The archery competition can last for hours, and only a well-conditioned body can stand up to the strain. Darrell Pace's bow has a pull of forty-eight pounds, which launches his arrows at a rate of 200 feet per second.

Forecast: Moscow

MEN

1976 Champion: Darrell Pace, USA
1980 Favorites: Darrell Pace, USA; Richard McKinney, USA; Rod Baston, USA; Giancarlo Ferrari, Italy; Michinaga, Japan; Sante Spigarell, Italy

WOMEN

1976 Champion: LuAnn Ryon, USA
1980 Favorites: Ryon, USA; Judy Adams, USA; Lynette Johnson, USA; Zebinisa Rustamova, USSR; Valentina Kovpan, USSR

Athletics (Track and Field)

In the modern games as in the ancient, the track and field events form the core of the Olympic structure. In Athens in 1896 twelve of the forty-two events were track and field competitions, and although some have been discontinued and others added over the years, the public's enthusiasm for and interest in track and field grows with every Olympiad.

The 1980 games will feature twenty-three track and field events for men and fourteen for women. The competition will begin on Thursday, 24 July, five days after the opening ceremonies, and will continue until 1 August. All of the events, except for the 20 km walk, the 50 km walk, and the marathon, will take place in Central Lenin Stadium.

Track and field events may be broken down into three categories: running, jumping, and throwing. For the men, the running events are the 100-meter, the 200-meter, the 400-meter, the 800-meter, the 1500-meter, the 5,000-meter, and the 10,000-meter runs; the 3,000-meter steeplechase; the marathon; the 110-meter and 400-meter hurdles; the 4x100 and 4x400 relays; the 20 km walk; and the 50-km walk. Women runners will compete in 100-meter, 200-meter, 400-meter, 800-meter, and 1500-meter runs; 100-meter hurdles; and 4x100 and 4x400 relays.

The jumping events for men are the long jump, the triple jump, the high jump, and the pole vault; for women, the long jump and the high jump.

The throwing events for men are the discus, the hammer, the shot put, and the javelin; for women, the discus, the javelin, and the shot put.

The men compete in one combination event, the decathlon; the women also compete in one combination event, the pentathlon.

Rules

As in Montreal, the track and field events in Moscow will span eight days. For each of the twenty-one individual men's events and twelve individual women's events, each country may enter up to three competitors, all of whom must have equaled or bettered the Olympic standard as set by the IOC. In the team relay events, each country may enter six competitors, but only four may compete.

The rules for most of the track and field events are basically quite simple. In the running events, interference is outlawed and can result in disqualification. In the sprints, runners cannot leave the starting blocks before the gun sounds. Jumpers must take off behind the designated marks.

Shot putters, discus throwers, and hammer throwers may not release outside of the launching rings, while javelin contestants may not release over the starting line. In the pole vault, the pole must conform to IOC standards.

Recently a controversy has arisen concerning women's track. The dispute stems from the fact that there are no distance events over 1500 meters for women in the Olympics. With the increased popularity of jogging and with the number of female distance runners, including marathoners, on the rise, it is a valid issue. I suspect that by the 1984 Olympics in Los Angeles, the longer races will have been added to the women's program—as well they should be.

Viewing Tips

The more you know about an athlete and his specific event, the more enjoyable the viewing becomes. For instance, the 100 meters lasts only ten seconds. For the most part, anyone can appreciate the raw power and phenomenal speed of Harvey Glance or Houston McTear. But if you understand the importance of a perfect start, if you know to look for the push out of the blocks, then a new dimension is added to the dash. In events where technique and timing are critical, your appreciation of a performance is greater if you know why, for instance, one discus thrower generates more speed and power than another, or why one high jumper goes over the bar belly first and another back first.

Most sports fans focus on a particular sport which they follow religiously. They are likely to become very knowledgeable about that sport and thus enjoy it more; they are transformed from passive spectators into "armchair quarterbacks." Well, there's nothing wrong with becoming an armchair football player, especially if it makes the game more interesting. My goal is to provide enough information about the various Olympic events to turn some of those quarterbacks into "armchair decathletes and milers."

The Sprints—100 and 200 Meters

Most coaches will tell you that an athlete either has speed or doesn't have it. A great sprinter must be naturally fast, but he must also have good technique. Valery Borzov, the exceptional Soviet 100- and 200-meter man, has spent years of postgraduate work studying technique and its application in the sprints. Obviously his scientific pursuits have paid off. Valery won the 100 and 200 in 1972, and he finished third in the 100 in 1976.

In the sprints, look for a high knee kick. The higher the knee comes up, the more force it generates on the way down. Sprinting motions must always point straight ahead. Any sideways movement, like the arms swinging across the body or the toes pointing outward, causes the runner to lose speed.

According to most coaches the start is half the race—especially since the winning margin is rarely more than one meter. At the sound of the gun, the sprinter drives off the mark, pushing mainly with the front foot. He tries to maintain a low angle out of the blocks. Runners can no longer anticipate the gun and get a "rolling start" by leaving the blocks a split second before the gun actually fires, because the pistol and the starting blocks are now wired to a sensing device. The blocks have switches held open by the force of the runner's foot against them. If a sprinter moves before the shot, the electric device automatically detects it.

Jimmy Hines of the United States set the world record in the 100 meters in Mexico City when he went the distance in 9.9 seconds. That figures out to about twenty-eight miles per hour.

The techniques and theories that apply to the 100 meters are also valid in the 200. Consider that since 1896, seven runners have won gold medals in both the 100 and 200 in the same Olympic games. Four of those doubles were scored by Americans. The 200 is also a flat-out sprint. The strategy is simple—go as fast as you can. In Moscow the 200 will be run on a curve. Notice how the sprinters hug the inside of the lane on the curve so that they can save precious inches. A slight inward lean on the curve is also essential.

400 Meters

When Harry Hillman won the 400 meters at the 1904 games in 49.2 seconds, the 400 was considered a strategic race in which pace and position would affect the outcome. Lee Evans destroyed that notion, and his fellow competitors as well, when he ran a blistering 43.8 in the 400 meters in Mexico City in 1968.

In terms of what to look for in a 400-meter athlete, Alberto Juantorena is not a bad place to start. Tall, 6′2″, and powerful, 185 pounds, he has the two essential elements, a long stride and good foot speed. Endurance is no longer really crucial in the 400, but natural speed and stamina are required to sustain the swift pace over the entire distance. I've always said that to win the 400 you must be able to beat "the Bear"—the invisible animal that waits for you at the 300-meter mark and jumps all over your back. He's so heavy that you want to stop running so he'll leave you alone. But if you can ignore the Bear and keep on digging, then you have a chance of winning the race.

Athletes who run the 400 must make a few adjustments. For one thing, the knees are kept lower and the arms don't sway as much as in the shorter sprints. Also, as a viewer, look for the runner who seems to be moving with a relaxed stride. During the 400 some athletes actually allow the heel to touch the ground lightly before the toes push off so that they can ease the pressure on the calf.

The Middle Distances—800 and 1500

The 800 is run as two circuits of the 400-meter track. Although, the 800 is called a middle distance race, which would indicate that strategy is a factor, Juantorena changed the thinking in track circles when he ran the 800 at Montreal as though it were a quarter-mile. Incredible as it seems, Juantorena ran his first 800 only three months before the 1976 games. But what he lacked in technique he made up for in sheer natural speed and power.

In the 800, look for a runner with a long stride, but not so much of a stretch as to appear to be jumping. A great half-miler must be careful to avoid getting boxed in by runners beside and in front of him. Passing should be done quickly, and when the leaders least expect it. To determine whether a front-runner has enough strength left to actually win, see if he is able to hold off the first man who attempts to pass. If he can stay ahead at that point , then he probably will take the race.

The 1500 meters, or "metric mile" (it actually measures 4921 feet, 359 short of a mile), is considered by many to be the showpiece event of the track and field competition. Traditionally, the times of the milers are used by historians to measure track and field progress over the years. Mel Sheppard won the 1500 in London in 1908 in 4:03.4. John Walker took the gold in Montreal with a 3:39.17, which was five seconds off the world record set by Kip Keino in 1968. Walker's philosophy, however, was that his primary objective was to win. If he broke the record while doing so, well then all the better. Perhaps one of the reasons that John's time was not record-breaking was the absence of top-flight competition. Most of the African nations had boycotted the Montreal games, which left some of the great names out of the 1500. Hopefully, politics can be kept out of the Moscow games—though that is an unlikely prospect. I have a suggestion, however: I think we should take all of the politicians and make them run ten miles at the beginning of the games. Then they'll be so tired they won't be able to interfere and everyone will have more fun.

For the Moscow games, familiarize yourself with the different styles of the 1500-meter men. Know, for instance, who prefers to lead a race, who likes to come from off the pace, who has the strong finishing kick. It is useful to understand the significance of the split times—the clockings at the 400-meter mark, the halfway mark, the three-quarter mark. There is nothing in sports more exciting than the last 400 meters of the 1500. And the way the field is shaping up for Moscow, the last lap of the 1500 should be one of the great ones.

Long Distances—5,000 and 10,000 Meters

The 5,000-meter (slightly more than three miles) race is a beautiful event. Every element of running is involved in the contest. A great long distance runner must have endurance, which comes with training. He must also have the speed to stay out of trouble and the strong kick when he needs it. The distance man must be "heady," a thinker, with a feel for pace and a sixth sense that tells him when to make a move and when to conserve energy.

The strategies and training methods of the 5,000 apply equally to the 10,000 meters. Often the 5,000 winner will come back to double in the 10,000. But only if the endurance is there is the double victory possible. In 1972 and 1976, the amazing Lasse Viren of Finland won both the 5,000 and 10,000. And in 1976 he went on to run in the marathon, where he finished fifth.

The 3,000-Meter Steeplechase

The steeplechase is a 3,000-meter (almost two miles) event, seven times around the 400-meter track. A great steeplechaser must possess endurance and speed, but he must also be an excellent hurdler. The steeplechase contains twenty-eight, three-foot-high hurdles, seven of which are followed by water hazards. By paying close attention to the way a runner negotiates the hurdles, you can usually get a good idea of how tired or how strong he is at any point in the race.

In the steeplechase no penalty is assessed for stepping on the top of the hurdle. In Moscow you can expect somewhere around an 8:15 time.

Road Events—20-Km Walk, 50-Km Walk, and the Marathon

There are three road events: the 20-km walk, the 50-Km walk, and the 26-mile, 285-yard marathon. As with the steeplechase, the 5,000, and the 10,000, these events are offered only for the men.

Athletes in this country have virtually ignored the walk race as an Olympic event. However, considering the jogging explosion, I expect that within the next five years there will be some spillover from running to walk racing, and that many excellent walk race prospects will emerge in the U.S.

The rules of the walk race are very important because they

prohibit a contestant from making any move that would simulate a run. A walker must always have a portion of one foot in contact with the ground. During the first lap of the walk race, which takes place inside the stadium before the walkers move out onto the road, you will see the track officials squatting alongside the track, keenly watching for ground contact. While one foot touches the ground, the other leg must be completely straight for a split second. The heel touches the ground first and the toe is the last part to leave. You might assume that such strict rules would result in numerous disqualifications, but surprisingly, that's not the case. The walkers have perfected their motions to the point where they rarely break their rhythm.

The marathon took its name from the plains of Marathon, the site of a victory by the Greek army over a superior Persian force in 490 B.C. Pheidippides, the first marathon man, ran the entire distance from Marathon to Athens to announce the great victory, after which he dropped dead from exhaustion. Though no runner in the history of the games has actually died during a marathon, just about every other calamity imaginable has befallen the hundreds of competitors.

In terms of what type of athlete it takes to win the event, the marathon defies categorizing. Where sprinters are likely to be stocky and powerful and milers thin and lanky, runners of all shapes and sizes have won the marathon.

Obviously, stamina and endurance are the key factors in the race. However, a strong mental attitude and the ability to block out pain over an extended length of time are other essential attributes.

Almost every continent of the world has fostered a marathon champion. The wild terrain of Ethiopia, where barefooted runners train over thorny, rocky hills, has brought forth runners like the two-time Olympic gold-medalist Abebe Bikila, while the concrete jungles of Boston and New York, where runners train amidst mazes of skyscrapers, have produced superb marathoners like Bill Rodgers.

The marathon is one of the few events which you will actually be able to experience more fully by viewing it on television than by being there in person.

Hurdles

There are two hurdling events, the 110 and the 400 meters, for men and one event, the 100 meters, for women. The 110-meter hurdles for men has ten hurdles, each 3½ feet (1.08 meters) high, which are set ten yards apart. The 400 meters race also has ten hurdles, but they are 3 feet high and set thirty-five meters apart. The women race over eight hurdles, 2½ feet (1.6 meters) high.

Generally, the best hurdlers are tall and lanky, on the order of Greg Foster or Edwin Moses. While watching the actual races, look for hurdlers who seem to be either maintaining a constant speed or increasing their speed as they move towards, over, and beyond each hurdle. A great hurdler strives for a fluid motion that smoothly incorporates the jump into his stride.

For the 110 the hurdlers normally take eight steps to the first hurdle and three steps in between. In the proper hurdling form the lead leg is extended fully and straight ahead. The leg is parallel to the ground over the hurdle, but swings down immediately afterwards to maintain speed. The trail leg must be kicked into a position with the thigh and foot parallel to the hurdle on the way over. The lower the hurdler's profile, and the shorter the time in the air, the faster the overall time. The same procedure applies to women.

The 400-meter hurdles obviously requires stamina as well as speed; it is a grueling race. Unlike the 110, in which the hurdlers maintain the same number of steps between hurdles, in the 400 the competitors usually take more steps between the last hurdles because they are tiring. Unfortunately for the other hurdlers who competed in Montreal, the brilliant American 400 man, Edwin Moses, actually maintained the same number of steps throughout the race and simply destroyed his rivals.

Long Jump

Both men and women compete in the running long jump. A good broad jumper must generate sufficient runway speed for his takeoff. The runway usually measures between 100 and 140 feet. The higher the body on the takeoff, the better the jump. On the landing the body should be pitching forward with the knees flexed. It is essential that a long jumper not fall backwards on the landing, since the distance of the jump is measured from the takeoff board to the mark in the sand closest to it. Notice how most of the jumpers appear to be riding a bicycle in the air; it is a style that many feel adds distance to their efforts.

High Jump

Men and women also compete in the high jump. The first time that women were allowed to compete in the modern games was 1928 in Amsterdam. In those games a Canadian high jumper, Ethel Catherwood, went over the bar at 5'3". In a dual meet in 1978 between Italy and Poland, Sara Simeoni cleared 6'7". In fifty years the women have improved their record by almost a foot and a half.

Generally, tall athletes with long legs make the best high jumpers, but of course there are exceptions to every rule. Consider the U.S. hope for the gold in Moscow, Franklin Jacobs. Jacobs stands only 5'8", but in the Millrose Games in 1978 he went 7'7¼", almost two feet over his head. What Franklin lacks in height, he more than makes up for in leg spring.

There are several methods used by high jumpers these days. Jacobs prefers the "flop," a style developed by Dick Fosbury, who used it to win the gold medal in 1968. I also used the flop when I won the decathlon. I believe that it is the most natural way to jump. The head and shoulders are the first over the bar and the body just follows, rag-doll fashion. The only thing the jumper really has to concentrate on is getting the hips over the bar. After that, everything else is in good shape.

The other predominant method is the straddle, a variation of the "western roll." Here the jumper kicks the leg farthest from the bar as high as possible, and when that leg clears the bar, he rolls over it, face down.

Most high jumpers wear special shoes, with the sole of the shoe on the lead foot built up for leverage.

Triple Jump

In one form or another the triple jump has been a part of the Olympics almost from the seventh century B.C. In the Paris Olympics in 1900, Ray Ewry won the standing hop, step and jump with a jump of 34'8½". Through three Olympics Ewry won ten gold medals, more than any man in the history of the games. In the rarefied air of Mexico City, Viktor Saneyev of the USSR went 57'¾" in the triple jump.

Contestants in the triple jump must be careful to maintain control through each of the moves (hop, step, jump) so that their balance is intact for each maneuver.

Pole Vault

Through the years the pole vault has undergone some significant changes, particularly with respect to equipment. The most dramatic improvement came with the switch from bamboo to fiberglass in the construction of the poles. Since the introduction of the fiberglass pole with its graduated levels of flexibility, pole vaulters have soared to eighteen-foot heights. To get the most out of the new poles, new techniques, utilizing the exaggerated whipping action, had to be developed. The vaulters learned quickly that a higher grip on the pole increased the vaults by almost a foot and a half. The pole vault is the most difficult of the field events to master.

Notice how the vaulters seem almost to climb up the pole after they plant, then push themselves into a handstand, stomach to the bar; as their feet go over they push the pole away, raise their arms, and attempt to land feet first.

Shot Put

The men's shot weighs 16 lbs. (7.2 kg). The women's shot weighs 8 lbs., 13 oz. (4 kg). The shot putter may not touch the top of the wooden circle which surrounds the pit, or the ground outside the circle. However, he may touch the inside of the toeboard without fouling. The actual put must be made from above the shoulders.

Obviously, size and strength are essential in a shot putter.

But agility and quickness cannot be discounted. The object in the shot is to keep your weight low and have as much of the mass of your body behind the shot as you possibly can. You don't throw the shot, you push it. And you drive from the legs. Then you extend the throwing arm quickly with as much force as you can muster. The shot is held in the fingers and rests against the ridge at the base of your fingers.

Discus

The men's discus weighs 4 lbs., 6.5 oz. (2 kg). The women's weighs 1 kg. As with the shot, size is critical in the discus thrower. To excel in the discus requires even greater speed and coordination than in the shot put.

The discus thrower starts in the throwing circle with his back to the sector and the arm holding the discus extended straight out. He makes a full turn, then another half-turn at the exact moment of release.

In Athens, Bob Garrett tossed the discus 95'7½". In Montreal in the decathlon I threw it 164'1". Mac Wilkins won the gold with a heave of 222', though he had thrown it as far as 232'. Mac will be back in Moscow, and if the new technique he's been working on is perfected by then, you can look for a new Olympic record.

Javelin

Both men and women participate in the javelin, throwing the same relative spear. In the ancient games the javelin had a rubber thong attached to the handle which helped the athlete to catapult it. The rules for the javelin state that a contestant must run straight to the throwing line without turning before he makes his toss.

Notice that javelin throwers are generally tall and lanky and have long, sinewy arms. Strength is not as much of a factor in the javelin as it is in the other throwing events. In a way you don't really throw the javelin as much as pull it over your shoulder. You start the motion with your weight on your back foot and then you complete the transfer on your follow-through. It is advantageous to release the javelin at a 45-degree angle. Most of the throwers take their run at only three-quarter speed so that they can maintain good body control.

Hammer

Only the men compete in the hammer throw. The total weight of the hammer is sixteen pounds. It consists of a ball with a four-foot wire and handle attached to it. The hammer circle is seven feet in diameter.

In recent years the USSR athletes have dominated the event. In the hammer the contestants take two turns and then release the projectile in what looks like controlled frenzy.

In 1900 John Flanagan of the U.S. heaved the hammer 167′4″. In 1978 Karl-Hans Riehm of West Germany threw the hammer 263′6″.

Supposedly, the hammer originated in Ireland, where the young farm lads used to amuse themselves by seeing how far they could toss the heavy sledgehammers used in their work.

Combination Events—The Decathlon and the Pentathlon

The modern decathlon is actually a derivative of the ancient pentathlon. It consists of ten events that take place over two days. The first day's events are the 100 meters, the long jump, the shot put, the high jump, and the 400 meters. On the second day come the discus, the pole vault, the javelin, and, finally, the 1500 meters. They say that the decathlon is the truest test of athletic ability in the world. I don't know. I do know that it must certainly be one of the most demanding competitions in the world. There are other events, perhaps, which require an athlete to endure more pain, but there are none that require such precision and excellence over as long a period of time.

I have always said that the decathlon shows no mercy— that no one ever beats it, because just one mistake, one tiny error, and you can blow the whole thing. That is especially true in the Olympics. If you are a fraction of a second off your best time in the 100 meters, or if you sling the discus a half-foot short of what you know you're capable of, then it will kill you. There is always some place in the decathlon where you could have picked up an extra twenty-five points or so, and those points could have meant the difference between the gold and the silver. After a meet I used to dream about all of the times I could have picked up an extra twenty points and didn't. I'm glad I won the decathlon in Montreal; otherwise I might still be thinking of those extra points.

At 6'2" and 200 pounds, I was fortunate to be an excellent size for a decathlete. Through the years other Olympic champions have also had similar builds: Bill Toomey was 6'2", 190, and Avilov is 6'3" and 190. Having the proper build is very important since the decathlete must actually be a sprinter, a middle distance man, a weight thrower, and a jumper.

Balance is the key to a good overall performance. If you perform well enough in every event, you can actually win the decathlon without winning one individual event. In 1960 C.K. Yang of Formosa won seven of the ten decathlon events, but Rafer Johnson took the gold when he surpassed Yang by great margins in the throwing events.

Personally, I have always believed that a strong second day is an excellent tactical weapon. Since my opponents were constantly aware of my strength in the pole vault and the 1500, they knew that no matter where we stood after the first day, they were going to have to look over their shoulders on the second.

In watching the decathlon, see if you can determine how each athlete is handling the pressure. The mental strain of the event is intense, and the decathlete who can best cope with it will most likely maximize his performances.

The pentathlon is the combination event for women. The five events take place in this order: 100-meter hurdles, shot put, high jump, long jump, 200-meter run.

Relay Events

There are two team relay events, the 4x100 meters and the 4x400 meters. In the 4x100 each competitor runs 100 meters (one-quarter of the way around the track) and then passes the baton to his teammate. In the 4x400 each competitor runs one lap and then passes the baton.

The key to the relay events, besides sprint speed, is a smooth baton exchange. The first three members of the team must pass the baton within the designated twenty-yard zone. Watch to see that neither the incoming runner nor the outgoing runner slows down during the exchange; both should be traveling at the same speed when the pass is made. The exchange should be made right hand to left, or vice versa, to avoid a collision. The relays demand a lot of practice and perfect coordination between team members.

Forecast: Moscow

MEN
100 Meters
1976 Champion: Hasely Crawford, Trinidad
1980 Favorites: James Sanford, Clancy Edwards, Houston McTear, Harvey Glance, USA; Silvio Leonard, Cuba; Don Quarrie, Jamaica; Crawford, Trinidad; Pietro Mennea, Italy

200 Meters
1976 Champion: Don Quarrie, Jamaica
1980 Favorites: Clancy Edwards, Steve Williams, James Sanford, USA; Pietro Mennea, Italy; Quarrie, Jamaica; James Gilkes, Guyana

400 Meters
1976 Champion: Alberto Juantorena, Cuba
1980 Favorites: Juantorena, Cuba; Billy Mullins, Willie Smith, USA; Tony Dardin, USA

800 Meters
1976 Champion: Alberto Juantorena, Cuba
1980 Favorites: Juantorena, Cuba; Sebastian Coe, Great Britain; Steve Ovett, Great Britain; James Robinson, USA; Olaf Beyer, East Germany

1500 Meters
1976 Champion: John Walker, New Zealand
1980 Favorites: Walker, New Zealand; Coe, Ovett, Great

Britain; Eamonn Coghlan, Ireland; Steve Scott, USA; Thomas Wessinghage, West Germany

3,000-Meter Steeplechase
1976 Champion: Anders Garderud, Sweden
1980 Favorites: Henry Rono, Kenya; Bronislaw Malinowski, Poland; Patriz Iig, West Germany; Ismo Tuokonen, Finland

5,000 Meters
1976 Champion: Lasse Viren, Finland
1980 Favorites: Rono, Kenya; Marty Liquori, USA; Markus Ryffel, Switzerland; Venanzio Ortis, Italy

10,000 Meters
1976 Champion: Lasse Viren, Finland
1980 Favorites: Rono, Kenya; Martti Vaino, Finland; Brendan Foster, Great Britain; Ortis, Italy

Marathon
1976 Champion: Waldemar Cierpinski, East Germany
1980 Favorites: Bill Rodgers, Jeff Wells, USA; Leonid Moseyev, USSR; Toshiko Seko, Japan; Cierpinski, East Germany

20-km Walk
1976 Champion: Daniel Bautista, Mexico
1980 Favorites: Bautista, Mexico; Roland Wieser, East Germany; Pyotr Pochenchuk, USSR

50-km Walk
1976 Champion: (New Event)
1980 Favorites: Raul Gonzales, Mexico; Jorge Llopart, Spain; Venyamin Soldatyenko, USSR

110-meter Hurdles
1976 Champion: Guy Drut, France
1980 Favorites: Renaldo Nehemiah, Greg Foster, USA; Alejandro Casanas, Cuba; Thomas Munkelt, East Germany

400-meter Hurdles
1976 Champion: Edwin Moses, USA
1980 Favorites: Moses, James Walker, USA; Harald Schmid, West Germany

400-meter Relay
1976 Champion: USA
1980 Favorites: USA; USSR; Poland; East Germany

1600-meter Relay
1976 Champion: USA
1980 Favorites: USA; USSR; West Germany; East Germany; Kenya; Nigeria

High Jump
1976 Champion: Jacek Wszola, Poland
1980 Favorites: Vladimir Yaschenko, USSR; Rolf Beilschmidt, East Germany; Franklin Jacobs, USA; Greg Joy, Canada

Pole Vault
1976 Champion: Tad Slusarski, Poland
1980 Favorites: Mike Tully, USA; Vlad Trofimyenko, USSR; Antii Kalliomaki, Finland; Wladimir Kozakiewicz, Poland

Long Jump
1976 Champion: Arnie Robinson, USA
1980 Favorites: Robinson, James Lofton, Larry Myricks, USA; Nenad Stekic, Yugoslavia; Jacques Rousseau, France

Triple Jump
1976 Champion: Viktor Saneyev, USSR
1980 Favorites: Joao Oliveira, Brazil; Saneyev, USSR; James Butts, Ron Livers, Willie Banks, USA; Anatoly Piskulin, USSR

Shot Put
1976 Champion: Udo Beyer, East Germany

1980 Favorites: Beyer, East Germany; Al Feuerbach, Dave Laut, USA; Aleksander Barishnikov, USSR; Reiji Stahlberg, Finland

Discus

1976 Champion: Mac Wilkins, USA
1980 Favorites: Wilkins, USA; Wolfgang Schmidt, East Germany; Markku Tuokko, Finland; Imrich Bugar, Czechoslovakia

Hammer

1976 Champion: Yurity Syedekh, USSR
1980 Favorites: Syedekh, USSR; Karl Riehm, West Germany; Roland Steuk, East Germany; Boris Zaichik, USSR

Javelin

1976 Champion: Miklos Nemeth, Hungary
1980 Favorites: Michael Wessing, West Germany; Nikolay Grebnyev, USSR; Wolfgang Hanisch, East Germany; Bob Roggy, USA

Decathlon

1976 Champion: Bruce Jenner
1980 Favorites: Guido Kratschmer, West Germany; Aleks. Grebenyuk, USSR; Daley Thompson, Great Britain

WOMEN
100 Meters

1976 Champion: Annegret Richter, West Germany
1980 Favorites: Richter, West Germany; Marlies Gohr, East Germany; Evelyn Ashford, USA

200 Meters

1976 Champion: Barbel Eckert, East Germany
1980 Favorites: Marita Koch, Gohr, East Germany; Ashford, USA; Ludmila Krondrateva, USSR

400 Meters

1976 Champion: Irena Szewinska, Poland

1980 Favorites: Christine Brehmer, Koch, East Germany; Rosalyn Bryant, USA; Maria Kulchunova, USSR

800 Meters
1976 Champion: Tatyana Kazankina, USSR
1980 Favorites: Tatyana Providokhina, Nadezhda Mushta, USSR; Anita Weiss, East Germany

1500 Meters
1976 Champion: Tatyana Kazankina, USSR
1980 Favorites: Giana Romanova, USSR; Natalia Maracescu, Rumania; Kazankina, USSR; Francie Larrieu, Mary Decker, Jan Merrill, USA

100-meter Hurdles
1976 Champion: Johanna Schaller, East Germany
1980 Favorites: Schaller, East Germany; Grazyna Rabsztyn, Poland; Deby LaPlante, USA; Tatyana Anisimova, USSR

400-meter Relay
1976 Champion: East Germany
1980 Favorites: East Germany; USSR; West Germany; USA; Great Britain

1600-meter Relay
1976 Champion: East Germany
1980 Favorites: East Germany; USA; Poland; USSR

High Jump
1976 Champion: Rosemarie Ackerman, East Germany
1980 Favorites: Ackerman, East Germany; Sara Simeoni, Italy; Andrea Matay, Hungary

Long Jump
1976 Champion: Angela Voigt, East Germany
1980 Favorites: Voigt, East Germany; Vilma Bardauskiene, USSR; Jarmila Nygrynova, Czechoslovakia

Shot Put
1976 Champion: Ivanka Khristova, Bulgaria
1980 Favorites: Helena Fibingerova, Czechoslovakia; Ilona Slupianek, East Germany

Discus
1976 Champion: Evelin Schlaak, East Germany
1980 Favorites: Schlaak, East Germany; Faina Feleva, USSR

Javelin
1976 Champion: Ruth Fuchs, East Germany
1980 Favorites: Kate Schmidt, USA; Fuchs, East Germany; Nikanorova, USSR

Pentathlon
1976 Champion: Sigrun Siegl, East Germany
1980 Favorites: Jane Frederick, USA; Nad. Tkachenko, USSR; Diana Konihowski, Canada

Basketball

Occasionally, historical accounts read like fairy tales. The story of the invention of the game of basketball is one of those accounts. As a bedtime story it ranks somewhere between *Br'er Rabbit* and *The Little Engine That Could.*

One winter day in 1891 a thirty-year-old Canadian physical education instructor, who was teaching an exercise class at the Springfield, Massachusetts, YMCA, decided that it was too cold to take the kids outside into the yard to play. Bored with watching his students do their calisthenics, Dr. James Naismith sent the gymnasium's janitor off in search of two cardboard boxes. The janitor, unable to locate any boxes, returned instead with two peach baskets. The substitution turned out to be a fortunate one: had the janitor found what he was looking for, the NBA seasonal championship would be in boxball.

Naismith hung the baskets at opposite ends of the gym and told his students to put the soccer ball into them. Meanwhile the janitor had the unenviable task of climbing a ladder and retrieving the ball whenever one of the students happened to get lucky. Apparently he didn't have to work very hard, because the early basketball scores at the Y were usually 2 to 1, or 3 to 2.

Dr. Naismith put nine men on a side in the first game at the Y. A distinctive feature of the early game was the sideline scramble—when the ball went out of bounds, possession went to the first player who controlled it, a situation which, with eighteen players on the floor, frequently resulted in a mass free-for-all. After viewing some of the recent Olympic basketball games—the 1972 final in Munich, for example— some people would say that the sport hasn't changed much. But in fact, quite a few new rules have been adopted.

In 1894 Naismith changed the mass jump ball into a one-on-one (center versus center) jump ball. Each time a basket was scored a jump ball ensued. It wasn't until 1937 that the rule was dropped. After 1937 the center jump was used only at the beginning of the game, at the half, and if two players had possession of the ball simultaneously.

From a spectator's standpoint, basketball is basically a simple game. Certainly, that is one of the reasons for the phenomenal growth it has experienced in such a relatively short time. While many of the Olympic sports can trace their origins back to Java man, basketball is only ninety years old. One of the most interesting and touching episodes in the Olympic history of the sport took place in 1936 in Berlin. That year the seventy-four-year-old Dr. Naismith traveled to Germany to see his sport inducted into the program of the XI Olympiad. Unfortunately, the Olympic debut was something of a debacle, mainly because the tournament was played outside on clay courts. It rained throughout the last day and the finals between the U.S. and Canada looked more like a qualifying heat in the 100-meter butterfly than a basketball game. The U.S. won the mud-plagued affair, 19–8. It was the first in a long line of American victories.

In 1923 a uniform set of rules, essentially the same as those adhered to today, was adopted. Up until 1923 infractions like double-dribbling and traveling had awarded free throws to the opposing team instead of possession.

During the 1920s and 1930s basketball enjoyed most of its popularity in the Western Hemispher. Besides the U.S. and Canada, Mexico and Puerto Rico fielded excellent squads. When World War II erupted, American GI's were sent all over the globe. Along with their pinups of Betty Grable, they took their baseball mitts and rubber basketballs. By the time the war ended, the rest of the world had been exposed to the layup and the jump shot.

Though basketball was a part of an exhibition at the 1932 games in Los Angeles, it wasn't until four years later in Berlin that it officially became part of the program. It took twelve more years for the rest of the world to offer anything resembling a legitimate challenge to the American supremacy. In the 1948 games in London, the U.S. had one close call against Argentina before it captured the gold. That year four members of the University of Kentucky team, the NCAA champions, played on the Olympic team: Alex Groza, Wah Wah Jones, Ralph Beard, and Cliff Barker. Almost thirty years later, Dean Smith used some of the same strategy when he organized and coached the 1976 Olympic team. In Montreal, Smith used four players from his own University of North Carolina squad: Phil Ford, Mitch Kupchak, Tom La Guarde, and Walter Davis.

Since entering the Olympic competition in Helsinki in 1952, the Russians have provided most of the competition for the U.S. in the finals. But until their 1972 upset victory, that competition wasn't very stiff.

In 1956 Bill Russell and K.C. Jones of the University of San Francisco spearheaded a team which disposed of the Soviets 89–55. In the Rome games of 1960 the U.S. fielded a squad of awesome basketball talent. Many journalists still believe that it was one of the finest teams, pro or amateur, ever assembled. The 1960 lineup featured Jerry West and the "Big O," Oscar Robertson, at guard, with Terry Dischinger, Walt "the Bell" Bellamy, and Jerry Lucas up front. Also on the team were Darrell Imhoff, Jay Arnette, Adrian Smith, Bob Boozer, and Les Lane. The Russians finished a distant second in Italy.

From 1960 until 1972 the U.S. rolled to titles without much

perspiration. In 1968 a U.S. squad of relative unknowns, including Spencer Haywood, Mike Barrett, JoJo White, Charlie Scott, and Mike Silliman, went into the tourney as underdogs to the Yugoslavs. In the finals they trampled the Yugoslavians by fifteen points.

Then, in 1972, the American team of Tom Henderson, Doug Collins, Kevin Joyce, Tom Burleson, Dwight Jones, and Tom McMillen swept all of their preliminary games by huge point margins. The Russians, after sneaking past the Cubans, 67–61, were again the opponents in the finals. In the game for the gold the Soviets took the lead early and, surprisingly, kept it until the last moments of the contest. But with six seconds left Doug Collins picked up a loose ball at midcourt and drove for the basket. He missed the lay-up but was knocked down and fouled. With three seconds left he went to the line for his two free throws. He made both of them and the U.S. took the lead 50–49.

Alexander Belov then attempted to inbound the ball for the Russians. The clock was started. He could not find an open man and with one second left the Brazilian referee signalled a time out, believing that the protesting Russian officials had blocked the scorer's view. At this point William Jones of Great Britian, chairman of the FIBA rules committee, illegally rushed up to the official time keeper and signalled that the clock should be reset to three seconds because the Russians had called time out before Collins's second free throw. But before the clock could be reset play was resumed. With one second left the Soviets took a desperation shot that missed and the U.S. team mobbed the floor believing they had won.

But the U.S. celebration was short-lived. Jones demanded the clock be reset to three seconds (something he had no power to actually do). After several minutes of arguing the officials complied. Again the Russians threw a full court pass. This time huge Alexander Belov shook off Kevin Joyce and Jim Forbes, both of whom landed on the floor, and then sunk the layup as the buzzer sounded. Pandemonium broke out, this time Soviet-style. The U.S. team lodged a protest. The IOC spent all night and until 5:30 the next morning reaching a decision. But in the end the tainted USSR victory stood. The U.S. players voted to boycott the awards ceremony and they refused the silver medal.

The U.S. went to Montreal in the summer of 1976 anxious to prove that American basketball players were still the best in the world. Dean Smith, the successful coach of North Carolina, had put together a talented squad of young players. In the days before the games, the U.S. press harped on the relatively small size of the team (they averaged 6'6"). Smith's team-oriented philosophy, however, demonstrated that height was not a prerequisite to winning. Except for one close call against the Puerto Ricans, the U.S. rolled to the gold. The score in the final was Yugoslavia, 74, the U.S., 95. It was the seventy-seventh victory in seventy-eight Olympic games for the U.S., and the eighth gold medal.

In 1976, for the first time ever, women competed in the basketball competition. The match-up in the finals was a familiar one—U.S. versus USSR. This time the superior Soviet height and experience paid off, as the Russians took the gold. Bulgaria finished third.

Rules

The International Federation of Amateur Basketball (FIBA) is the governing body for Olympic basketball. The FIBA has set the number of teams that may qualify to play in Moscow at twelve for the men and six for the women. The men's teams will be divided into two groups of six each. The top four teams in each group move on in an elimination series. The women will play a straight round-robin tourney.

Olympic basketball is basically the same game that is played at the amateur level in the U.S. with a few exceptions. Under international rules the free throw lane is cone-shaped, twelve feet wide at the free throw line and sixteen feet wide at the baseline. The American lane measures twelve feet at both lines. In the Olympics a shot must be put up within thirty ssconds, and the clock is reset after a shot is taken. The shot clock prevents slowdown tactics. Another difference is that bonus free throws come after ten fouls instead of seven.

Viewing Tips

You should expect to see a rougher style of play in the Olympics. Fewer fouls are called for offenses like pushing off and moving picks. The rebounding can get very physical. It is usually a real meat market under the boards in the Olympic games. Strength and size are often substituted for skill in international play.

The European and Caribbean teams are older and much more experienced in international competition than the American teams. The foreign squads have played together for years, while the U.S. men play together only after the Olympic trials. The team play of the Russians and South Americans is immediately apparent; each player seems to know exactly what his teammates are thinking. For pure shooting and ball handling, however, the U.S. teams are still unequaled. Basketball anytime is a great sport to watch, but the Olympic version is especially thrilling.

Forecast: Moscow

MEN

1976 Champion: USA
1980 Favorites: USA; Russia; Yugoslavia

WOMEN

1976 Champion: USSR
1980 Favorites: USSR; USA; Bulgaria; Cuba

Boxing

In terms of popularity, boxing has made quite a comeback in recent years. It is difficult these days to turn on the television on a weekend afternoon and not find one of the three networks broadcasting a prizefight. In the 1940s and 1950s boxing developed a reputation as the "dirty kid on the block," as a sport that was inundated with shady underworld characters and fixed contests. Terms like "taking a fall" and "setup" were part of the vernacular of the ring. The suspect integrity of the sport turned the spectator off. However, in the mid-1960s the sport began to recover some of its lost appeal, and today it is not only a tremendous attraction professionally, but also one of the most popular events on the Olympic program.

It's no secret that much of the credit for the renewed interest in the sport goes to the 1960 light-heavyweight Olympic champion from Louisville, Kentucky, Muhammed Ali. When the scrawny, likable kid, then named Cassius Clay, beat Poland's Pietrzykowski in the Olympic finals in Rome, and then went on to take the world heavyweight crown from the "Big Bad Bear," Sonny Liston, a new era had arrived for pugilism.

Olympic boxing gave Ali his first real taste of fame, and it also helped launch the careers of such champions as Floyd Patterson, who fought in Helsinki as a middleweight, Joe Frazier, and George Foreman. In Montreal the Spinks brothers, Sugar Ray Leonard, and Howard Davis emerged as the latest in a line of tough U.S. ghetto kids who boxed their way to the gold at the Olympics.

Amateur boxing is now bigger than ever, and the quality has never been higher. The boxing events in Moscow will span twelve days; it takes that long to pare down the huge number of contestants.

In one form or another, boxing has been a part of the Olympic program since 688 B.C. In those days contestants wore abbreviated headguards and wrapped their fingers with leather straps. For the early Greeks, it was a dangerous sport guaranteed to excite the spectators. The blood that filled the dirt pits was graphic testimony to the sport's brutality. But as brutal as it was in the sixth century B.C., it got just that much more savage when the crazed Romans introduced the cestus, an iron-studded knuckle cover. These early "brass knuckles" assured that at least one of the contestants, if not both, would be maimed or killed. Fortunately for the present-day pugilists, Olympic boxing no longer allows the use of the spiked gauntlet.

The first boxing competition in the modern games took place in St. Louis in 1904, and as it did in the rest of the events that year, the U.S. won all the medals. Except for the Stockholm games of 1912, boxing has been on every subsequent Olympic agenda. The U.S. has traditionally fared well in Olympic competition, especially in the heavier weight classes. However, unlike many of the sports in the games, boxing has never been dominated by any one country. For example, in the bantamweight competition since 1924, there have been twelve champions from eleven different countries. That doesn't mean that some countries don't place more emphasis on the sport than others. The Iron Curtain countries have tremendous amateur boxing programs, and in recent years these extensive programs have paid dividends. In 1972, nine boxers from communist countries won medals. It is easy to account for those impressive results if one realizes that in 1971, while there were approximately 10,000 amateur boxers in the U.S., there were 400,000 in Russia.

To combat the superior recruiting programs of other nations, the 1976 U.S. coaches developed a training and competition plan that eventually produced the most explosive show of boxing force and finesse since the 1900 games. In Montreal the U.S. fighters took thirty-five of forty-one bouts. What the U.S. coaches did was schedule more pre-Olympic international bouts than ever before. These fight cards gave the "green" U.S. kids valuable experience against tough, seasoned opponents. The U.S. squad got a chance to see, firsthand, the styles of the Europeans and Cubans. The coaches also made sure that each boxer received personal attention and worked to encourage a feeling of closeness among team members—a feeling that manifested itself in Montreal, where each member of the squad spoke of the team and coaches as a "family." By the time the Forum boxing ring had emptied, the new U.S. "family" had taken home a miner's payday—five gold medals.

The first-ever set of Olympic boxing brothers, Michael and Leon Spinks, devasted the opposition. Leon stopped his light-heavyweight opponent, Soria the Cuban, in the third round, while Michael TKO'd the Russian Riskiev. Howard Davis, now a top pro, took the lightweight crown even though his mother had died of a heart attack two days before the games began. Sugar Ray Leonard, a household name these days, stopped a tough Cuban in the finals, despite sore hands. And flyweight Leo Randolph garnered his gold by a decision.

One Cuban who was not to be denied his gold medal was awesome Teofilo Stevenson. Stevenson, the 1972 Olympic champion, chased the Rumanian challenger, Mircea Simon, all over the ring before finally decking him—proving along the way that Joe Louis was right when he said, "They can run, but they can't hide." The Moscow games should provide another dynamic display of boxing.

Rules

There are eleven weight categories in the Olympic program:

Category	Weight Limit
Light-Flyweight	Up to 48 kg—106 lbs.
Flyweight	Up to 51 kg—112 lbs.
Bantamweight	Up to 54 kg—119 lbs.
Featherweight	Up to 57 kg—126 lbs.
Lightweight	Up to 60 kg—132 lbs.
Light-Welterweight	Up to 63.5 kg—140 lbs.
Welterweight	Up to 67 kg—148 lbs.
Light-Middleweight	Up to 71 kg—156 lbs.
Middleweight	Up to 75 kg—165 lbs.
Light-Heavyweight	Up to 81 kg—179 lbs.
Heavyweight	Over 81 kg

Each country may enter one boxer for each division. The contestants must be over seventeen years old. Each bout consists of three three-minute rounds with one minute's rest between rounds. The winner is determined by either a knockout or a decision. In the case of a decision, the judgment of the five ring judges is final. The judges score the fight on a "twenty-point must system." Which means one boxer must be awarded twenty points for a round; if the round is even, then both fighters receive twenty points. If one boxer dominates the round, he receives twenty points, while his opponent gets anywhere from nineteen to fifteen points. A rough foul (a low blow) is a two-point deduction. A lesser foul is a one-point deduction. Either the referee or the judges can call a foul. Knockdowns are worth two points if they are clean, one point if the falling fighter was off-balance when he was hit.

A loss eliminates a contestant from the competition. The winners continue to square off until only four are left in each division. The two winners of the semifinals fight for the gold and silver. Both losers in the semifinals receive bronze medals.

The Olympic gloves weigh eight ounces—four ounces for the leather and four ounces of padding.

Viewing Tips

To the inexperienced spectator, boxing may appear to be a very random sport. Compared to the precision of an archer or the controlled routine of a gymnast, the movements of a boxer often look crude and undisciplined. Do not be misled. Boxing is as scientific a sport as just about any of those on the Olympic program. Watch how straight the boxer keeps his arm when he jabs; notice how his head is in constant motion, making it a difficult target to hit. A superior fighter will assess his opponent's strengths and weaknesses, and then capitalize when the opportunity is there. A good fighter will throw his jab often, and when he spots an opening he'll throw his power punch. Pay attention to the stamina of the athletes: when a boxer tires he drops his guard and his punches are thrown in a swinging manner instead of straight ahead. The U.S. fighters are generally faster than the Europeans and move around the ring in a circling motion, looking for an opening. The Europeans are less mobile; they move straight in, forcing their opponents to the ropes.

In professional fighting a judge scores a round according to who he thought "won" it. In the Olympics the judges score each individual set of punches. Contestants score points by landing punches on the trunk of the body from the waist up and on the head. There are no points for the arms. The Olympic gloves are painted white on the tips to allow the judges to better score the punches. A blow must be landed with the white part of the glove. If the fist is not clenched, the blow is ruled a slap and no points are awarded.

Boxing is an exciting event, and if you watch several matches, by the time the finals roll around on Saturday, 2 August, you should be a well-educated viewer.

Forecast: Moscow

Light-Flyweight
1976 Champion: Jorge Hernandez, Cuba
1980 Favorites: Stephen Mushoki, Kenya; Richard Sandoval, USA

Flyweight
1976 Champion: Leo Randolph, USA
1980 Favorites: Jorge Hernandez, Cuba; Alexander Mikhilov, USSR; Jerome Coffee, USA; Henry Srednicki, Poland

Bantamweight
1976 Champion: Yong Jo Gu, North Korea
1980 Favorites: Stefan Forster, East Germany; Jackie Beard, USA; Adolpho Horta, Cuba

Featherweight
1976 Champion: Angel Herrera, Cuba
1980 Favorites: Herrera, Cuba; Bernard Taylor, USA

Lightweight
1976 Champion: Howard Davis, USA
1980 Favorites: Andeh Davidson, Nigeria; Davey Armstrong, USA

Light-Welterweight
1976 Champion: Sugar Ray Leonard, USA
1980 Favorites: Lemuel Steeples, USA; Hugo Fernandez, Argentina; Valeri Lvov, USSR

Welterweight
1976 Champion: Jochen Bachfeld, East Germany
1980 Favorites: Rachkov, USSR; Miodrag Permunovic, Yugoslavia

Light-Middleweight
1976 Champion: Jerzy Rybicki, Poland
1980 Favorites: Viktor Savchenko, USSR; Jeff Stoudemire, USA; Louis Martinez, Cuba

Middleweight
1976 Champion: Michael Spinks, USA
1980 Favorites: Jose Gomez, Cuba; Vlad. Shapkivov, USSR; Tony Ayala, USA

Light-Heavyweight
1976 Champion: Leon Spinks, USA
1980 Favorites: Herbert Bauch, East Germany; Mik. Erofeev, USSR

Heavyweight
1976 Champion: Teofilo Stevenson, Cuba
1980 Favorites: Stevenson, Cuba; Jurgen Fanghaenel, East Germany

Canoeing

Archaeologists tell us that canoes have been around since prehistoric times, apparently an invention of the Stone Age. It is not difficult to imagine how the first one might have come into being; the scene probably went something like this:

A lazy Cro-Magnon man, resting on the bank of a swiftly flowing river, notices a log moving along on the current. Since he has a ways to travel downriver to the next cave, he decides to hitch a ride on the log. The idea works out pretty well, except that his perch is a bit precarious, and so it occurs to him to hollow out a place to sit. The canoe is born, and it is only a matter of a few thousand years until the American Indians refine the log into a sleek bark vessel rather similar in design to those used today.

The North American Indians were the first people to build canoes manageable enough to be raced. In the mid-1500s

Jacques Cartier, the French explorer who discovered the St. Lawrence River, devoted long passages in his diary to descriptions of "Indians gliding over the smooth surfaces in their canoes made of birch bark."

The kayak is the Alaskan Eskimo version of the canoe. Kayaks were originally made of sealskin stretched over a whalebone frame, and were used primarily for hunting.

For the purposes of Olympic competition, a canoe is a boat, pointed at both ends, propelled by a crew that kneels, facing forward, and uses a single-bladed, unfixed paddle.

A kayak is paddled from a sitting position using a double-bladed paddle.

The man who is credited with popularizing canoeing as a modern sport was a London Scot named John MacGregor. MacGregor was a fascinating nineteenth-century character who built a boat very similar in design to the Eskimo kayak and named it the Rob Roy. MacGregor journeyed all over the lakes and rivers of Europe and then wrote books about his adventures. His enthusiasm and intriguing stories inspired many other young men of the time to build similar Rob Roys and set off for exciting new vistas.

In 1865 the Royal Canoe Club was formed, and the Prince of Wales became its first commodore. The New York Canoe Club was organized in 1871, and in 1880 the American Canoe Association was founded. Efforts were made on the part of the IRK (Internationella Representantskopet fir Kanotidrott), the international governing body, to place a canoe on the 1928 Olympic program. The attempt was unsuccessful, and the group failed again in 1932. Canoeing finally made it into the Olympics in 1936 in Berlin. Twelve years later in London, women were allowed to compete in a kayak event.

American athletes have not fared well in the Olympic canoeing and kayaking competitions, although in Munich in 1972 the U.S. managed a bronze in the canoe slalom event. There were eleven events on the 1972 program, five of which were conducted on the slalom course. The concrete course was fed by the River Lech. It was an extremely challenging setup that wound its way around spectator stands accommodating thirty thousand. The Eastern European countries, especially Russia, East Germany, Hungary, and Poland, placed very well.

The slalom events were excluded from the Montreal games because the cost of building an artificial white-water course was prohibitive. There were, however, nine events on the men's program and two on the women's. The East Germans and Russians captured nine of the eleven events. The U.S. paddlers did not place.

Rules

Each country may enter one boat per event. Seventeen competitors from each country are allowed to participate. The eleven events on the Moscow program are:

MEN
500-meter Kayak Singles
500-meter Canoe Singles
500-meter Kayak Pairs
500-meter Canoe Pairs
1,000-meter Kayak Singles
1,000-meter Canoe Singles
1,000-meter Kayak Pairs
1,000-meter Canoe Pairs
1,000-meter Four-man Kayak

WOMEN
500-meter Kayak Singles
500-meter Kayak Pairs

Each race is begun from a standing start.

Viewing Tips

There is really very little pacing or strategy in the 500- and 1,000-meter canoe and kayak races. The competitors basically go all out from start to finish, and this is why the event is so physically demanding. Consider that the paddlers propel the boats 1,000 meters in three minutes, which means they are moving almost twelve miles an hour. To sustain that pace, they must average about 125 strokes per minute. It is an awesome rate.

The canoes are approximately seventeen feet long and thirty inches wide. The kayaks are a little narrower. Obviously, in a boat so small, balance is a genuine concern. The canoeists guide their boats by altering their strokes; while the kayaks have foot-controlled rudders.

Notice the stroke of the canoeists. There are basically three parts to each stroke: the "catch," when the blade cuts the water; the pull through the water; and the pull out of the water, where the blade must remain close to the surface on the return so that little motion is wasted. The stroke uses the muscles in the arms, as well as those in the chest, back, and legs.

Forecast: Moscow

MEN
500 meters–Single Canoe
1976 Champion: Aleksander Rogov, USSR
1980 Favorites: East Germany; USSR; Canada; Yugoslavia

1,000 meters–Single Canoe
1976 Champion: Matija Ljubek, Yugoslavia
1980 Favorites: USSR; Yugoslavia; Rumania

500 meters–Canadian Doubles
1976 Champion: USSR
1980 Favorites: USSR; Hungary; Rumania; Poland

1,000 meters–Canadian Doubles
1976 Champion: USSR
1980 Favorites: USSR; Hungary; Rumania

500-meter Kayak Singles
1976 Champion: Vasil Diba, Rumania
1980 Favorites: Rumania; USSR; East Germany

1,000-meter Kayak Singles
1976 Champion: Rudiger Helm, East Germany
1980 Favorites: East Germany; USSR

500-meter Kayak Doubles
1976 Champion: USSR
1980 Favorites: East Germany; USSR; Norway

1,000-meter Kayak Doubles
1976 Champion: USSR
1980 Favorites: Hungary; East Germany; USSR

1,000-meter Kayak Fours
1976 Champion: USSR
1980 Favorites: USSR; Spain; East Germany

WOMEN
500-meter Kayak Singles
1976 Champion: Carola Zirzow, East Germany
1980 Favorites: USSR; East Germany; Rumania

1,000-meter Kayak Doubles
1976 Champion: USSR
1980 Favorites: USSR; East Germany; Hungary

Cycling

The birth of the bicycle is placed tenuously in France in the late seventeenth century, but since it was impossible to keep the original machine balanced and in motion at the same time, it apparently died an ignominious death. A century later the apparatus was reincarnated as the tricycle. In 1790 a Frenchman, Count de Siviac, resurrected the two-wheeled concept. The count's contraption had wooden wheels and a crossbar, but you couldn't guide, pedal, or stop it. Nevertheless, it was a bicycle.

Around 1816 Baron Drais von Sauerbronn, chief forester for the duchy of Baden in Germany, invented a pivoting front fork which allowed the rider to steer the machine—a welcome improvement. In 1834 an English blacksmith attached pedals to connecting rods so the bicycle could be self-propelled. The addition of working pedals to the frame made the cycle much more stable and certainly faster, but with the wooden wheels the ride remained a bit bumpy. In fact, those early wooden-wheeled bikes were often called "bone-shakers." In 1888 J. B. Dunlop, the same Dunlop of automobile tire fame, developed air-filled pneumatic tires; at the time, Dunlop was a veterinary surgeon.

In 1890 the Michelin brothers introduced a removable tire. The inventions of Michelin and Dunlop raised bicycling to a new level of popularity. And with its acceptance as a legitimate form of transportation came its acceptance as a sport. The roads at the time were still crude and rough, but the sidewalks were smooth. So the racers took to the sidewalks, terrifying pedestrians and claiming more than a few casualties along the way. By the turn of the century, thousands of bicycle clubs had sprung up all over the world. With the advent of the automobile, though, the popularity of bicycle racing in the U.S. declined. On the Continent, however, it has remained a key sport, and today bicycle racers are among the most revered European sports heroes.

Cycle racing has been in the Olympics since the Athens games. In 1896 the Frenchman Emile Masson won three gold medals. In the seventeen Olympic games that have followed, the riders from the nations of Western Europe have captured just about all of the medals. U.S. cyclists have won only two medals, a gold in the 1,500-meter team pursuit in 1900 and a bronze in the 1912 road race.

Cycling, like all of the Olympic sports, has had its share of bizarre moments. In 1936 the Frenchman Lapebie led the pack for most of the road race, but near the end of the race, a teammate actually caught up to him, grabbed his jersey, and held on just long enough to sling past Lapebie to victory. In 1960 Knud Jensen, the Danish racer, died after collapsing during the road race. Later it was determined he had died as a result of a drug injection by the team trainer.

In 1972, the USSR, Poland, and Austria won three medals each, while eighteen other countries also participated in the victory ceremonies. During the road race the Dutch team was disqualified after officials discovered traces of illegal drugs in their urine samples.

In Montreal, Johansson of Sweden pulled off a minor upset in the grueling 160-mile road race. Martinelli of Italy finished second, and Nowicki of Poland, third. The USSR took the team time trial; and West Germany won the 4,000-meter team pursuit.

Rules

The six events on the Moscow cycling program are divided into two categories: road and track. The two road races are the individual road race and the team time trial. The individual road race will take place over the new Krylatskoye circuit, which can be altered to accommodate any distance between 200 and 300 km. There are supply points along the route where a rider may pick up spare parts.

The team time trial is usually a 100-km race. Four riders per nation are entered, three must finish the event for a team to be eligible for a medal. The start is staggered at intervals of three to four minutes.

The four track events will take place in the Krylatskoye Velodrome. There are three individual races—the 1-km time trial, the sprint (3 laps), and the 4,000-meter pursuit—and one team event—the 4,000-meter team pursuit. There are no cycling events for women.

In the time trial each rider races the clock. The racer starts from a stationary position with his assistant holding the bike upright. If a rider makes a false start, he is allowed a second chance after five other cyclists have competed.

The sprint is considered the most prestigious track event. Each nation may enter one rider. There are three laps to the sprint. Three or four riders compete in the preliminary heats. As in wrestling, judo, and rowing, there are repechage heats, which give losing riders a second chance. After the preliminaries fastest eight riders are matched up, one on one. The eight quarter-finalists are pared down to four semifinalists and then to two finalists. Each one-on-one is a best of three series.

In the individual pursuit the fastest eight riders are determined by time trials. The riders pair off for a series of elimination races. In the pursuit, the riders start from opposite sides of the track. The design of the pursuit race means that the riders must actually go all out over the entire, exhausting 4,000 meters. If one rider overtakes the other, the race is over. Failing that, the rider who crosses the finish line first wins.

The team pursuit follows the same basic procedure. Two teams of four line up at opposite ends of the track. To save energy and capitalize on the wind draft created by the lead rider, the cyclists alternate taking the lead. When one rider tires of breaking the wind, another rider moves up to take his place. The winning time is determined by the third rider of the team across the finish line.

Viewing Tips

The two different types of races require two different types of bicycles. The track bikes are extremely light (17–20 pounds). They utilize a single, fixed, noncoasting gear, which means that the pedals turn every time the wheel turns. This guarantees maximum acceleration over a short distance.

The road bikes are slightly heavier and are of a sturdier construction. They must be able to absorb the punishing grind of the road. The road bikes have ten derailleur gears, consisting of two sprockets on the front and five on the rear hub.

Each type of race requires a different and unique strategy. In the track sprint you won't see the riders pedaling all out until the final lap or two. Often a rider will stand virtually motionless, just balancing his bike, waiting for the otr rider to take the lead. During the first lap, they'll check each other out, cruising high and low while looking for the right time and place to make a move. It is a nerve-racking race which demands split-second decision making. By the Olympic rules, the rider who takes the lead on the first lap must set a pace no slower than a walk. Sometimes a rider will tire of playing the waiting game and will take off early, trying to "steal" the race.

In the time trials, look for the riders with raw speed and endurance. These events are to cycling what the 800 and 400 meters are to track. The road races are grueling tests of stamina and skill. Sometimes teammates may work together during the individual road race. By that I mean that if one racer is obviously superior to another, the weaker rider may try to pace his teammate—a tactic sometimes used in the 1500 meters in track.

Forecast: Moscow

200-km Individual Road Race
1976 Champion: Bernt Johansson, Sweden
1980 Favorites: East Germany; Sweden; USSR; Italy; Poland

100-km Team Time Trial
1976 Champion: USSR
1980 Favorites: USSR; Poland; East Germany; Denmark

Match Sprints
1976 Champion: Anton Tkac, Czechoslovakia
1980 Favorites: Czechoslovakia; East Germany; France; USSR; Poland

1,000-meter Individual Time Trial
1976 Champion: Klaus Grunke, East Germany
1980 Favorites: West Germany; USSR; East Germany; Belgium

4,000-meter Individual Pursuit
1976 Champion: Gregor Braun, West Germany
1980 Favorites: West Germany; USSR; Holland; East Germany

4,000-meter Team Pursuit
1976 Champion: West Germany
1980 Favorites: West Germany; USSR; East Germany; Great Britain

Equestrian Sports

The equestrian competition is the one event in the Olympic games where the athlete is not solely responsible for his or her ultimate success. To win a gold medal, the rider's execution must be nearly flawless, but he must also have the cooperation of his animal. When horse and rider move as one, the result is a synergistic ballet which makes the event one of the most beautiful of all to watch.

The first time horses were introduced into the Olympics was in 680 B.C. In that year the equestrian events included a four-horse chariot race, a mounted horse race, and a loose horse race. In those Ben Hur days, not only did the horses not receive any of the rewards, but the winning chariot drivers also went without prizes. The wreaths of victory were reserved for the wealthy stable owners. The Greeks were not the only people to stage equestrian events during the seventh century B.C.; the Romans, Assyrians, and Egyptians had also harnessed the horse for racing.

Contemporary equestrian sports are to some degree derived from specific military maneuvers developed over the centuries in which the horse was an instrument of warfare. Since World War Two, when the Polish and Soviet cavalries made their tragic and futile last stands against German tanks, the horse has had no place in combat, but the equestrian skills associated with military horsemanship survive.

The development of horsemanship as a sport dates back to the middle of the sixteenth century, when superb riding schools emerged in Italy. Federico Grisone and Giovanni Pignatelli opened an equitation academy in Naples during that time. The sport was further refined in the French, Austrian, and Swedish schools of the eighteenth century.

Riding events were scheduled for the first modern Olympics in 1896, but because of economic problems they were never held. Four years later in Paris, a jumping competition did take place, and the Belgian riders swept all the gold and silver. In Stockholm in 1912, the Swedes struck gold in four of the five events on the card. For the next twenty years, the

Swedes and the Dutch dominated the sport, although the Italian riders did fare well in the Grand Prix jumping in Antwerp in 1920.

The equestrian competition is one of only three Olympic events (the others being shooting and yachting) in which men and women compete on an equal basis. Teams are comprised of the best riders from their respective nations, regardless of sex. In 1972 the best of England's riders included the daughter of the queen, Princess Anne, who acquitted herself well, though she failed to win a medal.

Through the Olympic years the anthems of many different nations have been played in the soft dirt arenas. In 1932 the U.S. sent some outstanding competitors to the games. In 1968 in Mexico City, the U.S. copped one gold, two silvers, and a bronze. Canada, West Germany, the USSR, and Great Britain have also produced world champion horsemen.

In Montreal in 1976 the U.S. riders were very successful; Coffin and Plumb took first and second in the three-day event, and the U.S. also swept the gold in the team three-day. The West Germans, the Swiss, and the French took firsts in the other four events.

Rules

There are two events in each of the three specific areas of equestrian competition—dressage, jumping, and cross-country. The six events are individual and team three-day (cross-country), individual and team jumping, and individual and team dressage.

Three riders and horses from each nation may enter the dressage and three-day events. In the jumping, four riders may be entered in the team competition.

Grand Prix Dressage

In the dressage competition the rider must lead his mount through a set of intricate maneuvers, including, among others, the walk, the canter, the trot, the change-of-lead-leg canter, the false counter-canter, the piaffer, and pirouettes. The sight of an impeccably groomed horse carrying his stiff-backed, skilled rider through these unusual movements is one of the aesthetic delights of the Olympics.

In the dressage event there are some interesting rules concerning the horses. For instance, no horse may compete in more than three Olympic games—which gives you an idea of the importance of the animals in the competition. Also, no one besides the official rider may train the horse after its arrival at the games.

The judges evaluate the performances according to the position of the rider, the subtlety of the rider's control, and the execution of the maneuvers. Points are awarded on a scale of ten: ten is excellent; one is poor; a zero is a nonperformance. Each entry is allowed ten minutes to complete the program.

The Three-Day Event

The three-day is a combination of dressage, jumping, and cross-country elements. The first day is the dressage event. Though less complicated than the Grand Prix dressage, it is nevertheless a difficult segment. The three-day has a military flavor, and the purpose of the first day's competition is to determine if the rider can control his mount.

The second day is devoted to the grueling cross-country steeplechase. Over a course that covers twenty-one miles, the stamina of both horse and rider are severely tested. The course is divided into four sections, and each section must be completed within a specified time—bonus points are awarded for beating the clock. The first phase is approximately five miles over mostly wooded trails. The second phase is a two-and-a-half-mile steeplechase, with hurdles in the form of fences and hedges. The third phase is ten miles over trails and roads. After the third phase, there is a compulsory ten-minute rest. The fourth phase covers five miles and an average of thirty obstacles. The cross-country competition tests the endurance, stamina, and jumping ability of the horse, and the rider's sense of pace.

On the third day is the jumping event. Essentially, the purpose of the final day is to determine whether or not the horse and rider have something left after the brutal cross-country segment. The hurdles of the jumping event are not as high as those of the Grand Prix jumping, but each of the ten to twelve obstacles does measure almost four feet.

After the third day, all of the penalty points are totaled, the bonus points are deducted, and the rider with the lowest score wins the gold medal.

The Grand Prix Jumping

The Grand Prix jumping is a spectacular event. The contestants must clear obstacles that are five and six feet high, and there is a water jump that is five meters wide. The competition consists of two consecutive circuits around the course which must be concluded within a specific time limit. A knockdown of an obstacle adds four penalty points to a rider's score. A first refusal of a horse to jump is three penalty points, and a fall costs ten penalty points. The gold medal, as in the other equestrian events, is awarded to the rider with the fewest penalty points.

Viewing Tips

In the dressage events watch for the control exercised over the animal by the rider. Also pay attention to how graceful the horse appears while being guided through the delicate maneuvers.

The jumping and three-day events are exciting and often filled with sensational spills. For the equestrian events, familiarize yourself with the rules and then sit back and appreciate the beautiful moves of the horses and the courage and skill it takes to guide those magnificent animals over the demanding courses.

Forecast: Moscow

Three-Day Individual Event
1976 Champion: Tad Coffin, USA
1980 Favorites: Coffin, Bruce Davidson, USA; Helmut Rethmeir, West Germany; John Watson, Ireland

Three-Day Team Event
1976 Champion: USA
1980 Favorites: USA; West Germany; Canada; Australia

Grand Prix Dressage–Individual
1976 Champion: Christine Streckelberger, Switzerland
1980 Favorites: Streckelberger; Switzerland; Harry Boldt,
West Germany; Uwe Schulten-Baumer, West Germany

Grand Prix Dressage–Team
1976 Champion: West Germany
1980 Favorites: West Germany; USSR; Switzerland

Grand Prix Jumping–Individual
1976 Champion: Alwin Schockemoehle, West Germany
1980 Favorites: Michael Matz, USA; Gerd Wiltgang, West
Germany; Johann Heins, Holland

Grand Prix Jumping–Team
1976 Champion: France
1980 Favorites: USA; Holland; West Germany; France

Fencing

There is a sculpture on the wall of the twelfth century
B.C. temple of Pharaoh Rameses III that depicts two fencers
engaged in a sporting contest, wearing complete suits of
protective gear. It is the first known recorded account of
fencing as a sport, although it can safely be assumed that the
history of fencing as a means of combat goes back many
thousands of years.

For twenty-six hundred years after Rameses built his temple, the sword was primarily a military weapon. Then the
rifle was invented, and it didn't take long before fencing was
practiced solely as a sport.

A fourteenth-century German manuscript mentions the
sport of fencing, describing the weapons as heavy, double-
bladed instruments with large hand guards. The German
manuscript aside, there is considerable disagreement about
the modern genesis of the sport. The Spanish claim to have
introduced it, and then passed it onto the Italians. The Italians vociferously deny that the Spanish had anything to do

with the origin of the sport. The Italians point to a manuscript of Fiore dei Liberi which details certain fencing styles as proof that they were the first modern swordsmen. One thing is for certain; the methods and techniques used by the fencing masters today are very similar to the techniques chronicled in the early Spanish and Italian writings.

The épée was developed in the early 1500s, and its design has remained basically the same since then. A century later the foil, a slightly lighter but similar weapon, was invented. And as best as can be determined, the Italian fencing master Giuseppe Radaelli introduced the saber shortly thereafter.

The Olympic history of the sport dates from the Athens games. Both the foil and saber were part of the 1896 program. Four years later in Paris, the épée competition was added. In the eighty years of Olympic fencing competition, Cuba and the U.S. are the only two non-European countries to have won medals. The Cuban fencers put on an outstanding exhibition in the 1904 games in St. Louis, winning nine medals. The last American to win a medal was Albert Axelrod of New York, who captured a bronze in the foil in 1960.

Women have participated in the individual foil since 1924 and the team foil since 1960. Fencing is the only combat sport in the Olympics in which women compete.

From the 1920s through the 1950s France and Italy dominated the foil competition. Since then Russian and Polish fencers have done extremely well in the event, although in 1968 Drimba of Rumania took the individual foil and France garnered the team title.

The gold medals for the saber competition have rested quite peacefully in Hungarian trophy cases for most of the eighty years of the competition. When the Hungarian fencers have faltered, the USSR saber competitors have gladly picked up the slack. The winners in the épée have been a more diversified group, but since 1928 the gold medals have not left the Continent.

The West German fencers surprised everyone in Montreal by winning the team foil competition, placing second in the épée team, and taking first and second in the individual épée. The Russian fencers placed well in the saber, sweeping the individual honors. Hungary had to be satisfied with a gold in the women's individual foil event.

Rules

In Moscow there will be a total of six competitions for the men and two for the women. Each country may enter three competitors for each event, and one team for each weapon, with four competitors constituting a team. Both the individual and the team competitions are divided into pools. The pools are conducted round-robin style, so that every competitor faces all others in the same pool. The winners advance and are ranked in the next set of pools according to the number of hits they scored in the first set of matches. In the men's qualifying rounds matches are won by the first fencer scoring five touches. The winner in the women's matches is the first to make four touches. After the initial qualifying rounds, the matches are contested as the best two out of three, with five touches for a win. There is a six-minute time limit.

The women's second round is a four-hit match with a five-minute time limit. All of the fencers wear masks, gloves, and protective body covering.

The Foil

The basic foil is forty-three inches long and weighs approximately eighteen ounces. It has a flexible, four-sided blade, and the hand guard is saucer-shaped. Hits can be scored only with the tip of the blade and only by touching the trunk of the opponent. Hits on the head, arms, hand, etc., are not counted.

The Épée

The épée is similar to the foil except that the blade is triangular. The point is circular with a flat tip. The épée weighs approximately ten ounces more than the foil, owing in part to its larger hand guard. The entire body of the opponent is a legal target, but with the point only.

The Saber

The saber is approximately the same weight as the foil, but is an inch shorter. The blade is flat and the hand guard looks like a quarter-moon. Hits may be scored with both the point and the blade, and the body from the waist up is the legitimate target area.

Viewing Tips

One of the first things you will notice about the fencers is the wire attached to the back of their jackets at foil and épée. The electrical circuit actually runs from the blade of the foil or épée through the suit, comes out the back of the jacket, and winds onto a spool. As the fencers advance and retreat, the spool lets out or takes up the slack. The purpose of the electrical wiring, which was introduced in the foil competition in 1936, is to aid the judges in determining when a hit is actually made. When a hit occurs, the contact between the point of the blade and the opponent's jacket completes the circuit and an indicator light and a bell are set off. The elevated fencing area is called the piste. It is covered in a metallic substance which conducts electricity. For the foil the piste is 46 feet long and 6½ feet wide. It measures 14 feet longer for the épée and saber.

The key thing to watch in the fencing competition is the footwork, which is usually dazzling. The Olympic fencers are quick and dexterous, and they have terrific reflexes. They must also be very quick thinkers, since they constantly have to adjust their strategy. In the foil, which is the classic event, the "right of way" must be given to the attacker until the defender "parries" (blunts) the thrust, then the defender may counterattack (the riposte). In the foil, speed and strategy are everything. In the épée, the first to hit scores the point, and the épée is far less subtle than the foil. The saber is the most flamboyant fencing event, and for that reason it is often the favorite of the novice spectator. The movements and hits are also decidedly easier to detect than are those of the épée and foil.

Forecast: Moscow

MEN
Individual Foil
1976 Champion: Fabio Dal Zotto, Italy
1980 Favorites: Dal Zotto, Italy; D. Flament, France; A. Romankov, USSR

Team Foil
1976 Champion: West Germany
1980 Favorites: West Germany; Italy; Poland; France

Individual Épée
1976 Champion: Alexander Pusch, West Germany
1980 Favorites: Pusch, West Germany; Philippe Riboud, France; Johann Harmenberg, Sweden

Team Épée
1976 Champion: Sweden
1980 Favorites: Sweden; USSR; Hungary

Individual Saber
1976 Champion: Victor Krovopouskov, USSR
1980 Favorites: Krovopouskov, Mikail Burzev, USSR; M. Maffei, Italy

Team Saber
1976 Champion: USSR
1980 Favorites: USSR; Hungary; Italy

WOMEN
Individual Foil
1976 Champion: Ildiko Schwarczenberger, Hungary
1980 Favorites: V. Sidorova, USSR; Katarina Razcova, Czechoslovakia; Kornelia Hanisch, West Germany

Team Foil
1976 Champion: USSR

Field Hockey

It has the same number of men per side as American football. It is played on approximately the same size field. The equipment used by the players is very similar to that of ice hockey, and so is the goal area. The strategy of the game is very much like the strategy used in lacrosse and soccer. It requires the precision passing of basketball. As in baseball, a man taken out for a substitute cannot return to play. It is the national pastime of one specific country. The sport is field hockey and the country in which it is a national pastime is India.

Between 1928 and 1956 India won six straight Olympic titles in the truly ancient "stick and ball" game. In 1960 Pakistan upset India, but in 1964 in Tokyo, India returned to the top rung of the victory stand. Remarkably, though, in 1976 India was shut out of the awards ceremony for the first time in its years of Olympic participation in the sport.

The field hockey competition in Moscow is scheduled to begin on 20 July 1980. It will run for thirteen straight days, and judging by the 1976 tournament, in which New Zealand scored an upset victory, thirteen days will barely be enough time to figure out which country does indeed have the best squad.

A hybrid form of field hockey was first played by the Persians, who passed it on to the Greeks in about 1200 B.C. The origin of the modern version of the game dates back to 1839 or so, when the game as played by the Europeans merged with the British Isles games of hurling (from Ireland), shinty (from Scotland), and bandy (from Wales). By 1840 the Blackheath Hockey Club had been founded in England. In 1883 a code of rules was established by the Wimbledon Hockey Club, and in 1908 field hockey was included in the London games. The British sponsorship of the new event was a bit self-serving, as the British team romped through the three-game tournament, outscoring its opponents 23–3.

The British army was primarily responsible for spreading

the gospel of field hockey to the Far East, where it enjoys its greatest support. The Western Hemisphere has never really noticed or accepted the game. The U.S. has won only one medal in field hockey, a bronze, and that in 1932. In 1976 the U.S. team failed to qualify a squad for the Montreal games. It's not difficult to understand why when you realize that most Americans think of the game as a schoolyard exercise for girls. However, after watching a few Olympic matches, one immediately realizes that field hockey is not a docile form of recreation.

Rules

Under the Olympic rules, there are eleven players per team, with seven alternates. The lineup generally consists of five forwards, three halfbacks, two fullbacks, and a goalie. The goalie wears almost exactly the same padding, including the face mask, as an ice hockey goalkeeper. He may kick or stop the ball with his body while he is in the striking circle, but he is the only player allowed to do so—all others must use only their hands or stick.

A maximum of sixteen teams may compete in the Olympic tournament. As in the volleyball tournament the teams are divided into two pools. The teams of the A pool play off against each other, and those of the B pool do the same. The winners of the two pools play each other for the gold. The runners-up in each pool play for the bronze.

The hockey field is 100 yards long and 55 yards wide. It is divided into four quarters. At each end of the field is a net seven feet high and twelve feet wide. A semicircle called the striking circle extends out from the goal. A goal is scored when the ball goes into the net after being touched by the stick of an attacking player who is standing within the striking circle. The goals count one point each. The ball is generally made of plastic, though some balls have cork centers covered by leather. The ball weighs around six ounces and is approximately the same size as a standard baseball. The sticks are usually thirty-six to forty inches in length. The blade must be no longer than seven inches.

The game is played in two 35-minute halves, with a 10-

minute break in between. If the game ends in a tie, there are two 7½-minute extra periods. If the score is still tied, the next overtime period is sudden death, with the team scoring the first goal winning. Three sudden-death periods may be played, and if the teams fail to score, there is a penalty shoot-off, in which the teams choose five players to take alternate penalty shots. The team that scores the most goals wins.

Viewing Tips

When watching field hockey you can think of it as "ice hockey on the dirt" or "soccer with sticks." The game begins with a face-off, called a bully, in the center of the field. The forwards handle the bulk of the offensive work. The passing of the superior teams is precise and sharp. The players primarily pass the ball until they find an open man in the striking circle. The play in the circle, like the action in the ice hockey crease, is very rough. The defensive ballplayers are not likely to leave a man unguarded in the striking circle for very long. Players are not allowed to trip, hook, or raise the stick higher than the shoulders. When an infraction is called, the ball is given to the other team at an advantageous spot on the field.

In recent years defense has been the key to winning field hockey. The championship squads load up as many defensemen as possible into the striking circle. With the defense so tenacious, a great deal depends upon a team's passing style. In Munich in 1972, no team scored more than three goals in the final two rounds.

Forecast: Moscow

MEN
1976 Champion: New Zealand
1980 Favorites: Pakistan; Holland; West Germany; Australia

WOMEN
1976 Champion: (New Event)
1980 Favorites: Holland; West Germany; USA; Wales; Great Britain

Gymnastics

From the Greek word *gymnazein*, meaning "to train naked," comes the term gymnastics, and the Greeks gave us not only the word but the sport. In ancient Greek training facilities called gymnasia, students performed various series of systematic exercises. The purpose of these exercises was to develop their bodies. As with almost every physical discipline practiced by the Greeks, the recreational sport soon became a competitive one. Other ancient cultures, including the Chinese, the Persians, and the Indians, also practiced specific exercises as a supplement to their warfare training. The Romans, for instance, developed the wooden horse as a device for teaching their cavalry advanced mounting and dismounting techniques.

Gymnastics developed as a modern sport in the early nineteenth century. At that time, Ludwig Jahn, a German physical education instructor, introduced the pommel horse, side bar, parallel bars, and balance beam. By the late nineteenth century, U.S. athletes were heavily into the sport, and a team from Milwaukee actually competed in a German meet in 1881. Gymnastics was part of the program of the first Modern games in Athens; in all, five countries sent seventy-five gymnasts to Greece. From 1896 through 1932, the European countries, most notably Italy and Switzerland, fielded strong squads. The U.S. gymnasts won quite a few medals at the St. Louis Games of 1904, but many of the Americans were actually members of European clubs. In 1932 in Los Angeles, the U.S. gymnasts won medals in the special events of tumbling, rope climbing, and Indian club competition, plus the rings and horizontal bars.

However, from 1932 through 1976, the U.S. won only one medal, while the Russian and Japanese gymnasts rarely failed to take home a pocketful of gold, silver, and bronze. Occasionally, East Germany and Rumania have interrupted the Russian-Japanese dominance, but not very often.

The Eastern European and Japanese reigns may fall prey to a revolution of sorts in Moscow. The men's and women's teams from the U.S. are planning a coup in Russia, and their chances of success have never been better.

Why are the U.S. athletes suddenly back in contention for Olympic medals? Because in the last ten years two tiny, muscular athletes captured the attention of the entire world. In 1972 diminutive Olga Korbut of the USSR sprang upon the Olympic scene and, like a magnet, drew the Olympic spotlight to her. From the moment Olga smiled into the ABC cameras as she performed the splits on the balance beam, the front lawns of suburban houses from Bethesda to Beverly Hills began filling with schoolgirls in leotards and tights, cartwheeling their way through summer afternoons.

Then in 1976, fourteen-year-old, eighty-six-pound Nadia Comaneci dazzled the crowds of Montreal as she performed on the uneven bars and bebopped to jazz strains on the huge floor exercise mat. Her grace and ponytail captivated the spectators, while her routines bewitched the judges, who awarded her seven perfect scores (10) during the competition.

Olga and Nadia became the idols of thousands of budding gymnasts. But in Moscow, those idolators hope to become iconoclasts. The 1980 games will be the first chance for this new wave of superstars to strut their stuff. The kids who were twelve years old in 1976 are now sixteen, and they're ready to harvest a few of those Olympic medals.

Although Olga and Nadia were undoubtedly the impetus for the recent gymnastics explosion, they weren't the only stars down through the years. The superb Soviet gymnast Larisa Latynina won a total of seventeen Olympic medals before she hung up her leotard in 1966. Boris Shakhlin of the USSR won six gold medals during his brilliant career. Sawao Kato of Japan captured seven medals, and in 1976 the electrifying Nikolai Andrianov won seven medals—four golds, two silvers, and a bronze.

The gymnastics competition in Moscow should be thrilling. The level of international competition has never been higher. We can expect that after the games are over and the new stars have emerged, more young athletes than ever will be getting into the sport.

Rules

In the gymnastics competition the men and women compete in both compulsory and optional routines on each apparatus. The men have competed in the gymnastics competition since 1896. The women have participated in team competition since 1928, and in individual competitions since 1952.

The six events for the men are floor exercises, side horse (pommel), vault, parallel bars, horizontal bars, and the rings.

The women compete in the vault, uneven bars, balance beam, and floor exercise.

After the competitors perform their compulsory and optional routines, the athletes with the highest total scores advance to the finals. For each event there is a panel of four international judges. Each judge grades the performance, the highest and lowest scores are tossed out, and the other two are averaged to determine the score for the event. The judges rate each performance using a scoring scale of 10. Deductions for faults may range from as little as a tenth of a point to as much as one point. Understand that, as in boxing, diving, and wrestling, the scoring in gymnastics is based on the judge's opinion and is therefore essentially subjective. Throughout the Olympics there have been charges of biased judging. The charges are not always unfounded.

In the individual combined events the thirty-six highest-scoring gymnasts must perform an optional exercise on each apparatus. Added to their score on each apparatus is half the number of points they scored in the team competition. Obviously, the highest scorer wins.

In the team competitions, six members of each team perform an extra compulsory exercise on each apparatus. The five highest scores are added together to determine the team total.

Floor Exercise

The women have sixty to ninety seconds to execute thirteen compulsory exercises, plus their own optional moves, on a large mat. The women's routines are accompanied by music of the performer's choice. The women's floor exercise is a meticulously choreographed ballet.

The men's floor exercise is basically the same as the

women's, except the men must perform almost twice as many compulsory moves.

The Vault
In the women's vault, the competitors run to a vault 3½ feet high, launch themselves by jumping onto a springboard, then push off the horse with one or both hands into a handstand, twist, or horizontal vault. The men's vault follows the same procedure on a horse that is eight inches higher.

Uneven Bars—Women
One of the bars is 7½ feet above the floor, the other is 4 feet, 11 inches. The women execute maneuvers as they swing from one bar to the other.

Beam—Women
The balance beam is 16 feet long, 4 inches wide, and 3 feet, 11 inches, above the floor. The gymnasts execute a series of tumbling, dance, and jumping moves on the beam.

Side Horse—Men
The side or pommel horse (named for the pommelled hand grips) is 3½ feet high and 5½ feet long. The gymnasts perform eighteen compulsory exercises in addition to their own optional maneuvers. They are expected to use every part of the horse.

Rings—Men
The two rings hang 8 feet off the ground. Grasping one ring in each hand, the gymnasts perform eighteen compulsory moves, including two handstands.

Parallel Bars—Men
The two bars rest parallel to each other, 5 feet, 3 inches, off the floor. During the routine the gymnast must release both hands from the bars at least twice—one time above the bars, once below them.

Horizontal Bar—Men

On a bar 8 feet above the ground the men swing and vault through thirteen compulsory exercises.

Viewing Tips

As the gymnasts perform, the judges look for a certain fluidity of motion and a feeling of confidence. Obviously, falls, mishandled moves, and slips are mistakes for which points will be deducted from the athlete's score. More subtle flaws, such as hesitations and stopping and starting again, also result in point deductions.

Different countries take different approaches to the sport of gymnastics. The athletes from the countries which have been the most successful in recent Olympic competitions— Russia and Japan—have vastly different styles. The Japanese are known for the grace and finesse of their routines, which are filled with artful exercises. The Soviet style can be characterized as relying on feats of strength. The Soviet men are less acrobatic than the Japanese, but they counter with exercises that require tremendous power. The U.S. athletes seem to be developing a hybrid style, taking a little bit from both the Russians and the Japanese.

The floor exercise is actually an exercise in free-form tumbling. The women's routines are accompanied by music, which contributes to the impression that the entire routine is a modern dance recital. In the floor exercise, you can expect cartwheels, backflips with twists, pivots, and handstands. The performer should try to use all of the large mat in the course of the routine.

In the events involving apparatuses, keep an eye on the mounts and dismounts of the contestants. Landings are especially important. At all costs the athlete must avoid falling or slipping; it is acceptable, however, for a competitor to take a step backwards on landing in order to keep his balance.

The balance beam is an exquisite event to watch. On the four-inch-wide beam, the gymnasts perform incredible feats, including complete somersaults and sideways cartwheels, in which the entire body leaves the beam. In recent world championships gymnasts have executed consecutive somersaults and handless cartwheels on the beam. Splits and handstands are also often part of the action. The routine should utilize the entire beam, and the contestant should avoid too many moves which involve lying or resting on the beam.

Forecast: Moscow

MEN

Individual All-Around
1976 Champion: Nikolai Andrianov, USSR
1980 Favorites: Andrianov, Alexander Ditiatin, USSR; Kurt Thomas, USA

Individual Floor Exercise
1976 Champion: Nikolai Andrianov, USSR
1980 Favorites: Andrianov, USSR; Thomas, USA; Stoyan Deitchev, Bulgaria

Individual Side Horse
1976 Champion: Zoltan Magyar, Hungary
1980 Favorites: Andrianov, USSR; Thomas, USA; Junichi Shimizu, Japan

Individual Rings
1976 Champion: Nikolai Andrianov, USSR
1980 Favorites: Andrianov, Ditiatin, USSR; Samatsu, Japan

Individual Vault
1976 Champion: Nikolai Andrianov, USSR
1980 Favorites: Ditiatin, Andrianov, USSR; Shimizu, Japan

Individual Parallel Bars
1976 Champion: Sawao Kato, Japan
1980 Favorites: Stoyan Deltchev, Bulgaria; Thomas, USA; Ditiatin, USSR

Individual Horizontal Bar
1976 Champion: Mitsuo Tsukahara, Japan

1980 Favorites: Yoichi Tomita, Japan; Andrianov, Ditiatin, USSR; Thomas, USA

Team
1976 Champion: Japan
1980 Favorites: USSR; Japan; East Germany

WOMEN

Individual All-Around
1976 Champion: Nadia Comaneci, Rumania
1980 Favorites: Comaneci, Rumania; Elena Mukhina, Steila Zakharova, USSR

Individual Floor Exercise
1976 Champion: Nadia Comaneci, Rumania
1980 Favorites: Comaneci, Rumania; Zakharova, USSR; Leslie Pyfer, USA

Individual Vault
1976 Champion: Nelli Kim, USSR
1980 Favorites: Rhonda Schwandt, USA; Comaneci, Rumania; Maxine Gnauck, East Germany

Individual Uneven Parallel Bars
1976 Champion: Nadia Comaneci, Rumania
1980 Favorites: Marcia Frederick, USA; Mukhina, USSR; Comaneci, Emilia Eberle, Rumania

Individual Balance Beam
1976 Champion: Nadia Comaneci, Rumania
1980 Favorites: Comaneci, Rumania; Eberle; Shaposhnikova, USSR

Team
1976 Champion: USSR
1980 Favorites: USSR; East Germany; Rumania

Handball

When most of us think of handball, we imagine either a four-walled court at the local YMCA or three walls of concrete at an outdoor playground. We expect to see two or four men, their hands protected by half-fingered gloves, slapping a ball not much larger than a plum against the walls. Team handball as it's played in the Olympics is actually much closer in form to soccer or hockey than it is to the sport which keeps four to five million Americans in shape during the winter months.

First played in 1895, team handball was an outgrowth of a Scandinavian game, in which every part of the body except the feet could be used to advance the ball towards the goal. At the time it was an outdoor sport, then in 1920 it was adapted for indoor play. Handball was included in the Berlin Olympic program in 1936, and the host nation captured the gold. It was another thirty-six years, again in Germany, before handball returned to the games. In Munich Yugoslavia defeated Czechoslovakia for the gold, 21–16. The U.S. team qualified for the Olympics in 1972, but did not win a single game. The Munich finals were watched by over twelve thousand spectators, a graphic demonstration of the popularity of the sport, especially in the middle European nations.

In 1976, the USSR defeated Rumania for the title, while Poland took the bronze. In the women's competition the Soviet team also triumphed, with East Germany finishing second, and Hungary third. Both men and women will compete in team handball in Moscow.

Rules

In team handball the court is 131 feet, 4 inches long by 65 feet, 8 inches wide (40 meters by 20 meters). There is a center line and a free throw line, and the netted goal area is 6'6¾" x 9'10¼". In Olympic competition there are seven men on a side, including the goaltender. When the game is played outside, there are eleven men per side. The ball is about the size of a cantaloupe and looks something like a volleyball.

The players may advance the ball using any part of the

body above the knee. Once a player takes possession of the ball, he has three seconds in which to determine a course of action—a pass or a shot. While he has the ball, he may take three steps in any direction. Players may not shove, hold, or tackle each other, which theoretically makes team handball a non-contact sport. But then pro basketball is theoretically a non-contact sport.

Viewing Tips

For identification purposes the goalies wear numbers 1 and 12, the forwards, numbers 2 through 11 and 13 and 14. As with the Olympic volleyball tournament, there are two pools of teams and the winners of each pool play for the gold medal.

Handball matches are high-scoring affairs, since the players are able to throw the ball with considerable accuracy and the goalie has such a large area to protect. No one may shoot from within a line which extends 24 feet in a semicircle around the goal, the "goal area line." Penalties in the game draw penalty shots from the 24-foot line.

Team handball combines many of the elements of soccer, ice hockey, and basketball. It is not a difficult sport to follow, and the furious and often rough action is very exciting to watch.

Forecast: Moscow

MEN
1976 Champion: USSR
1980 Favorites: USSR; East Germany; Rumania; Poland

WOMEN
1976 Champion: USSR
1980 Favorites: USSR; East Germany; Hungary

Judo

Literally translated, the word "judo" means "the soft or gentle way." It is not likely, however, that anyone who has seen a judo match or exhibition would call it a gentle sport.

The name is accurate only with reference to the types of combat in which weapons are used.

In medieval times members of certain pacifistic Oriental religious sects developed hand-to-hand combat moves to protect themselves against armed highwaymen. At the same time the elite Samurai warriors practiced a fighting discipline called jujitsu which they employed in unarmed combat. The rigid feudal class structure of Japan helped to stimulate the popularity of jujitsu because the peasant classes were forbidden to carry swords. Jujitsu helped them to overcome superior strength by using leverage, quickness, and elusive defensive moves (conquering by yielding).

In the nineteenth century jujitsu became associated with hoodlums and delinquents. Consequently, it experienced a decline in popularity. In 1875 a slightly built young man who had been a student of jujitsu began experimenting with the discipline. After making certain changes, he realized that the easiest way to overcome an opponent was to use the opponent's own moves against him. In that way the opponent could be set off balance and then pulled or pushed to the ground. In 1882, the young man, Jigoro Kano, founded a school to teach his own innovative style of the martial art. To gain notoriety for his new technique, which he called "Kodokan judo," Kano challenged other jujitsu schools in Japan to a series of combat matches. His students emerged victorious in almost every instance, and from that time on, Kodokan judo was accepted as the superior style.

Kano was elected to the IOC in 1909 for his accomplishments in the sport, but, ironically, it took another fifty-five years for judo to become part of the Olympic program. In 1964 Japan exercised its prerogative as the host nation and added a sport—judo—to the agenda of the games. That year the Japanese swept three out of four gold medals, while Anton Geesink of the Netherlands won the other.

Judo was excluded from the 1968 games in Mexico City, but it was reinstated in the program in Munich in 1972. Japan captured two gold medals in Munich; Shota Chochoshvili won a gold in the light-heavyweight category; and the remarkable Wim Ruska of the Netherlands took two golds, one in the heavyweight and one in the open division. In the open division, Ruska lost an early match to Vitali Kusnezov of Russia, but in the repechage (second-chance) matches he worked his way back up to meet Kusnezov in the final, where he pinned the Russian in three minutes and fifty-eight seconds.

In Montreal the lightweight category was won by Hector Rodriguez of Cuba, and the Russian Nevzorov took the light-middleweight. Japan copped three golds, including one in the open category. And the surprising American, thirty-three-year-old Allen Coage brought home a bronze in the heavyweight division.

Rules

A judo contest is won when one man throws his opponent to the mat with "appreciable force." If the judges decide that the thrower had good form, then he receives one point. If the throw is not executed with correct form, he receives a half-point and needs another half-point to secure the win. If an opponent is held on his back for thirty seconds, the attacker receives one point (a win); twenty seconds brings a half-point. If a man submits because he is being held in a powerful hold, he loses by one point. Each match lasts ten minutes. If the match goes the limit with no point awarded, the judges and referee decide the outcome.

Each nation may enter one contestant per event. The repechage system allows a loser to have a second chance, so in effect the tournament is what is commonly called a double elimination. The competition mat is 16 meters by 16 meters. The center area is called the shiaijo and is 9 meters by 9 meters. There is a one-meter-wide red area and a five-meter border to protect the combatants.

Viewing Tips

The competitors wear the judogi, the traditional white, baggy suit. To distinguish between Olympic contestants, one athlete wears a red belt, the other a white belt. In training and in all other competitions except the Olympics, the judokas, as judo practioners are called, wear colored belts which represent different degrees of accomplishment. The lowest-ranking judoka wears a white belt, then come three degrees of brown, and finally, ten degrees of black.

If you watch the competition closely, you will notice that the competitors use several different types of throws. The five basic throws are the tewarza, a hand throw; the koshi-waza, hip throw; the yokosutemi waza, a throw with one's side on the mat; masutemi waza, a throw with one's back on the mat; and the ashiwaza, the foot and leg throw. In addition, there are many variations of each throw.

Forecast: Moscow

Lightweight
1976 Champion: Hector Rodriguez, Cuba
1980 Favorites: Cuba; South Korea; Hungary

Light-Middleweight
1976 Champion: Vladimir Nevzorov, USSR
1980 Favorites: USSR; Japan; France

Middleweight
1976 Champion: Isamu Sonoda, Japan
1980 Favorites: Japan; USSR; Yugoslavia

Light-Heavyweight
1976 Champion: Kazuhiro Ninomiya, Japan
1980 Favorites: Japan; USSR; Great Britain

Heavyweight
1976 Champion: Sergei Novikov, USSR
1980 Favorites: USSR; Japan; USA; West Germany

Open
1976 Champion: Haruki Uemura, Japan
1980 Favorites: Japan; Great Britain; USSR

Modern Pentathlon

The modern pentathlon is a fascinating event, but for a variety of reasons, it hasn't drawn much attention from sports fans in this country. For Americans, it is a foreign sport—foreign not only to our way of thinking, but literally a sport that has its roots in other countries. Moreover, it is a military event. To this day all of the U.S. Olympic competitors in the modern pentathlon have been members of the armed forces.

The prime force behind getting the modern pentathlon on the Olympic program was the founder of the modern games, Pierre de Coubertin. As far as de Coubertin was concerned, the decathlon, which was already on the program, was not the measure of the complete athlete. He felt the decathlete's prowess was limited to only one specific area—track and field. The baron considered the modern pentathlon the test of the true renaissance athlete, since its five events try the athlete in completely diverse areas.

The tenacious Frenchman fought with the IOC, the group he had founded, for several years about including the modern pentathlon on the program. Finally he enlisted the aid of the prestigious Swedish Sports Military Federation, and in 1912 the modern pentathlon was added to the agenda of the Stockholm games.

The five events of the modern pentathlon are riding, fencing, shooting, swimming, and running. In concept, the modern pentathlon recreates a series of challenges that a military courier might encounter under conditions of war. Imagine that each contestant is a military courier for his country and that the message he must deliver could mean the difference between victory and defeat. The courier commandeers a horse, any horse, and begins galloping off towards his destination. He is pursued. The enemy successfully shoots his horse out from under him. The courier grabs his sword and engages his pursuers. He defends himself well, but his sword is broken. He must resort to his pistol. His excellent marksmanship delays the enemy until he can make his escape. He flees, but soon encounters a river, which he swims across, and then, in the tradition of the marathoner, he runs cross-country until he reaches his destination. Regardless of the fact that the premise is altogether fictional, I think it gives the event a terrifically romantic flavor.

The zealous baron actually wanted the athlete to perform all of the feats on the same day. Fortunately for the contestants, the IOC decided differently and allocated five days for the modern pentathlon.

For the most part, the Olympic history of the sport is a history of Russians, Swedes, and Hungarians marching to the victory stand. However, in 1976 in Montreal, that historical trend finally came to an abrupt and surprising halt. A country which had never even won a medal in the event produced the individual gold medalist, Pyciak-Peclak of Poland. The team title, which had been won every year since its inception by either Hungary or Russia, was captured by Great Britain, with Czechoslovakia second, and Hungary third. The U.S. came in fourth.

In recent Olympics there have been some very controversial episodes in the event. In 1968 the bronze medal winner forfeited his prize when traces of alcohol were found in his blood. And in 1972 in Munich an astonishing number of contestants, sixteen, were found to have traces of an outlawed tranquilizer in their systems before the pistol competition. It seems that the tension takes its toll on the pentathlete's nervous system. The embarrassed Olympic officials, choosing not to disqualify such a large number of competitors, instead determined that the athletes had not "officially" been warned to abstain from the drug.

Rules

Each country may enter four contestants in the pentathlon; however, only three are allowed to compete. The scoring in the five events—riding, fencing, shooting, swimming, and running—is based upon a standard 1000-point system, and in some events, an 1100-point system. If a pentathlete performs above the Olympic standard, he may actually score more than the allotted points.

Riding

The riding course measures 800 meters (a half-mile). At one time in the history of the games, the riding segment was conducted over a cross-country course that was often over 3,000 meters long, but in order to accommodate the spectators, the event was moved into the ring. Amazingly, the modern pentathlete must ride a horse that is unfamiliar to him. Twenty minutes before the riding competition begins, the riders draw lots for their mounts, which are supplied by the organizing committee.

The course contains fifteen obstacles, including a water jump, a double, and a triple jump, and must be negotiated in two minutes. No one jump may be higher than 3'9". Penalty points are deducted for mistakes during the round. If either horse or rider falls, the pentathlete is assessed 64 points; a first refusal by the horse to jump costs 24 points, a second refusal, 48 points, and a third, 72 points.

Fencing

The modern pentathlon fencing competition is conducted along the same lines as the regular Olympic fencing tourney, except that only one "hit" is required to win a match. The matches are three minutes long, and if no one scores a hit in three minutes, the match counts as a double default. Electrically wired épées are used by the competitors. Each competitor must face all the others one time. To score the standard 1,000 points the athlete must win 70 percent of his matches; if he wins more than 70 percent, points are added to his score; if he loses more than 30 percent, points are deducted.

In Montreal the Soviet modern pentathlon team endured an outrageous embarrassment: Boris Onischenko, the silver medalist in Munich, was disqualified when it was discovered that he had wired his épée to record a hit when he hadn't actually made contact. He proclaimed his innocence and swore the épée was not his, but his pleas fell on deaf ears, and the teacher at the Dynamo Sports Institute in Kiev was ordered home by the Russian government.

Shooting

The pistol shooting competition takes place on the third day, with the men firing at silhouette targets from a distance of 25 meters. The targets pivot in such a way that the broadside view is visible for three seconds and then disappears for seven seconds. The pistol is drawn from an angle of 45 degrees (with the body). The contestant must score 194 points out of a possible 200 to receive the 1,000 points for the event. Each point over 194 is worth an additional 22 points, while each point below 194 is a minus 22.

Swimming

If the pentathlete swims the 300 meters in 3:54 or less, he receives 1,000 points. Five seconds below or above the 3:54 is worth plus or minus five points. In Montreal the fastest time posted was a 3:13.60, which was worth 1300 points.

Cross-country Run

The rugged cross-country course is 4,000 meters (2½ miles) long, with hills that may be as steep as 300 feet. The runner must clock a 14:15 time to receive the 1,000 points. For each second below that time, he gains three points; for each second above, he loses three points. In Montreal Adrian Parker's cross-country run of 12:09.50 was good for 1378 points. His outstanding last-day performance helped Great Britain to its first team gold medal.

Viewing Tips

Americans have never shown particular enthusiasm for the modern pentathlon, perhaps because it is an event little publicized in this country. But if one makes it a point to know the origins of the sport and to learn something about the athletes who are competing in it, then the modern pentathlon is a thrilling event to follow.

Every country that competes in the modern pentathlon has its own preferred training methods. The U.S. coaches believe that the keys to victory are the shooting, swimming, and running events. They feel that if an athlete is strong in those three areas, he can score well enough to win. The Hungarians, who have always excelled in the sport, emphasize the fencing, riding, and shooting segments. The Soviets teach the opposite; find strong runners and swimmers and then teach them to ride, fence, and shoot. Regardless of which training method is used, the modern pentathlete must eventually display proof that he is a superior all-around competitor.

Forecast: Moscow

Individual
1976 Champion: Janusz Pyciak-Peclak, Poland
1980 Favorites: Pyciak-Peclak, Poland; Pavel Lednev, USSR; Jan Bartu, Czechoslovakia

Team
1976 Champion: Great Britain
1980 Favorites: USSR; Poland; Hungary; Czechoslovakia

Rowing

Archaeological evidence indicates that certain prehistoric tribes of Asia held actual boat-racing competitions. Egyptians of the fourteen century B.C. practiced a sport they called "oarsmanship." In the writings of the poet Virgil, many lines allude to the "oarsmen with their naked shoulders, moist with oil." When the Romans invaded England in 54 B.C., they traveled in boats propelled by oars pulled through the water by the sweat-soaked biceps of slaves.

In England in 1715, the Irish actor Thomas Doggett sponsored the first modern rowing contest on the Thames River. The prize, "Doggett's Coat and Badge," was awarded to the first boatman to row his boat the 4½ miles from the London Bridge to Chelsea. The Doggett race was an outgrowth of the friendly competitions between the various water taxis that plied their trade on the river.

In 1811 an English crew manning a gig from the British

ship *Hussar* traveled to New York to race against the crew of the *American Star*. As reported in several New York City newspapers, the race from Bedloe's Island to Hoboken was viewed by 60,000 spectators. The *American Star* pulled off a minor upset. In 1829 crews from Oxford and Cambridge staged the first intercollegiate rowing race. The Henley Royal Regatta, initiated ten years later in 1839, became the first amateur race to achieve international status. Following the example of the two outstanding English universities, Harvard and Yale squared off on Lake Winnipesaukee in New Hampshire in 1852 in the first American intercollegiate competition. Harvard won the inaugural.

A coxless pairs event was scheduled on the program of the 1896 Athen games, but it had to be canceled due to poor rowing weather. So the first Olympic competition was actually held at the Paris games of 1900. There were five events on the Paris program. Surprisingly, the English, who were the finest rowers in the world at the time, sent only a single sculler. In the eight oar event the U.S. team from the Philadelphia Vesper Boat Club won what was to be the first of many gold medals. Since the Paris games, the U.S. has captured eleven gold medals in the men's coxed eights, though in Montreal in 1976, the U.S. failed to make the finals in the event for the first time in Olympic history.

1976 wasn't the only off year for America's rowers. London in 1908 and Stockholm in 1912 were also lean years for the U.S. But in Antwerp in 1920, John Kelly, who would later come to public attention as the father of Grace Kelly, won the single sculls. He then teamed with his cousin, Paul Costello, to win the double sculls. Four years later, in Paris in 1924, Kelly and Costello again took the double sculls. Costello found a new partner for the '28 games, but the result was still the same, a gold medal. In 1956 Kelly's son, John Kelly, Jr., earned a bronze in the singles, which so far has made him the last U.S. medalist in the event.

In recent years the USSR and East Germany have been extremely strong in the rowing competition. Since 1952 Russian rowers have captured ten gold medals. In 1976 the East

Germans exploded with victories in the quadruple sculls, the pairs with coxswain, pairs without coxswain, fours without coxswain, and the eights with coxswain.

In Montreal women competed in the rowing competition for the first time. Joan Lind of Long Beach, California, took the silver medal behind Scheiblich of East Germany in the single sculls, and the U.S. women's team regained some of America's lost pride by capturing the bronze in the eights with coxswain.

Rules

There are two classifications in the sport, rowing and sculling. In rowing the oarsman handles one oar with both hands; in sculling, the oarsman works a pair of oars, one in each hand. In Moscow there will be eight events for men: single sculls, double sculls, pair oars without coxswain, pair oars with coxswain, four oars without coxswain, four oars with coxswain, eight oars with coxswain, and the new event, added in 1976, quadruple sculls.

For the women there are six events: single sculls, fours with coxswain, double sculls, pairs without coxswain, quadruple sculls, and eights with coxswain.

The still-water course is 2,000 meters long. Six crews eventually make it to the finals after a series of heats, including repechage heats, in which a crew that has lost one match receives a second chance to make the semifinals.

The races start with the bows of the boats directly on the starting line. Adding a touch of glamor to the proceedings, the instructions are given in French: "Êtes vous prêt?" (are you ready?); "Partez" (go). A crew is allowed two false starts before being disqualified.

Single Sculls

Single sculls is generally considered to be the most difficult division. The boat is built for one man weighing approximately 185 pounds. The boat (shell) itself weighs only about 30 pounds. Single sculls is man-to-man competition in its purest form.

Double Sculls

The boat in the double sculls competition weighs about 65 pounds. It is rowed by two men with two oars each.

Pair Oars without Coxswain (Coxswainless Pairs)

In the pair oars, two men row with one oar each. The boat weighs about the same as the double sculls boat.

Four Oars without Coxswain (Coxswainless Fours)

The shell weighs 130 pounds. There are four men, but no coxswain to steer. The oarsman in the bow guides the boat with his right foot by pushing on a pedal attached to a rudder. However, he avoids using the rudder at all costs because it tends to slow the boat down; instead he calls for his oarsmen to put forth more effort on one side of the boat than the other.

Pair Oars with Coxswain (Coxed Pairs)

Two men plus a coxswain man this shell. The boat weighs about 85 pounds and is three feet longer than the boat used in the other pairs event. The coxswain sits in the rear (stern), steers the boat, and keeps an eye on the competition. He must weigh at least 110 pounds.

Four Oars with Coxswain (Coxed Fours)

Four oarsmen and a coxswain man the boat, which weighs 160 pounds and is 45 feet long.

Eight Oars with Coxswain (Coxed Eights)

Coxed eights are to rowing what the 1500 meters is to track and field. It is the favorite event of the fans, and justifiably so. Eights have been timed at almost fourteen miles per hour over the mile and quarter. For nine men moving a 300-pound boat through the water with only eight slim sticks of wood, that is a remarkable speed.

Quadruple Sculls

The quadruple sculls is four men without a coxswain, using eight oars.

Viewing Tips

Rowing can be a very exciting event, but as in all sports, certain aspects of it are more glamorous than others. For instance, the single sculls and the coxed eights are the true crowd-pleasers. The single sculls is raw one-on-one competition—the "prize fight" of rowing. The coxed eights is a beautiful and thrilling event, a fluid study in timing and power. Only after years of working together does a coxed eight crew jell. The finals are a "don't miss."

The pair oars without coxswain is also a spectator favorite. Again, timing is critical, since there must be perfect synchronization between the two rowers. Both the pair oars with coxswain and the four oars with coxswain are considered to be primarily power events, since the crews must have the strength to propel an extra, nonrowing man through the water. Neither of the events is known for attracting the best oarsmen.

You may hear the commentators speak of the "run." The run is the distance the shell is propelled by one stroke of the crew. The seats in the sculls slide back and forth about sixteen inches, which allows the sculler to push off the foot braces and transfer the pulling action from the arms to the legs. In the rowing competition, teamwork is more than important, it is essential. Without it, the rowers cannot generate any speed.

Forecast: Moscow

MEN

Single Sculls
1976 Champion: Pertti Karppinen, Finland
1980 Favorites: West Germany; Yugoslavia; East Germany; USSR

Double Sculls
1976 Champion: Norway
1980 Favorites: Norway; Great Britain; East Germany

Quadruple Sculls
1976 Champion: East Germany
1980 Favorites: France; West Germany; East Germany

Coxed Pair
1976 Champion: East Germany
1980 Favorites: East Germany; Poland; Czechoslovakia

Pairs without Coxswain
1976 Champion: East Germany
1980 Favorites: East Germany; USA; France; Holland

Coxed Fours
1976 Champion: USSR
1980 Favorites: USSR; East Germany; Great Britain

Fours without Coxswain
1976 Champion: East Germany
1980 Favorites: East Germany; USSR

Eights
1976 Champion: East Germany
1980 Favorites: East Germany; West Germany; New Zealand

WOMEN

Single Sculls
1976 Champion: Christine Scheiblich, East Germany
1980 Favorites: East Germany; USSR; USA; Hungary

Double Sculls
1976 Champion: Bulgaria
1980 Favorites: Bulgaria; USA; East Germany

Quadruple Sculls
1976 Champion: East Germany
1980 Favorites: East Germany; USSR; Rumania

Pairs without Coxswain
1976 Champion: Bulgaria
1980 Favorites: East Germany; Canada

Coxed Fours
1976 Champion: East Germany
1980 Favorites: Bulgaria; East Germany; USA; USSR

Eights
1976 Champion: East Germany
1980 Favorites: East Germany; USA; USSR; Canada

Shooting

It was inevitable that shooting should have been included in the Olympic program of the first modern games in Athens, for although man has yet to become civilized enough to eliminate weapons of combat, he long ago reached the point where he saw other uses for them besides killing. From spear throwing came the javelin competition; from military bow and arrows came archery; and the Olympic shooting events also evolved from military competition.

The first guns were long-barreled weapons, rifles of a sort, developed during the fourteenth century. The handgun was invented in the early fifteenth century by Camillo Vitelli, whose hometown, Pistoia, Italy, was the inspiration for the word "pistol." Vitelli's pistol was a simple metal tube fixed to a straight stock of wood, having a touchhole through which the powder was ignited with a slow match. The wheel lock was invented almost a hundred years after Vitelli's pistol, and it was at that time that firearms were adopted for sporting purposes. The weapons that will be used in Moscow by the marksmen of some seventy countries are a long way from Vitelli's crude but effective instrument.

In the shooting competition at the 1896 Athens games, the

host Greeks won three gold medals, and the U.S. team won two. The medalists for the U.S. were two brothers, John and Sumner Paine. The Paines' victories forged a path of success for other American marksmen that continued through the 1920 games at Antwerp. After that, the Swedes and the Norwegians moved to the fore. However, since 1952, the USSR's many outstanding competitors have garnered more than their share of medals. East Germany and Poland have also fostered many excellent marksmen.

Interestingly, the shooting competition has undergone possibly more changes than any other Olympic event. There were five events in Athens and six, including trap, at Paris. Team competitions were added in St. Louis. In 1912 the Swedes capitalized on their prowess in the sport and offered up twelve divisions in Stockholm. In the 1920 games there were an amazing nineteen categories in the shooting competition, a testimony to the growing popularity of the sport. By 1972 the number of divisions had been pared down to a workable eight, and in Montreal seven categories were contested, the same number scheduled for Moscow.

The shooting story in Montreal was very dramatic. The U.S. scored a gold in trap shooting and another in the crowd-pleasing three-position–small-bore-rifle competition. It was the three-position competition that captured the headlines. Lanny Bassham, a captain in the U.S. Army, had finished second to his compatriot, John Writer, in Munich. The confident, loquacious Bassham arrived in Montreal prepared only for victory. His teammate was Margaret Murdoch, a stocky ex-WAC with outstanding credentials, including the Pan-American championship. Murdoch was the first woman to represent the U.S. in the Olympic shooting competition.

Throughout the arduous, nerve-straining match, Murdoch held a slim lead over Bassham and the West German, Siebold. But towards the end of the competition, Murdoch faltered slightly, just enough to let Bassham catch her. In the case of a tie, the judges turn back to the last ten shots to make their decision. There, Bassham had barely bested Murdoch. At the awards ceremony the two mounted the victory stand. As the flag was raised and the first strains of the national anthem sounded, Bassham leaned over and grabbed Margaret's hand and pulled her up to the higher step. Together they stood at attention as the anthem was played. Later Bassham said, "I didn't do it as an act of defiance, I just believed Margaret shot as well as I did."

Rules

A participating country may enter two contestants for each of the categories. The weapons used in the competition must meet specific requirements concerning caliber or gauge, barrel length, weight, ammunition, and type of sight. Telescopic sights are not allowed.

.22 Caliber Small-Bore Rifle—Three Positions

The three positions of the competition are standing, kneeling, and prone. From each position, forty shots are fired at a distance of 50 meters from the target. In the standing and prone positions the contestants have two hours to fire the forty shots. For the kneeling position they are allotted one hour and forty-five minutes.

The target is approximately 6¼ inches wide, and the bull's-eye is three-quarters of the size of a dime. It is worth ten points, and the concentric circles and lines around the bull's-eye are worth from nine points down to one.

Small-Bore Rifle—Prone

This event, often called the English match, is conducted in the same manner as three-position, except that only the prone position is used. There are sixty shots fired, ten shots per series, with a two-hour time limit.

Rapid-Fire Pistol

Here the shots are fired in two courses, with a course comprising six five-shot series. In all, sixty shots are fired at five targets from a distance of twenty-five meters. The five targets are revealed simultaneously, and the shooter fires one shot per target. In the first two series, the five shots must be fired within eight seconds; in the next two series, within six seconds; and in the last two series, within four seconds.

Free Pistol

The target distance is fifty meters. A total of sixty shots—six ten-shot series—must be fired within a 3½-hour time period.

Moving Target

A target resembling a boar moves across an open space of ten meters at a constant speed. Two speeds are used. In the fast run the target is available for 2.5 seconds. In the slow run it is exposed for 5 seconds. Three ten-shot series may be fired at each target. The distance is fifty meters.

Clay Pigeon—Trap

Each competitor fires a total of 200 shots in eight rounds of 25. The weapons used are 12-gauge shotguns. In the trap event the shooter maintains a constant position while the birds are thrown up from different angles.

Clay Pigeon—Skeet

The specifics of the skeet competition are the same as for the trap, except that in the skeet event the birds are thrown up from two positions, while the shooter fires from several locations.

Viewing Tips

The 1976 Olympic champion, Lanny Bassham, called his event—the small-bore rifle—a sport of "controlled non-movement." It is a perfect description. Olympic marksmen must be able to control their bodies over an exhausting, six-hour period. The slightest movement while the trigger is being pulled will cause an errant shot. And in the Olympic events, two or three errant shots and the marksman can forget about winning a medal. A missed bull's-eye can be costly, but a score of eight or below is usually fatal to a competitor's chances.

When you're watching the shooting competition, pay close attention to the pace of the shooters. Notice how they utilize the entire two hours to fire the forty shots. They will wait until conditions are perfect before firing. Optimum conditions mean the right lighting and no wind.

Part of Bassham's Olympic preparation included not eating for twelve hours before the competition. It assured him his digestive system would not be working. Even the movement of his stomach could have affected his aim. Lanny spent years training his body for the Olympic competition. His pulse rate was an exact sixty beats, which left him a full second between beats, and in that second he pulled the trigger. The triggers used in the competition can be set off with as little as two ounces of pressure.

The rifles used in the Olympics may weigh as much as seventeen pounds, so holding one steady over a two-hour period requires strength and stamina. Shooting is a somewhat esoteric sport, but if as a spectator you know what to look for, it can be fascinating to watch.

Forecast: Moscow

Small-bore Rifle—Prone
1976 Champion: Karl Smieszek, West Germany
1980 Favorites: Margaret Murdoch, Lones Wigger, USA; Malcom Cooper, Great Britain

Small-bore Rifle—Three Positions
1976 Champion: Lanny Bassham, USA
1976 Favorites: Bassham, USA; Stephen Thynel, Sweden; Gottfried Kustman, West Germany

Rapid-fire Pistol
1976 Champion: Norbert Klaar, East Germany
1980 Favorites: Dan Iyuga, Rumania; Ian Tripsa, Rumania; Ragnar Skanaker, Sweden

Free Pistol
1976 Champion: Uwe Potteck, East Germany
1980 Favorites: Mauritz Minder, Switzerland; Harald Vollmar, East Germany

Moving Target
1976 Champion: Alexsander Gazov, USSR
1980 Favorites: Ranniko, Finland; Carlos Silva, Guatemala;
Giovanni Mezzani, Italy; Christoph Zeisner, West Germany

Trap Shooting
1976 Champion: Don Haldeman, USA
1980 Favorites: Haldeman, USA; Athos Pisoni, Brazil;
Michel Carrega, France

Skeet Shooting
1976 Champion: Josef Panacek, Czechoslovakia
1980 Favorites: Elie Pinot, France; Gert Bengtsson, Sweden;
Luciano Brunetti, Italy; Fiermo Roberti, Argentina

Soccer

Major league baseball calls its climactic end-of-the-season tournament the World Series, and the National Football League brings us the Super Bowl, the championship of professional football. Realistically, though, the World Series isn't really the championship of anything except professional baseball in the United States, and the Super Bowl is seldom super. There is only one major sport in which the championship is truly the championship of the world—soccer.

The world championship tournament of soccer is held, like the Olympics, every four years; it is called the World Cup and it is the pinnacle of success in professional soccer. If the projected viewing figures for the Moscow games hold up, the 1978 World Cup—with its one billion viewers—will have attracted the second largest viewing audience for a sporting event in the history of the world. What the World Cup is to professional soccer, the Olympics are to the amateur version.

Today more than 150 nations field soccer teams for international competition. And though the British lay claim to being the fathers of the sport, it is more likely that at least ten different ancient cultures played a game which involved kicking a ball around a field. We know for certain that both the Romans and the Chinese engaged in such games. Some archaeologists claim to have unearthed evidence that in early cultures the "balls" were actually the heads of hated enemies who had been defeated in combat.

By the fourteenth century the sport had become so popular in England that King Edward II outlawed it, hoping to encourage the pursuit of more gentlemanly and practical sports, such as archery. Edward wasn't very successful in discouraging his subjects, and neither were any of his successors, including Elizabeth I, who banned the sport in 1572.

Almost three hundred years later, in 1863, the English Football Association was born. Within a decade the sport was being played on almost every continent. The word "soccer" comes from a bastardized version of "association football," the term used to differentiate the game from Rugby football, which was also popular during the late 1800s. When the newspapers reported the matches, they often shortened that to "assoc. football," and from there it is not difficult to see how the word "soccer" evolved.

Up until the 1930s the British were the masters of the game. Then in one great ten-year wave, the South American teams became competitive. By 1955 the European countries of Hungary, Yugoslavia, Italy, Germany, and Spain were challenging for the World Cup and the Olympic gold medal.

Soccer was included on the Olympic program for the first time in Paris in 1900, though only two countries competed that year. Similarly, in St. Louis in 1904, only two teams, the U.S. and Canada, were represented. Canada won, but the silver medal that went to the Americans is the only one this country has ever received. Except in 1924 and 1928, when Uruguay won the tournament, the gold medal has always gone to a European nation. In 1972 in Munich, Poland defeated Hungary for the championship by a score of 2–1. The U.S. made it into the final sixteen teams that year, which for the American squad was a significant accomplishment. In 1976 East Germany beat Poland 3–1, to take the gold.

Rules

Since so many nations have soccer teams, and since the

Olympic competition is limited to sixteen teams, the International Amateur Football Federation conducts a worldwide elimination tournament on several continents during the year prior to the games. Fourteen teams are chosen by this means, and the representation is geographical. In 1980 two countries from North and Central America will go to the Olympics; two will be there from South America; three from Asia, Australia, and New Guinea; three from Africa; and four from Europe. The defending champion, East Germany, and the host country, Russia, automatically receive invitations. The United States will be conspicuous only by its absence in Moscow; Mexico eliminated the U.S. squad in early 1979.

After the sixteen teams have been decided, the field is divided into four groups of four teams. The four teams then play each other one time. The two leaders of each group advance into the quarterfinals. Eventually, the eight teams are reduced to only two, and the finalists play for the gold. In 1980 the soccer finals will be held in Central Lenin Stadium, while the quarterfinals and semifinals will be played in Minsk, Kiev, and Leningrad.

Each team is allowed to bring seventeen players, of whom eleven are on the field at one time. The teams are allowed only two substitutions per game. A team consists of a goalkeeper, two fullbacks, three halfbacks, and five forwards. No one except the goalie may use his hands, except on throw ins from out of bounds, and the goalie may use his hands only in the penalty area in front of the net. Also he must bounce the ball after taking four steps. When the ball goes out of bounds off a player's foot, a player from the opposing team throws the ball back in play using a two-hand overhead toss. If the ball goes out of bounds behind the net, it is put back into play with either a corner kick by a player from the defending team or a goal kick from a player of the offensive team.

The Olympic soccer field is 105 meters long by 68 meters wide. It is slightly larger than an American football field. The goal is 24 feet wide by 8 feet high. The ball weighs between 14 and 16 ounces, and is 8½ inches in diameter. The game is played in two 45-minute halves (no timeouts).

Depending upon the infraction, different penalties are assessed; they range from loss of possession to a free kick at the goal from twenty yards out.

If a game ends in a tie, two 15-minute overtime periods may be played. If the game is still tied, the winner is decided by a series of five penalty kicks, with the teams taking alternating shots at the goal.

Viewing Tips

Soccer is an extremely fast-paced game with constant action at both ends of the field. In many ways it is similar to ice hockey, with offensive men rushing towards the goal, defensive men trying to thwart the assault, and the goalie moving around, intently watching the ball, always preparing to cut down the angle the shooter will have at the net.

American spectators have always been hungry for high-scoring games. They seem to equate lots of scoring with outstanding play. And since soccer games often end with the score 2–1 or 3–2, they cite the low scores as evidence that the game is slow and boring. However, if you consider that in American football the touchdown, which is the unit of scoring, counts for six points even though it is only one score, you'll see that the scoring in soccer is often comparable to that of American football. If a touchdown counted only one point, many NFL games would end with 3–2 and 4–3 scores.

Soccer is a relatively easy game to follow, which partially accounts for its tremendous popularity. To get a sense of which team is dominating the game, notice which end of the field most of the action is taking place in, and which side is taking the most shots. It's an old—but accurate—axiom that a team can't score if it can't get the ball out of its own territory.

It is thrilling to watch the great Olympic players control the ball; they are as deft and agile with their insteps (the toe is rarely used for kicking) as most athletes are with their hands. They fake, stop, dribble, and shoot with uncanny accuracy. Another exciting move is the header, in which a goal is scored by a player's heading the ball into the net. Obviously, it takes a strong neck and excellent coordination to head the ball with the force required to score a goal.

Forecast: Moscow
1976 Champion: East Germany
1980 Favorites: Poland; East Germany; USSR; Brazil

Swimming and Diving

In no other Olympic sport have the times of the performances improved as much as they have in swimming. Compare, for instance, the improvements in the performances of
track and field athletes with those of swimmers. In the 1896
Athens games the fastest man in the world over 100 meters
of cinder track was Tom Burke. He covered the distance in 12
seconds. In 1976 Hasely Crawford of Jamaica traveled the
100 meters in 10.06 seconds. In a span of eighty years, the
times of the best sprinters in the world improved by less than
two seconds.

In 1896 a Hungarian swimmer named Alfred Hajos won
the 100-meter freestyle in 1:22.2. Undoubtedly, the 1980 gold
medalist in the same event will break the 50-second barrier.
That's an improvement of over half a minute within a distance of 100 meters. Since the first games of the modern era,
swimming performances have improved by approximately
30 percent. Not all of the reasons for the dramatically faster
times have to do with the abilities of the athletes. Technical
advances certainly have accounted to some degree for speed-
ier clockings. In the Athens games the swimmers competed
in the Bay of Zea, where the course was simply marked off
with ropes. The ocean currents and pounding waves made
the going slow and rough. Contemporary competition swimming pools are labeled "fast" or "slow" depending on specific
factors. Fast pools—and the one in Moscow is expected to be
superfast—have a uniform depth of at least eight to nine
feet, so the water doesn't rebound off the bottom and cause
added turbulence. A fast pool has a good gutter system, which
laps up the overflow caused by the swimmer's arm and kicking action, and a continuous feed of new water into the system at the bottom of the pool, which maintains the same
water level throughout the race.

The skintight, modern-day swimming suits eliminate unnecessary drag. And it's to the point now where many men have even shaved their heads in search of a few milli-seconds of shaved time.

Though new equipment and faster pools have had a tremendously positive effect on the racers' times, most of the credit for the improved performances still goes to the athletes. The Olympic swimmers of the 1980s have better training methods, stronger bodies, and more advanced stroke technique than their predecessors.

For all the changes that have taken place in the sport, a few things have remained the same. Swimming, like gymnastics, continues to be a sport for the youngsters of the world, especially as far as the women are concerned—world class female swimmers are rarely out of their teens. In 1968, the golden girl from Sacramento, Debbie Meyer, won three gold medals. She was fifteen years old. Debbie's time in the 400-meter free was 4:31.8, 33 seconds faster than Johnny Weissmuller's gold medal clocking in the 400 in the 1924 games. This year in Moscow, Tracy Caulkins and Cynthia "Sippy" Woodhead will carry on the Olympic teenager tradition.

The exact origins of swimming as a sport are as elusive to pin down as the mermaids of ancient Greek mythology. From Roman historians we know that Julius Caesar was quite a skillful swimmer. Ancient Egyptian artifacts depict women swimmers practicing a style that is similar to the present-day breaststroke. And more than once, the Old Testament mentions people swimming in the Nile.

Japan was the first country to develop a national swimming program. In 1603 the Japanese emperor decreed that certain privileged private schools would compete against each other in swimming matches. In 1837, two hundred years after the Japanese, the English formed a national swimming association. The association spent its time organizing competitive races, most of which were won by breaststrokers or sidestrokers, those being the earliest strokes used in the sport. The British also developed huge "swimming tanks" for indoor swimming; by 1830 there were six such tanks in London.

Other countries followed suit, and as swimming became more organized, the competitive emphasis shifted from long distance races to events which emphasized speed rather than endurance. Accordingly, a variety of strokes were developed and refined, with those that constitute the modern repertoire—the breaststroke, the backstroke, the butterfly, and the freestyle (Australian crawl)—eventually accepted as the most efficient and effective means of propelling the body rapidly through water.

Swimming has been a part of the Olympic program from the very beginning of the modern games, but it was at the 1912 Olympics in Stockholm that the sport really came of age, largely through the exploits of Duke Kahanamoku, an Hawaiian swimmer with skin like tanned leather and a weightlifter's body. Kahanamoku had honed the flutter kick into a precisely timed up-and-down movement, streamlined the turn, and perfected a bilateral breathing method. His techniques left his opponents floundering and marked the beginning of a new era in competitive swimming. It was in Stockholm also that women competed in Olympic swimming for the first time.

American swimmers—male and female—have compiled a brilliant record in Olympic competition, yielding dominance from time to time only to the Australians and more recently, in the women's events in 1976, to the East Germans.

In Munich in 1972, the U.S. team took gold medals in seventeen of the twenty-nine events—nine for the men and eight for the women. Then in Montreal, the U.S. men's team completely overwhelmed the opposition. In an unprecedented near sweep, the American men won twelve gold medals, and twenty-five of thirty-seven total medals. In only one race did they fail to finish first, and in the course of the competition they set eighteen new world records. The women's team, stunned by the power of the East German squad and its leader, Kornelia Ender, managed only one gold. The young women now preparing to test the water in Moscow have no intention of allowing that particular bit of history to repeat itself.

Although it is likely that man was diving into water about the same time he began swimming in it, it wasn't until 1895 that diving as a sport came into being. In that year the Royal Lifesaving Society of Great Britain sponsored several "diving competitions" throughout the country.

Diving was first introduced into the Olympic games in St. Louis in 1904. On the program that year were both springboard and platform competitions. G. E. Sheldon, an American diver, won both events. From 1904 until Antwerp in 1920, the German and Swedish divers demonstrated their superiority. But from Antwerp to the 1964 Tokyo games the U.S. divers reasserted themselves. In that span of forty-four years, American divers won every platform event except one, and every single springboard. Some of the great U.S. divers during that period were Albert White, Pete Desjardins, Sammy Lee, Bob Webster, David Browning, Ken Sitzberger, and Bernard Wrightson in 1968. Among the outstanding women divers were Elizabeth Becker, who won the springboard in 1924, then married the men's champion, Clarence Pinkston, and Pat McCormick won the springboard *and* the platform in 1952 and then remarkably came back to duplicate the feat in Melbourne in '56.

In 1972 Micki King, who won the springboard competition, was the only U.S. woman diver to capture a medal. Four years earlier in Mexico City, Micki appeared to have locked up the gold in the springboard, but she broke her arm on the next to last dive and ended up fourth.

Also in Munich, the great Italian diver, twenty-four-year-old Klaus Dibiasi, competing in his third Olympics, won the platform competition for the second straight time. Incredibly, in Montreal, Klaus won the platform for a third time, narrowly edging the tough American youngster, Greg Louganis. Louganis shrugged off the defeat; after all, he was beaten by Dibiasi. Phil Boggs of the U.S. took the springboard. Jennifer Chandler, also of the U.S., finished first in the women's springboard.

Rules

There will be thirteen swimming events for men, thirteen for women, and two diving events for each in the 1980 games. The programs for men and women are almost identical: both will swim in 100-, 200-, and 400-meter freestyle events; in 100- and 200-meter competitions in the breaststroke, the backstroke, and the butterfly; and in the 400-meter individual medley. The men will compete in a 1500-meter freestyle race; the women in an 800-meter race. In the team competitions the men swim a 4x200 freestyle and a 4x100 medley relay; the women swim a 4x100 freestyle and a 4x100 medley relay. The diving events for both are the 3-meter springboard and the platform.

Each country may enter a total of thirty-three men and thirty women in the swimming and diving competition. Three competitors may be entered for each event, and one team per country may be entered in the relays. In the freestyle competition any stroke is legal, but the crawl is almost always used.

The breaststroke must be executed with the arms and legs in the water at all times. The butterfly is a variation of the breaststroke, but the arms are flung out of the water, over the head, and pulled back through the water to the sides of the torso.

The competitions take place in a fifty-meter pool divided into eight lanes. The contestants must stay within the boundaries of their lanes. All races except the backstroke start with the swimmers on platforms at one end of the pool; at the starter's gun, they dive into the water. The backstrokers start in the water, leaning back as they hold onto the side.

In the diving events the springboard is three meters high, the platform is ten meters. The diving competition is evaluated by seven judges, who must consider two factors on each dive, execution and degree of difficulty.

Each dive is given a score by each judge. The scores range from 10 (a perfect score) down to 0, using half-point increments. After a dive is completed, each judge registers his score, the highest and lowest marks are tossed out, and the remaining five are multiplied by a degree of difficulty factor. There is a standard Olympic table which rates the degree of difficulty for all possible dives. The table rates dives from a low of 1.2 to a high of 3.0. For example, if a diver received a combined score of 30 from the five judges, and the degree of difficulty of the dive was 2.0, then his score for the dive would be 60.0. The diving competition is similar to gymnastics in that each competitor must perform a series of compulsory dives, after which he may perform his own optional dives. In the platform competition the men have ten dives, the women eight. In springboard the men make eleven dives, the women ten.

Viewing Tips

To enjoy watching the Olympic swimming competition, one does not necessarily need an extensive knowledge of the sport. The swimmer who finishes first wins. However, there are certain things to look for which can make the viewing more interesting.

The butterfly, for instance, is the most physically demanding stroke. A good butterflier must have strength and stamina. In the kick that accompanies the overhead arm motion—called the dolphin kick—the feet stay together and move up and down in the water, bending at the knees.

The breaststroke kick is a slight variation of the universal frog kick.

During the competitions pay particular attention to the starts and the turns. By watching the turns you can get a good idea of who's making up ground and who's losing it—and why. The new flip and somersault turns are major reasons for the faster times of today's athletes.

At the start the swimmers attempt to get off the mark as quickly as possible. They strive for full extension on the dive, but they must stay on the surface of the water. Any motion that cuts into the water costs precious seconds.

Diving is one of the most beautiful sports in the Olympics. It requires of its participants a combination of skills: the balance and tumbling ability of a gymnast, the strength of a swimmer, and the guts of a skydiver. The platform competition takes place from a tower thirty-four feet above the water. That's like jumping off a three-story building. When the diver hits the water he may be moving forty miles per hour, and that can result in a concussion severe enough to break more than one bone.

Notice the size of the splash the diver makes as he or she enters the water; generally, the smaller the splash, the smoother the entry. There are five basic types of dives—forward, backward, gainer (the diver faces the water on take-off but spins around to go in facing the board), cutaway (the diver faces the board but cuts forward and goes in facing the water), and twist (the diver spins like a ballet dancer, rotating on his head-to-toe axis)—and combinations of the five are also possible.

Don't expect the same divers to excel in both the springboard and platform competitions. The two disciplines demand different training techniques, and only rarely does a diver achieve full mastery of both.

Forecast: Moscow

SWIMMING—MEN

100-meter Freestyle
1976 Champion: Jim Montgomery, USA
1980 Favorites: Montgomery, Rowdy Gaines, David McCagg, USA

200-meter Freestyle
1976 Champion: Bruce Furniss, USA
1980 Favorites: Gaines, Brian Goodell, USA; Sergei Kopliakov, USSR

400-meter Freestyle
1976 Champion: Brian Goodell, USA
1980 Favorites: Goodell, USA; Vladimir Salnikov, USSR

1500 Freestyle

1976 Champion: Brian Goodell, USA
1980 Favorites: Goodell, USA; Salnikov, USSR

100-meter Backstroke
1976 Champion: John Naber, USA
1980 Favorites: Bob Jackson, Peter Rocca, Clay Britt, USA; Viktor Kuznetsov, USSR

200-meter Backstroke
1976 Champion: John Naber, USA
1980 Favorites: Jesse Vassallo, Peter Rocca, USA; Kuznetsova, USSR

100-meter Breaststroke
1976 Champion: John Hencken, USA
1980 Favorites: Hencken, Steve Lundquist, USA; Gerald Moerken, West Germany; Graham Smith, Canada

200-meter Breaststroke
1976 Champion: David Wilkie, Great Britain
1980 Favorites: Lundquist, Nick Nevid, Hencken, USA; Moerken, West Germany; Smith, Canada

100-meter Butterfly
1976 Champion: Matt Vogel, USA
1980 Favorites: Joe Bottom, USA; Roger Pyttel, East Germany; Par Arvidsson, Sweden

200-meter Butterfly
1976 Champion: Mike Bruner, USA
1980 Favorites: Bottom, USA; Pyttel, East Germany; Arvidsson, Sweden

400-meter Individual Medley
1976 Champion: Rod Strachan, USA
1980 Favorites: Jesse Vassallo, USA; Sergei Fesenko, USSR

400-meter Medley Relay
1976 Champion: USA

1980 Favorites: USA; USSR; Sweden

800-meter Relay
1976 Champion: USA
1980 Favorites: USA; USSR; Canada; West Germany

SWIMMING—WOMEN

100-meter Freestyle
1976 Champion: Kornelia Ender, East Germany
1980 Favorites: Cynthia Woodhead, Jill Sterkel, USA;
Barbara Krause, East Germany

200-meter Freestyle
1976 Champion: Kornelia Ender, East Germany
1980 Favorites: Woodhead, Kim Linehan, Sterkel, USA;
Krause, East Germany; Tracey Wickham, Australia

400-meter Freestyle
1976 Champion: Petra Thumer, East Germany
1980 Favorites: Woodhead, Linehan, Tracy Caulkins, USA;
Tracey Wickham, Australia

800-meter Freestyle
1976 Champion: Petra Thumer, East Germany
1980 Favorites: Woodhead, Linehan, Wickham, USA; Michele Ford, Australia

100-meter Breaststroke
1976 Champion: Hannelore Anke, East Germany
1980 Favorites: Julia Bogdanova, USSR; Tracy Caulkins, USA

200-meter Breaststroke
1976 Champion: Marina Koshevaia, USSR
1980 Favorites: Caulkins, USA; Lina Kachushite, Bogdanova, USSR

100-meter Butterfly
1976 Champion: Kornelia Ender, East Germany

1980 Favorites: Andrea Pollack, East Germany; Mary Meagher, Jill Sterkel, Caulkins, Joan Pennington, USA

200-meter Butterfly
1976 Champion: Andrea Pollack, East Germany
1980 Favorites: Meagher, Caulkins, USA; Pollack, East Germany

100-meter Backstroke
1976 Champion: Ulrike Richter, East Germany
1980 Favorites: Linda Jezek, Kim Carlisle, USA; Antie Stille, East Germany

200-meter Backstroke
1976 Champion: Ulrike Richter, East Germany
1980 Favorites: Jezek, USA; Stille, Kornelia Polit, East Germany

400-meter Individual Medley
1976 Champion: Ulrike Tauber, East Germany
1980 Favorites: Caulkins, USA; Petra Schneider, East Germany; Sharon Davies, Great Britain

400-meter Freestyle Relay
1976 Champion: USA
1980 Favorites: USA; Canada; East Germany

400-meter Medley Relay
1976 Champion: East Germany
1980 Favorites: USA; East Germany; Canada

DIVING—MEN

Springboard
1976 Champion: Phil Boggs, USA
1980 Favorites: Boggs, Greg Louganis, USA; Giorgio Cagnotto, Italy

Platform
1976 Champion: Klaus Dibiasi, Italy
1980 Favorites: Louganis, USA; Falk Hoffman, East
Germany; Carlos Giron, Mexico; David Ambartsumian,
USSR

DIVING—WOMEN

Springboard
1976 Champion: Jennifer Chandler, USA
1980 Favorites: Chandler, Cynthia Potter, USA; Irina
Kalinina, USSR

Platform
1976 Champion: Elena Vaytsehovskaia, USSR
1980 Favorites: Kalinina, USSR; Martina Jaeschke, East
Germany; Melissa Briley, Barb Weinstein, USA

Volleyball

Volleyball, like basketball, was invented in a Massachusetts YMCA gymnasium. In 1895 William Morgan, a physical
education instructor for the Holyoke YMCA, designed the
game, which he called "mintonette," for businessmen who
found basketball too rigorous. Two years after Morgan strung
the tattered tennis net across the gym floor, he set forth the
rules of mintonette in a handbook for the sport. A short time
later the name "mintonette" gave way to "volleyball," which
better described the way the players volleyed the ball back
and forth.

The first national tournament was held in a Brooklyn
YMCA in 1922. Six years later the United States Volleyball
Association became the single recognized governing body. In
1947 the International Volleyball Federation was formed un-
der the leadership of Paul Liband, a Frenchman. In 1949 the
U.S. Women's Collegiate Division was organized.

Volleyball made its entry into the Olympic games following
a 1957 exhibition match played before the IOC in Sofia,
Bulgaria. In the 1964 Olympic games in Tokyo, the USSR

men won the debut gold and the Japanese triumphed in the women's division. Interestingly, all of the women on the Japanese team were employees of the same company. During the four years prior to the games, they had devoted all of their free time to training and practice. Since 1964 the USSR and Japan have been the dominant forces in both men's and women's volleyball. In 1972 the Japanese men overcame the East Germans and the Soviet women successfully defended their 1968 title. In 1976 the Japanese women again prevailed, and Poland won the gold in the men's tournament.

Rules

The International Volleyball Federation supervises the qualifying procedure for the Olympic volleyball tournament. In the women's competition, automatic bids are extended to the defending Olympic champion, the current world champion, and the host country. The remaining berths are occupied by the North American–Central American champion, the South American champion, the Asian champion, and an at-large team.

The men's qualifying procedure is basically the same as the women's, except that three other teams are included— the African champion and the top two finishers in the qualifying tournament.

In the game itself two teams of six players occupy opposite sides of a net (8 feet high for men, 7 feet 4½ inches for women) on a smooth-surfaced court, 30 feet by 60 feet. The object of the game is for one team to get the ball over the net and have it touch the ground within the opponent's "fair" area. The ball may be struck up to three times on each side, but no player may touch the ball twice in succession.

Only the serving team may score a point. When the serve changes hands (side out), no points are awarded. The game is won by the first team to score fifteen points, and the winning team must win by two points. Olympic matches are decided in the best two out of three games.

Viewing Tips

Each time the serving point is won, the players rotate their position in a clockwise direction. The three players on the front line move one man to the right, the three on the back line move one man to the left. The things to watch for are the exciting spikes, where a player jumps above the net and hits the ball straight down into the opponent's court. Spikes by world class players have been timed at speeds in excess of 100 miles per hour. Also notice the diving saves, where the players save the ball from touching the ground by diving recklessly to the floor, stopping the ball inches from the ground.

In Olympic competition neither team may speak to the referee during play. Communication between the referee, who sits on a raised platform similar to that of a tennis referee, and the players is done by a complicated set of hand signals.

Forecast: Moscow

MEN

1976 Champion: Poland
1980 Favorites: USSR; Cuba; Brazil; Italy; Poland

WOMEN

1976 Champion: Japan
1980 Favorites: Japan; Cuba; USSR; USA

Water Polo

Water polo was developed in England in 1870. In many ways the game suggests soccer played in the water. Although it may not have started out as a very physical sport, water polo today is one of the roughest games in the world. In the early years of the sport, the players would swim or walk on the bottom of the pool, so the coaches merely recruited the largest and strongest athletes they could find, regardless of aquatic abilities. In recent years that practice has stopped, but the sport remains rough, tough, and bloody.

In the 1900 Paris games, England dominated the event. In

those rugged days it was quite acceptable to rip the ball from an opponent's hands using any method whatsoever. One such method involved holding the opponent's head under the water until he surrendered the ball. In later Olympic games, after the introduction of the fully inflated ball, such tactics were outlawed. Nevertheless, some of the tactics you will see in Moscow are not that far removed from the early drowning moves.

Italy, Germany, and, particularly, Hungary have been the dominant Olympic forces in water polo. In 1972 the USSR finally avenged many previous defeats at the hands of the Hungarians. The U.S. that year finished a surprising third.

In Montreal Hungary returned to the winner's circle. Italy copped the silver, the Netherlands the bronze.

Rules

The object of the game is to put the ball in the opponent's net, while prohibiting him from doing likewise. There are seven men on a squad. The goalie may handle the ball with two hands. Everyone else must use only one hand. The players may carry the ball in one hand while they are swimming, or they may pass the ball, or it may be dribbled (pushed along by the head, while the player swims with both hands).

Penalties allow the offended player an unobstructed pass to a teammate or a free dribble, but no free shot. The water polo pool should be 30x20 meters, and have a uniform depth of six feet. The goal is a net 9.9 meters wide by 1 meter high which floats on the water in a secured spot. The goalkeeper may not throw the ball more than half the length of the pool, and he must remain within four yards of the net.

Viewing Tips

A lot of the action in water polo, unfortunately, goes on under the water. The referees constantly try to monitor the players' underwater actions, but it is a difficult, if not impossible, job. Water polo requires tremendous stamina and endurance. The men literally are treading water or swimming for the entire game. The best players are those who can endure like distance swimmers and explode like sprinters.

1976 Champion: Hungary
1980 Favorites: Hungary; USA; USSR; Yugoslavia

Weightlifting

The origins of the Olympic sport of weightlifting can be traced to the turn of the eighteenth century, when the first modern barbells were used by carnival strongmen. Up to that time, the weights used in lifting were dumbbells— small, single, hand weights.

The strongmen who traveled the U.S. and Europe during the early nineteenth century putting on carnival and circus exhibitions were the modern extensions of ancient myths that have been a part of every culture. In that same way, Vasily Alexeiev of the USSR is the evolutionary successor to the crowns of Samson and Hercules.

Weightlifting was part of the rigorous training schedule of all the ancient Greek athletes, especially the implement throwers and the wrestlers. Oddly enough, weightlifting as a separate individual sport was never a part of the ancient games. Yet when the IOC established the modern games, weightlifting was included on the program of the 1896 Athens Olympics.

In Athens gold medals were awarded in two weightlifting categories—barbell and dumbbell. Lancaster Elliot, an Englishman, won the gold in the dumbbell when he lifted 156½ pounds over his head with one hand. Viggo Jensen of Denmark won the barbell competition with a lift of 248 pounds.

Weightlifting was dropped for the 1900 games, but returned to the program in St. Louis in 1904. There, American Otto Oshoff of Milwaukee lifted 191¼ pounds over his head with one hand to win the gold. The event was deleted from the next two programs, but surfaced again for the 1920 Antwerp affair. At that time the dumbbell competition was permanently discontinued.

Beginning in 1948 and continuing through 1956, the U.S.

dominated the sport. In the 1948 games the American weight-lifters won four gold medals, three silvers, and one bronze. It was the finest American performance ever.

In 1960 the era of Soviet domination began. The Russians swept five of six golds in Rome. Since 1964 the Eastern European nations have "owned" the competitions, and the U.S. athletes have won only four medals.

Rules

There are ten weight divisions in the 1980 competitions:

Weight Division	Weight Limit
Flyweight	Up to 114 lbs.
Bantamweight	Up to 123 lbs.
Featherweight	Up to 132 lbs.
Lightweight	Up to 148 lbs.
Middleweight	Up to 165 lbs.
Light-Heavyweight	Up to 181 lbs.
Middle-Heavyweight	Up to 198 lbs.
100-Kilo (new category)	Up to 220 lbs.
Heavyweight	Up to 242 lbs.
Super Heavyweight	Over 242 lbs.

Each country may enter ten competitors, with a maximum of two lifters in each category. The barbells used in the Olympic competition consist of a steel bar two meters long with discs on the end. The discs range in weight from 2¼ pounds to 55 pounds. The lifting platform is four meters square and the competitors may not step beyond its boundaries without being disqualified. Each contestant gets three attempts at each weight.

The two Olympic lifts are the snatch and the clean and jerk.

Viewing Tips

In the snatch lift the athlete grips the barbell palms down and in one motion lifts the barbell off the ground and above his head. He then must lock his arms. In the upward thrust the legs may be split or bent, but once the bar is above the head the feet must remain on the same line and the bar must be held motionless until the referee gives the signal that the lift is valid.

The clean and jerk is a two-part movement. In the first movement the lifter takes the bar off the ground and brings it to his shoulders. The bar may not touch the chest until the first position movement is complete, at which point it may rest on the chest with the arms bent for as long as the lifter chooses. Then the feet are moved into a straight line in preparation for the jerk. The lifter bends his legs into a squat and in one move thrusts the bar above his head, completely extending his arms. He must hold the weight motionless until the referee's signal is given.

The referee and the two judges each control two buttons— one red and the other white. If two of the officials push the white buttons, which light white bulbs, the lift is correct: two red lights indicate a "no count."

Forecast: Moscow

Flyweight
1976 Champion: Alexander Voronin, USSR
1980 Favorites: Voronin, USSR; Stefan Leletko, Poland; Belah Olah, Hungary

Bantamweight
1976 Champion: Norair Nourikian, Bulgaria
1980 Favorites: Tad Dembonczyk, Poland; Anton Kodjabasev, Bulgaria

Featherweight
1976 Champion: Nikolai Kolesnikov, USSR
1980 Favorites: Kolesnikov, USSR; Valentin Todoroy, Bulgaria; Takshi Salto, Japan

Lightweight
1976 Champion: Zbigniew Kaczmarek, Poland
1980 Favorites: Yanko Rusev, Bulgaria; Gunther Ambrass, East Germany

Middleweight
1976 Champion: Yordan Mitkov, Bulgaria
1980 Favorites: Mitkov, Nikolai Kolev, Bulgaria; Peter Wenzel, East Germany

Light-Heavyweight
1976 Champion: Valeri Shary, USSR
1980 Favorites: Boris Blagoev, Bulgaria; Yuri Vardanyan, USSR

Middle-Heavyweight
1976 Champion: David Rigert, USSR
1980 Favorites: Gennadiy Bessonov, USSR; Rolf Milser, West Germany

100-Kilo Class
1976 Champion: (New Event)
1980 Favorites: David Rigert, USSR; Manfred Funke, East Germany

Heavyweight
1976 Champion: Valentin Christov, Bulgaria
1980 Favorites: Jurgen Clezki, East Germany; Yurily Zaitsev, USSR

Super Heavyweight
1976 Champion: Vasily Alexeiev, USSR
1980 Favorites: Alexeiev, USSR; Gerd Bonk, East Germany

Wrestling

First introduced as part of the pentathlon in the eighteenth ancient Olympiad in 708 B.C., wrestling had actually been practiced by the Japanese, Chinese, Persians, and Egyptians for centuries before that. Often these ancient wrestling contests were held in conjunction with religious festivals. Many of the myths that were part of the religions of the Egyptians and Greeks were based upon famous wrestling matches between the gods, or between the gods and heroes with super-human strength.

Naturally, when Baron de Coubertin revived the games in Athens in 1896, he made sure that wrestling was included on the program. At the time most wrestlers were actually professionals, earning, if not handsome salaries, at least adequate livelihoods. Now the professional wrestler is purely an entertainer, part clown, part stuntman, and the Olympic-style amateur wrestler is the true embodiment of the sport. In 1896 the heavyweight category was the only division contested. The athletes wrestled Greco-Roman style, in which the contestants begin standing up and no holds below the waist are permitted. Historically, Greco-Roman wrestling has been dominated by the wrestlers from Europe and the Middle East. In fact, no American has ever won a medal in the event.

In 1904 in St. Louis, there were seven wrestling events, all of them freestyle, on the agenda. The U.S. won all seven. In 1908 both freestyle and Greco-Roman styles were contested in the games. In 1912 in Stockholm, the entire program was made up of Greco-Roman events. That year the longest final match ever staged in the Olympics took place. The match ended in a draw, after the two light-heavyweights—Anders Ahlgren of Sweden and Ivan Bohling of Finland—had fought for an incredible nine hours. Following that match, new rules were implemented.

In 1936 Kristjan Palusalu of Estonia accomplished a feat that has never been duplicated. He captured gold medals in the heavyweight category in both freestyle and Greco-Roman wrestling.

During the 1960s the U.S. suffered through a wrestling drought, winning only two silvers and a bronze in Rome and Mexico City. But in 1972 Ben Peterson, Dan Gable, and Wayne Wells all grappled their way to the gold, and Peterson's brother, John, Rich Sanders, and Chris Taylor grabbed a pair of silvers and a bronze. In the Montreal Olympics, John and Ben Peterson, sons of a Wisconsin dairy farmer, reversed themselves. This time twenty-seven-year-old John, a middleweight, won the gold medal in his division, and twenty-six-year-old Ben captured a silver in the light-heavyweight.

In the lightweight freestyle division, Butch Keaser of the U.S. Marines looked like he had things all wrapped up even before his final match. Keaser, aiming to become the first black American wrestler to take the gold, had built up an impressive point total in his preceding matches, and he was under the impression that even if he lost his last match by eleven points he would still be the winner. As it turned out, in a bizarre performance, he did lose in the final to the Russian, and by eleven points. But he had been mistaken; he could have lost the match and still retained the gold, but only if he lost by no more than seven points. It was a painful moment for the Marine.

In the rest of the divisions the Soviet wrestlers captured five of ten freestyle golds and seven of ten in the Greco-Roman.

Rules

The two styles of Olympic wrestling, Greco-Roman and freestyle, each have ten weight divisions.

Weight Division	*Weight Limit*
Paperweight	Up to 105½ lbs. (48 kg)
Flyweight	Up to 114½ lbs. (52 kg)
Bantamweight	Up to 125½ lbs. (57 kg)
Featherweight	Up to 136½ lbs. (62 kg)
Lightweight	Up to 149½ lbs. (68 kg)
Welterweight	Up to 163 lbs. (74 kg)
Middleweight	Up to 180½ lbs. (82 kg)
Light-Heavyweight	Up to 198 lbs. (90 kg)
Heavyweight	Up to 220 lbs. (100 kg)
Super Heavyweight	Over 220 lbs. (over 100 kg)

Each nation may enter one wrestler per weight division.

In the Greco-Roman style, the wrestlers begin standing up and all holds below the waist are illegal. The head may not be held by a hold that uses more than one arm. A wrestler may not be taken down face first. In the case of a takedown, the attacker's body must touch the mat before his opponent's upper body touches down. Obvious fouls include biting, scratching, hair pulling, tripping, and choke holds.

In freestyle almost any move is legal except the obvious fouls (as above), pressure holds on the throat and eyes, and twisting holds.

An international panel consisting of a three-man jury, three judges, and the referee decides each match using a point system similar to that used in boxing. Each set of moves which results in one wrestler's gaining an advantage over his opponent is worth a specific number of points. For instance, in freestyle, if a wrestler takes his opponent to the mat and maintains a moment of control, he is awarded one point. If his opponent then reverses the control (a reverse), the opponent is awarded one point. If a wrestler puts his opponent "in danger" by holding his shoulders at an angle of less than 90 degrees to the mat for five seconds, he is awarded three points; for less than five seconds, the hold is worth two points. A fall or pin occurs when a wrestler holds both his opponent's shoulders on the mat simultaneously. In the case of fouls, the wrestler who has been fouled receives one point.

Viewing Tips

Wrestling is a truly remarkable sport, because it requires such tremendous stamina and endurance. Wrestlers rarely have a chance to relax or coast—their bodies are under constant pressure and pain. Try remembering how exhausting it used to be when you wrestled for a few minutes in the grade school playground. Then imagine the amount of effort exerted by the Olympic athlete. Even marathoners do not expend the energy of the wrestler. Runners train their bodies to operate like machines; their moves become repetitive, which requires less energy than a constantly changing set of moves. Wrestlers do not have the luxury of allowing their bodies to gain a certain momentum and then having to concentrate only on maintaining it.

It is interesting to watch a wrestler play possum as he attempts to lure his opponent into believing he is vulnerable. Notice how the wrestler uses his body weight to wear down his opponent. Although a wrestler always tries to avoid overexerting himself, sometimes he must use more energy than he'd like to score a reversal or escape.

Wrestlers also employ fakes, wherein they appear to be making one type of move, when actually they are hoping to get their opponent to commit himself to a defensive posture. Some wrestlers rely on speed and quickness; others on superior strength.

Wrestlers are scored on what is termed a "bad-mark" system. The wrestler with the fewest bad marks at the end of the tournament is the winner. If a wrestler loses by being pinned, he receives four bad marks; a decision loss is three bad marks; a draw, two apiece. Winning by a decision counts as one bad mark and a win by a pin does not draw any bad marks. If a wrestler accumulates five bad marks, he is eliminated from the competition. That way each contestant is assured of at least two matches. The bad-mark system rewards aggressiveness and penalizes safe, defensive wrestling.

Forecast: Moscow

FREESTYLE

Paperweight
1976 Champion: Khassan Issaev, Bulgaria
1980 Favorites: Serge Kornilaev, USSR; Nobuo Fujisawa, Japan

Flyweight
1976 Champion: Yuji Takata, Japan
1980 Favorites: Takata, Japan; Anatoly Belogazo, USSR

Bantamweight
1976 Champion: Vladimir Yumin, USSR
1980 Favorites: Yumin, Viktor Alexeyev, USSR

Featherweight
1976 Champion: Jung-Mo Yang, South Korea

1980 Favorites: Kinichi Horii, Japan; Joseph Del'Aquila, Canada

Lightweight
1976 Champion: Pavel Pinigin, USSR
1980 Favorites: Pinigin, Seidi Saban, USSR

Welterweight
1976 Champion: Jichiro Date, Japan
1980 Favorites: Date, Japan; Lee Kemp, USA

Middleweight
1976 Champion: John Peterson, USA
1980 Favorites: Peterson, USA; Adolf Seger, West Germany

Light-Heavyweight
1976 Champion: Levan Tediashvily, USSR
1980 Favorites: Ben Peterson, USA; Une Neipert, West Germany

Heavyweight
1976 Champion: Ivan Yarygin, USSR
1980 Favorites: Harold Buttner, East Germany; Russ Hellickson, USA; Vasile Puscasu, Rumania

Super-Heavyweight
1976 Champion: Soslan Andiev, USSR
1980 Favorites: Jimmy Jackson, USA; Andiev, USSR

GRECO-ROMAN STYLE

Paperweight
1976 Champion: Alex Shumakov, USSR
1980 Favorites: Shumakov, USSR; Salih Bora, Turkey

Flyweight
1976 Champion: Vitaly Konstantinov, USSR

1980 Favorites: Nicu Ginga, Rumania; Moradali Shirani, Iran

Bantamweight
1976 Champion: Pertti Ukkola, Finland
1980 Favorites: Ukkola, Finland; Farhad Mustafin, USSR

Featherweight
1976 Champion: Kazimier Lipien, Poland
1980 Favorites: Lipien, Poland; Laszlo Reczi, Hungary

Lightweight
1976 Champion: Suren Nalbandyan, USSR
1980 Favorites: Nikolai Dirnoy, Bulgaria; Lars-Erik Skiod, Sweden

Welterweight
1976 Champion: Anatoly Bykov, USSR
1980 Favorites: Niteslav Macha, Czechoslovakia; Ferenc Kocsis, Hungary

Middleweight
1976 Champion: Momir Petkovic, Yugoslavia
1980 Favorites: Petkovic, Yugoslavia; Ion Draic, Rumania

Light-Heavyweight
1976 Champion: Valery Rezantsev, USSR
1980 Favorites: Petre Dicu, Rumania; Frank Anderson, Sweden

Heavyweight
1976 Champion: Nikolai Balboshin, USSR
1980 Favorites: Balboshin, USSR; Gheorghiu Petkov, Bulgaria

Super Heavyweight
1976 Champion: Aleksander Kolchinsky, USSR
1980 Favorites: Kolchinsky, USSR; Arne Robertsson, Sweden

Yachting

The 1980 Olympic Yachting competition is scheduled to begin on Monday, 21 July. It will run for seven days and end on 29 July. The twenty-fifth and twenty-sixth of July will be held open as reserve days, in case of inclement weather. The Olympic Sailing Center is located in Tallinn, on the Gulf of Finland, about 460 miles from Moscow.

The strait between Helsinki and Tallinn is only fifty miles wide, but on those seven days in July it will be the most conspicuous stretch of water in the world. Flagged with the colorful sails of some fifty-five nations, it is likely also to be the most beautiful.

Though man has transported himself across vast bodies of water with only the wind for an ally for thousands of years, the modern sport of yachting is only about three hundred years old. During the seventeenth century, to both avoid and track down pirate ships, the Dutch developed extremely swift and maneuverable vessels which they called *jaghtships*. Literally translated, the word meant "a hunting or tracking ship." The word "yacht" is simply a shortened English version of the Dutch name.

The man generally credited with popularizing yachting is King Charles II of England. Charles had left England for Holland after his father had been treated rather rudely and beheaded by Oliver Cromwell. While in Holland, Charles became acquainted and intrigued with the nifty pleasure craft of the Dutch. Just before he returned to England in 1660, Charles was presented a gift—a twenty-ton yacht—by the East India Company. Two years later he scheduled a race against his brother, the Duke of York, for a token prize of a hundred pounds.

For the next 200 years, prestigious yachting clubs sprang up on several continents. However, the very first was the Water Club of Cork Harbor in Ireland. In 1851 the 110-ton racing yacht, *America,* sailed across the Atlantic to compete in the Hundred-Guineas Cup race, a sixty-mile journey around the Isle of Wight. The *America* was triumphant, and the proud winners from the New York Yacht Club sailed home with the trophy on board. Once in the States, they renamed it the *America's* Cup, and today it is the prize in the most important yachting event in the world.

Yachting was included on the very first Olympic program, but bad weather reportedly caused cancellation of all the races. Ever since then, with the exception of 1904 in St. Louis, when the long journey to the U.S. was impractical for many nations, yachting competition has been a part of the games. In 1908 the English included powerboating on the schedule. By 1920 in Antwerp, thirteen classes were on the program. Only seven nations competed though, and the U.S. was not one of them. Through the years many different racing divisions have come and gone, and almost as many different countries have won medals. In 1976 in Montreal there were six classes of yachts. That year the sailors of Great Britain and the yachtsmen of Sweden, Denmark, and East and West Germany took home all of the gold medals, plus five of the twelve silver and bronze. The likable Englishman Reg White captured the gold in the Tornado class. In the Tempest class, John Albrechtson of Sweden, competing in his third Olympic games, captured the gold. David McFaull, a Hawaiian, copped a silver in the Tornado, edging Spengler of West Germany.

Rules

The six sailing classes in the Olympic Regatta are Soling (three-man crew); Tempest (two-man crew); Flying Dutchman (two-man crew); 470 (two/man crew): Tornado (two-man crew); and Finn (one-man crew).

All of the boats in the competition are of the same basic design and dimensions. Each country may enter only one yacht per class, and in every class except the Finn, the country supplies its own yacht. In the Finn class the Olympic Organizing Committee supplies the hulls, centerboard, and rudders, which are drawn for by lot.

To win an event, the crew must get its boat across the starting line, around a set number of buoys in the official order, and across the finish line before the rest of the boats. Only one race per division is sailed each day.

The start of a race is always crucial. A Race Committee boat gives visual warnings and starting signals at five-minute intervals. During this time the crews try to maneuver their boats into positions as close to the starting line as possible.

The higher a boat finishes the fewer points it is awarded. The boat with the lowest total number of points after seven races, with the worst race omitted, is declared the winner.

Viewing Tips

To get the most enjoyment from watching the yachting competition, it is important to understand the design differences of the boats in each class.

The Soling class is the largest yacht raced. It is 8.16 meters long, has a keel, and is sailed by three crew members.

The Tempest class yachts require two-man crews. The Tempest also has a keel. It is 6.70 meters long, and carries 23 square meters of sail.

The yachts of the Flying Dutchman class carry two-man crews, have a centerboard, and are 6.04 meters long. The 470 class, which replaced the 1972 Dragon class, has two-man crews and an overall length of 4.70 meters. It also has a centerboard.

The Tornado class replaced the Star Class of 1972. It is a catamaran with two hulls, and it is manned by a crew of two. A Tornado yacht is 6.09 meters long. The Finn is the smallest class. It is 4.5 meters long and is sailed by one man.

There are three marked courses: Alpha, on which the Flying Dutchman, Tempest, and Soling yachts compete; Bravo, for the 470 and Finn; and Charlie, for the Tornado. On three legs of the courses the boats sail towards buoys that are upwind, which means they have to zigzag back and forth (tacking is the proper term) into the wind at a 45-degree angle. The other legs are downwind, and while negotiating these legs, the yachts employ colorful spinnaker sails to increase their speed.

The sailing competition is tough, arduous, and exhausting. For seven days the various crews fight the elements and each other. Pay particular attention to the acrobatics performed by the crew members—they will do anything to keep their yacht righted. Times for each race are irrelevant, since the elements change each day. The only measure of performance is how a crew finishes in comparison to its competition.

Forecast: Moscow

Soling
1976 Champion: Denmark (Jensen)
1980 Favorites: Denmark; USA; East Germany; Sweden; Australia

Star
1976 Champion: (New Event)
1980 Favorites: USA; USSR; Sweden

Flying Dutchman
1976 Champion: West Germany (Diesch)
1980 Favorites: West Germany; Holland; France; Brazil

470
1976 Champion: West Germany (Huebner)
1980 Favorites: France; Spain; Holland; USA

Tornado
1976 Champion: Great Britain (White)
1980 Favorites: Great Britain; USSR; West Germany

Finn
1976 Champion: Jocken Schumann, East Germany
1980 Favorites: Canada; USSR; Great Britain; USA

The Story of Special Olympics

At this point, I would like to say something about an event which is in a class of its own: the Special Olympics.

Baron de Coubertin, father of the modern Olympics, said, "The important thing is not to win but to take part. . . . The essential thing is not to have conquered but to have fought well."

While this sentiment echoes the ideal of the Olympics, it expresses the reality of the Special Olympics, the world's largest program of sports training and athletic competition for the mentally retarded. All you have to do is attend the Special Olympics games as I have and you will see in its pucest form the true meaning of sports and the most meaningful expression of sportsmanship.

Eunice Kennedy Shriver, the founder of Special Olympics, expresses it best. She has said: "In the World Olympics, nation competes against nation. But in Special Olympics, nationality does not matter. We don't care.

"Age, size, speed, strength, these the world seems to value most. In Special Olympics, these qualities do not matter. We don't care.

"Beauty. Wealth. Brightness. These we are taught to prize. But in Special Olympics they do not matter. We don't care.

"What does matter in Special Olympics is courage and steadfastness. Striving rather than success. Determination rather than winning."

When I was training for the Olympic decathlon in Montreal, I noticed a group of mentally retarded youngsters practicing the 50- and the 440-yard dashes on the track where I was working out. At first I was somewhat reluctant to get close to what they were doing because I had never really come in contact with mentally retarded people before, but as I watched them practicing every day, I came to realize that the retarded have the same qualities we expect to find in every athlete: determination, courage, the ability to learn skills and to follow instructions, and a very strong desire to do their best. One thing stood out in my mind—there was no arguing, there was no fighting, there was no goofing-off. Every one of those boys and girls was determined each day to do better than the day before. And it wasn't long before I found myself talking to them, encouraging them, and even giving them some pointers whenever I thought I could.

A little while later there was a local Special Olympics meet on that same track and I went to see my athletes compete. Believe me, next to winning the gold medal in Montreal, my greatest thrill was seeing Special Olympians I had coached sprinting down the track with huge smiles on their faces, filled with the will to win but caring much more about how well they ran than where they finished. And I remembered something that my good friend Bill Toomey, who had won the Olympic decathlon a few years before I did, said about Special Olympics, "In an age of overcommercialization we have tended to become spectators. These special athletes with their dedication, enthusiasm, and competitive fire are showing us all the way back."

And so when I got back from Montreal, one of the first things I did was call Eunice Kennedy Shriver and ask her if I couldn't become a part of the Special Olympics organization and do what I could to encourage and train these gallant young athletes all over America. And it was a proud moment for me when, during dedication ceremonies for Bruce Jenner Stadium at Newtown High School in Connecticut, Mrs. Shriver announced that I had been appointed head coach of track and field for Special Olympics.

Special Olympics goes back to July 1968, when 1,000 mentally retarded youngsters gathered at Soldier Field, Chicago, for an historic event, the first international sports competition in which the retarded had ever been invited to take part. They had come from twenty-four states, the District of Columbia, Canada, and France. Their Olympic Village was the LaSalle Hotel in Chicago. The mayor of Chicago and the governor of Illinois welcomed them. A seventeen-year-old mentally retarded boy carried the Special Olympics torch into Soldier Field and ignited a forty-foot-high Special Olympics Flame of Hope. The Special Olympics flag was raised as one thousand balloons, each carrying the name of a Special Olympics athlete, rose colorfully into the bright July sky.

And then these athletes—age eight to sixteen—proved that they were true competitors. They ran the 50-yard and the 300-yard dashes. They threw the baseball for distance. They swam and played floor hockey and learned new skills in clinics and demonstrations taught by some of America's greatest amateur and professional athletes.

Two days later, when the torch was extinguished and the cheering died down, everyone there agreed that it had been the most important event in their lives. As Eunice Kennedy Shriver recalls: "I'll never forget the sight of two mentally retarded athletes—a boy and a girl—running proudly into that stadium in Chicago carrying the ceremonial Olympic torch. Mayor Daley turned to me and said, 'The world will never be the same.' And he was *right*. Because the world saw, for the first time, what its *most* neglected, *least* appreciated, *most* scorned and hidden citizens could accomplish."

That was the first Special Olympics games. And just organizing it and putting it on was an act of some daring because never before—*anywhere*—had retarded persons taken part in an event like this in a public arena.

In fact, until the first Special Olympics games were organized by the Joseph P. Kennedy, Jr., Foundation, few retarded children or young adults had ever taken part in a regular program of recreation or sports competition. Forty-five percent of all mentally retarded children received no physical education at all. Many communities actually had ordinances forbidding the retarded from using public gymnasiums, swimming pools, and playgrounds. And only about 25 percent of the retarded were given as much as sixty minutes of organized recreation per week. At that time, because many parents felt shame and guilt at having had a retarded child, the children were kept either hidden away at home or in institutions where they sat doing nothing, physically and mentally deteriorating because no one had faith or confidence in their ability to do anything of value.

That first Special Olympics games was the beginning of a movement that, since 1968, has become the largest sports program for the mentally retarded in the world; one of the world's largest volunteer organizations; one of the most widely respected, therapeutic activities for the mentally retarded; the catalyst for thousands of school, community, and institutional physical training and recreation programs; the gateway to public acceptance and self-esteem for the more than one million children and young adults who have taken part in Special Olympics sports training and athletic competition since 1968; and a vehicle for public understanding that has played a major role in changing the image of mental retardation and instilling an appreciation of the value of the retarded to our society.

But Special Olympics is much more than a story of courage and heroism among the mentally retarded and changing public attitudes toward them. It is, in every way, a sports program which demands the highest standards of coaching, timing, teaching, and training. In order to participate in state or international meets, athletes have to have participated in local or area competition. But unlike college or professional events or the Olympics themselves, Special Olympics is unique in that it accommodates competitors at all ability levels by assigning them to "competition divisions" based on both age and actual performance. Even athletes in the lowest divisions may advance all the way to the international games, because they are matched against their peers, not against the entire field. And so, in Special Olympics, there are athletes who can run the mile no faster than ten minutes. And there are those who, like Elee Bivens of Texas, who set the Special Olympics mile record in 1972, can run the mile in four minutes and forty-two seconds. What Special Olympics has proven beyond a doubt is that even an individual who has great difficulty with language or mathematics or with the power of reasoning can succeed in sports if he or she is given encouragement, training, and a regular opportunity to exercise the required skills and to experience the joys and the frustrations of competition. When it started in Chicago, Special Olympics consisted of only track and field activities, swimming, and one team sport, floor hockey, which had been imported from Canada where it had been developed for the mentally retarded. Today, Special Olympians are able to participate in fourteen official sports—track and field, swimming, diving, gymnastics, ice skating, basketball, volleyball, soccer, floor hockey, poly hockey, bowling, frisbee-disc, Alpine and Nordic skiing, and wheelchair events. Almost all other sports that take place in the world Olympics are offered as demonstration sports in Special Olympics. Because of the popularity of basketball and soccer, Special Olympics offers both team play and individual skills competition in these two sports.

World class athletes in every sport are attracted to Special Olympics because it gives them a real sense of the true meaning of athletics—which they sometimes lose as they concentrate on winning their own event. Rafer Johnson, who won a gold medal in the decathlon in the 1960 Olympics, has been head coach of Special Olympics since 1968, when the games began. And now the national coaching staff includes Julius Erving and John Havlicek in basketball, myself and Wilma Rudolph in track and field, Wilt Chamberlain and Linda Fernandez in volleyball, Pelé and Kyle Rote, Jr., in soccer, Bryan Watson and Stan Mikita in floor hockey, Kurt Thomas and Cathy Rigby in gymnastics, Jill Kinmont Booth and Billy Kidd in Winter Special Olympics, and many more of the most accomplished athletes in all the world. Muhammad Ali is a coach, and so are Rosey Grier, Carl Erskine, Don Meredith, Jan Stenerud, and JoJo Starbuck Bradshaw.

Ron Guidry, the great Yankee pitcher, is head coach of baseball. Ron, himself, has a mentally retarded brother, Travis, and he has said that even more than his own Cy Young Award, he and his family treasure the second-place ribbon his retarded brother, Travis, won in the Special Olympics softball throw.

I think of some of the Special Olympians whom I have met or whose stories have been told to me. Athletes like Toni Marie Chillemi, who, when she was ten years old, won a gold medal in gymnastics in the International Special Olympics games in Los Angeles even though she is a Down's syndrome child—the condition that, tragically and devastatingly, used to be called "mongolian idiocy." Thanks to Special Olympics and a mother who, because she was a dancer herself, recognized the value of physical activity to the development of every child, Toni Marie is not only an accomplished gymnast in her own right, but she also teaches normal children gymnastics in a community program. Or, there is Corrinne

Scruggs of Florida, who at age seventy won a silver medal in the wheelchair race in the international games at Mount Pleasant, Michigan, in 1975, as well as a bronze medal for the baseball throw. Corrinne had lived most of her life in an institution for the retarded and for thirty years had not said a word. But when Special Olympics came to her institution, she began to come out of herself, to communicate with others, and, finally, to become a skilled and joyous participant. Now she is out of the institution and living in a halfway house in her own community. And there is Mike Baker, who, in addition to being mentally retarded, was born with only one leg. Mike, too, is an accomplished gymnast, and in addition he runs, plays basketball, and is a model not only of courage but of skill. There is Melvin Hoover, one of the Special Olympians who was recognized by being awarded the Spirit of Special Olympics medal. When Melvin joined Special Olympics he had spent most of his years sitting at home. He couldn't walk. He had to be carried. But Melvin was not to be defeated. Bowling was his first Special Olympics event. He crawled to the lane and lunged forward, thrusting the ball down the lane, and landed spread-eagle across the floor. But he was determined to bowl, and in his division he came in first. Today, Melvin will try anything, and he'll stick with it and do his best. In one year he went from being carried to climbing on and off the school bus. His one wish is to walk and, thanks to his Special Olympics training and the faith of his parents and his coaches, with a little help, a little time, and a lot of courage, he will.

One of the most important things to me about Special Olympics is that it is almost 100 percent a grass-roots volunteer program. That tells me more about the kind of society we live in than all the federal funding and all the state grants and the high-priced coaches and the bureaucrats who run the various programs. The Joseph P. Kennedy, Jr., Foundation runs Special Olympics—with its more than one million athletes and its 250,000 volunteers throughout the world—with a headquarters staff of only five salaried people. The largest cash award it gives to any state or country is $750. It provides medals and ribbons and manuals and films for training and that is all. The rest of the money to operate year-round programs in more than 17,000 different locations comes from the communities themselves—from the generosity of corporations and individuals who understand the true value of Special Olympics. Actually, it takes more than $25 million each year to maintain the quality of the Special Olympics program and to provide some measure of growth. But somehow, even though that seems to be a massive challenge, the Special Olympics volunteers manage to come through.

The highlight, of course, of the Special Olympics program is the International Special Olympics games. Beginning in 1968 at Chicago's Soldier Field, the international games have been held in Chicago in 1970, in Los Angeles in 1972, in Mount Pleasant, Michigan, on the campus of Central Michigan University in 1975, and at the State University of New York College at Brockport in the summer of 1979. The first Winter International Special Olympics games took place in Steamboat Springs, Colorado, in the winter of 1978 and winter games will be held again in 1980–81.

Modeled on the Greek Olympics in spirit, ceremony, and competition, the international games provide a goal which is sought eagerly by the one million Special Olympians who participate in the year-round program each year. The Fifth International Summer Special Olympics games in 1979, for example, attracted 3,500 Special Olympians from every state in the United States, Puerto Rico, the District of Columbia, the Virgin Islands, Guam, American Samoa, and more than twenty other countries. ABC's "Wide World of Sports" carried a special program on the international games. Representatives from newspapers, magazines, and radio and television stations from around the world were present and reported this most unique and compelling event. Nearly 1,000 coaches and chaperones and over 2,000 volunteer students and townspeople from the Rochester-Brockport area of New York ran the games and provided a full, five-day program of athletic, cultural, social, educational, and recreational events for the athletes.

Since I first met those young athletes on the track where

I was working out, I've wondered why Special Olympics had such a hold on me. And then I heard Mrs. Shriver tell a story about another Olympic gold medal winner, Johnny Jones, who won his medal in Montreal representing the United States in the 400-hundred-meter relay. And when I heard what she said, I knew why I and so many other athletes and citizens throughout the world have responded so positively to the power and the beauty of Special Olympics. This is the way she told that story:

"When I attended the Texas Special Olympics in Austin, a very quiet, young, black man named Johnny Jones came up to me during the program and put something in my hand. It was a shiny leather box. I opened it and found the Gold Olympic Medal he had won in Montreal—a first place medal in world competition.

"He said to me, 'Mrs. Shriver—I want to give this to the Special Olympics of Texas.'

" 'The thing is,' he said, 'we athletes don't always appreciate our gifts. But coming out here makes you think. It makes you do whatever you can to help.'

" 'But why your *medal*?', I asked.

"And he answered, 'Right now I don't have a lot of money. But I have the medal. And by giving that I'm giving a part of myself. Other people can give money and time—but this medal that means so much. It seemed like the least I could do.'

"In your *own* lives, what will be *your* Olympic Medal? Will you hide it? Will you hoard it? Will you sell it to the highest bidder? Or will you give it away freely because it *is* a part of yourself. Because it *means* so much. Because it is the *least* you can do."

When I heard that, I realized, I think for the first time, through Special Olympics, what the Olympic ideal really signifies. And even more than the pageantry and the color and the symbolism and the magnificent performances, this meaning is symbolized to me by the very simple oath that all Special Olympians say before their games begin: "Let me win. But if I cannot win, let me be brave in the attempt."

Al Oerter won a gold medal in the discus competition in four consecutive Olympics. In 1977, at the age of forty, he came out of retirement and began throwing again and in 1979 is throwing the shot better than ever.

Bill Rodgers, winner of three Boston Marathons, will go to Moscow with an excellent chance of bringing back the gold medal. (United Press International Photo)

One of the most talented and publicized U.S. sprinters is Houston McTear who is acknowledged to have the fastest out-of-the-blocks start in the world.

Eamonn Coghlan of Ireland is one of the 1980 favorites in the 1500 meters. Here he takes his victory lap after setting a new world indoor record for the mile.

Henry Rono's three world records, in the 5,000 and 10,000 meters and the 3,000 meter steeplechase, earned him the honor of Track and Field's 1978 athlete of the year.

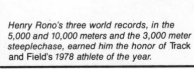

Mac Wilkins, 1976 Olympic champion in the discus, believes the Russians will "do anything possible to be successful," even resort to technology.

(United Press International Photo)

The most acclaimed U.S. rider in Moscow, by virtue of his back-to-back world championships in the three-day event, should be Bruce Davidson.

(United Press International Photo)

In the men's 100-meter freestyle, 6'5" Jim Montgomery, the 1976 gold medalist, is one of the best U.S. prospects.

(United Press International Photo)

Jane Frederick competes in the hurdles event of the pentathlon. Frederick holds the current American record in the pentathlon with 4,704 points. (United Press International Photo)

(United Press International Photo)

James Butts is one of the three U.S. hopefuls in the triple jump.

Margaret Murdock of Topeka, Kansas, won the silver medal in Montreal in the three-position small-bore (.22 caliber) rifle.

Franklin Jacobs finished first in the 1979 AAU high jump event and is the prime U.S. contender.

Evelyn Ashford has developed into the best woman sprinter in the country.

Brenda Morehead (right) is one of the likeliest candidates for a Moscow berth.

One of the reasons that the U.S. athletes dominate the archery competition is Darrell Pace, 1976 gold medalist and favorite in Moscow.

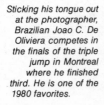

Sticking his tongue out at the photographer, Brazilian Joao C. De Oliviera competes in the finals of the triple jump in Montreal where he finished third. He is one of the 1980 favorites.

Lanny Bassham, the 1976 gold medalist in the small-bore rifle three positions competition, will surely be the 1980 pre-games favorite in the small-bore rifle event.

Arnie Robinson is expected to repeat his gold medal performance of 1976 in the long jump.
(United Press International Photo)

Three of the U.S. hopefuls in the women's 400 meter are (left to right): Shari Howard, Jennie Gorham, and Rosalyn Bryant.

Harvey Glance finished second in the 1979 AAU 100-meter event. As a college freshman he made the 1976 Olympic squad and finished fourth in Montreal.

Frank Shorter, the 1972 Olympic gold medalist, is a potential contender in the 1980 games.

(United Press International Photo)

In the 100-meter hurdles, Deby LaPlar of San Diego State is the front-runner.

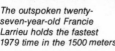

The outspoken twenty-seven-year-old Francie Larrieu holds the fastest 1979 time in the 1500 meters.

(United Press International Photo)

(United Press International Photo)

Renaldo Nehemiah is the most likely bet for the 1980 gold in the 110-meter hurdles.

Panoramic view of Lake Placid in the Adirondack Mountains of upstate New York. The Olympic stadium is on the left, the 400-meter speed skating oval is in the center, with Mirror Lake top right.

The old Lake Placid Olympic ice arena, used when Lake Placid hosted the 1932 winter games, has since been enclosed by local businesses. During the 1980 games, the village will be closed to traffic with spectators being bused in from distant parking lots.

An aerial view of the Olympic village in Lake Placid. The construction cost of the village has risen to nine times the initial estimate. After the 1980 Olympics the village will be converted to a minimum security prison for first-time offenders. (Wide World Photo)

When completed, the 90-meter ski jump tower will feature an outside glass-enclosed elevator. The 70-meter tower will have an inside stairway.

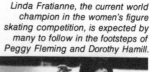

Linda Fratianne, the current world champion in the women's figure skating competition, is expected by many to follow in the footsteps of Peggy Fleming and Dorothy Hamill.

With recent victories in international competition, Jim Denney has established himself as a serious contender for a 1980 ski jumping medal.

The strongest medal hope on the U.S. women's ski team is Cindy Nelson who captured the bronze medal in the downhill in Innsbruck in 1976.

Peter Mueller will be out to defend his Olympic title in the men's 100-meter speed skating event.

Despite her obvious size disadvantage at 5'1" and 100 pounds, Beth Heiden must be ranked as the finest all-around woman speed skater in the world.

Lake Placid has the only luge run in North America.

Phil Mahre, the top slalom and giant slalom prospect and the most consistent skier in U.S. history, should fare well in Lake Placid in front of home country crowds.

Irina Rodnina and Alexsander Zaitsev, the 1976 gold medalists, are pairs figure skating's longest reigning titlists.

In 1976 Bill Koch stunned the frosty Nordic world when he captured a silver medal in the 30 km Olympic cross-country race.

Tai Babilonia and Randy Gardner are the current World Pairs Champions. They could make history in Lake Placid by becoming the first American twosome to win the Olympic pairs figure skating.

Leah Poulos-Mueller is the best woman ice sprinter in the world. The 500 meters is her specialty.

Steve Mahre, Phil's twin brother, is the number-two-ranked U.S. slalom skier.

With his eight straight World Championships in the past three years, Eric Heiden has become the premier speed skater in the world and the finest in U.S. history.

Sweden's Ingemar Stenmark seems a sure bet to win a 1980 gold medal in either the slalom or the giant slalom.

The Summer Games—
A Retrospective

The Ancient Games

The origins of the ancient Olympic games in the valley of Olympia are shrouded in the swirling mists of unrecorded time. Archaeologists believe that religious rites of some kind, perhaps even human sacrifice, were held in the valley at least as early as the year 1000 B.C.

The myths and legends recorded by ancient Greek poets and historians date the beginning of the games in the ninth century B.C. According to one tale, the Olympics were initiated by a young and stalwart warrior, Pelops, to celebrate his victory over King Oenomaus, the ruler of Pisa in the southwestern part of what is now the nation of Greece.

As the story goes, King Oenomaus had a gorgeous daughter, Hippodamia, who was much sought after by the young warriors of the region. Reluctant to give away his most prized possession, the king made the suitors of Hippodamia engage in a deadly game in order to obtain his daughter's hand in marriage. He decreed that the young warriors must whisk Hippodamia away in a chariot with the king himself in hot pursuit. Owing to the quality of the king's horses, thirteen of the suitors died at the end of Oenomaus's spear.

Pelops was the fourteenth suitor. As the king's chariot edged closer to his chariot and the young warrior seemed destined to become another victim of the race for Hippodamia, the axle on the king's chariot broke and Oenomaus was thrown to the ground and killed. According to legend, Pelops had bribed the king's charioteer to damage the axle, and so it is often said that the first Olympic contest was fixed.

To celebrate his victory over King Oenomaus and the acquisition of his kingdom, Pelops is said to have chosen a sacred site in the valley of Olympia where games and religious rites would be held for the glorification and appeasement of the gods.

Whether or not we believe the legend of Pelops, we do know that the first recorded Olympic games were held in 776 B.C. We even know that Coroebus of Elis became the Olympic champion in that year when he won the single event included in the games in those days—a footrace of about 200 yards.

To the Greeks, the Olympic games were much more than an athletic event. They were part of the worship of their pagan gods. The games were held once every four years during the sacred month of *Hieromenia,* when all hostilities between the continually warring city-states were halted to allow athletes and spectators to travel safely to Olympia.

The potential competitors in the games were required to prove that they had gone through at least a ten-month period of training prior to the games, and they were trained and watched over by the Olympic judges themselves for the thirty days immediately preceding the events. Only the best athletes were allowed by the judges to compete.

Over the years the number of Olympic events gradually expanded to include footraces of various distances, wrestling, boxing, chariot races, and other contests. The fame and prestige of the Olympics increased as well. Athletes from all the Greek city-states and eventually, after the conquest of Greece by the Romans, from the wide-ranging Roman Empire attended the games. The Olympics became an international event, a unifying force in the ancient world.

Olympic champions were treated as great heroes. When they returned to their homes, they were given money, houses, and other valuables. The most successful Olympians were immortalized by sculptors, poets, and historians. A few of the greatest Olympians were legends in their own time, and incredible tales of their physical prowess were circulated among the Greeks.

Perhaps the most famous of the ancient Olympians was a wrestler, Milo of Croton, who was known for both his great strength and his phenomenal appetite. Milo, who lived in the sixth century B.C., was said to have eaten an entire bull in one day. He was a six-time Olympic wrestling champion.

In their heyday, the Greek games were full of beauty, gaiety, and religious purity. The valley of Olympia contained beautiful temples filled with gigantic sculpture, an elaborate gymnasium, and a stadium that seated as many as 50,000 people on grassy hillsides. The athletic events were interwoven with religious ceremonies, and the athletes were required to please the gods by making pledges.

But as the power of the Greeks declined and the Romans began to control the Olympic games, they began to lose their ancient religious significance. The athletes were no longer content to be amateurs. They wanted to win money and other tangible rewards. The simplicity of the games was lost, and they took on a circuslike atmosphere.

The Olympic games reached perhaps their lowest point when the Roman emperor Nero built a palace in the valley in the first century A.D. and began entering the events himself. Because he was feared by the other contestants, Nero was very successful in the games.

In the year A.D. 394, the Olympic games, by then only tattered remnants of the glory they once had been, were halted by the Roman emperor Theodosius I. The Greek games, like the noble Hellenic civilization itself, faded into history.

The Modern Games

The revival of the Olympic games fifteen hundred years after the last contest at Olympia was brought about almost singlehandedly by a French aristocrat, Pierre de Fredy, the baron de Coubertin. The Greeks themselves had attempted to resurrect the ancient games twice in the nineteenth century—in 1859 and 1870—but both efforts had been badly attended and unimpressive. The Athens games failed to capture the imagination of the sports world.

But Baron de Coubertin, as it turned out, possessed the determination and the organizational skill to achieve what the Greeks could not. Born in Paris in 1863, he was educated at St. Cyr, the famous French military academy, and by family tradition would have been a military officer had he not developed an intense interest in education.

During a career devoted to the furtherance of public education, Baron de Coubertin concluded that physical fitness should be an important part of the education of French youth. Since he found enthusiasm for sports in the schools, and for amateur sports in general, at a low ebb, he became an outspoken advocate of amateurism.

The French aristocrat had visited the ruins of Olympia, studied the history of the ancient games, and become convinced that a new era in international athletic competition could be fostered through the revival of the Olympic games. He spoke of his desire for a new blossoming of international competition at a conference in Paris in 1892. He got little response that year, but at a subsequent conference on international sport two years later in Paris, he received approval for revival of the games.

The delegates at the Paris meeting agreed initially to hold the games in the French capital in 1900, but influenced by the delegates from Greece, they changed their minds and decided to schedule the revival for April 1896 in the Greek capital of Athens.

The decision, however, was only the beginning. As Dick Schaap notes in his *Illustrated History of the Olympics* (New York: Albert A. Knopf, 1963), an excellent source of Olympic information, carrying out the plan was another story altogether. In the first place, the Greek government, being virtually insolvent, could not afford to construct the stadium and other facilities that would be needed to make the games a success. In the second, there existed at that time no organization in the countries of the world for recruiting amateur athletes for the Olympic games.

The first problem was solved by the Greeks when Crown Prince Constantine enthusiastically supported the proposed Olympics, became honorary president of the Greek Olympic Committee, and began raising money. The fund-raising efforts culminated in a decision by a wealthy Greek philanthropist, George Averoff, to pay for the reconstruction of the ancient Panathenaic Stadium in Athens.

Lack of organization and enthusiasm in other parts of the

world was a problem that was not entirely solved. Participation at the first modern Olympic games was by no means universal. The athletes who did compete in the games often were not the best that Europe and America could offer. The New York Athletic Club, the most prestigious track and field organization in the U.S., took no part in the games. Still, athletes from eight countries assembled for the games.

1896—Athens

On 6 April 1896, when King George I of Greece formally opened the Olympic games, it was the beginning of a new era in amateur athletics. For the king was not only reviving the ancient Olympic games, he was resurrecting an international spirit of amateur sport that had disappeared for many centuries.

The American performance in 1896 was impressive. The thirteen-man Olympic team, which represented no official national athletic organization, won nine of the twelve track and field events. One of the most interesting championships won by members of the ragtag American team was captured by Robert Garrett, captain of the track and field team at Princeton University. While still at Princeton, Garrett had learned that there would be a discus throw in the Olympic games. Although he had never seen a real discus, Garrett trained on a facsimile modeled by a friend. When he reached Athens, he was given the real thing and he knew what to do with it. He won the event by seven inches on his last throw.

But it was not the Americans, it was the Greeks who won the most prestigious event at the first modern Olympic games. The planners of the revival had decided to hold a track and field event that was not part of the ancient Olympic games but was definitely a part of Greek history—a race from Marathon to Athens.

The event was staged to commemorate the dramatic run of Pheidippides over the same course in 490 B.C. The youth was a soldier in the Athenian army which repulsed and decimated the invading Persian army on the plains of Marathon. Immediately following the battle, Pheidippides took off his armor and began running toward Athens to inform the city of the great victory by the outmanned Athenian army. Although he had been a champion in the ancient games at Olympia, the race from Marathon to Athens was too much for the young athlete. He collapsed and died in the city after uttering the immortal words: "Rejoice—we conquer!"

In 1896, the marathon was also very important to the Athenians. Prior to the race, the home team had failed to win a single track and field event. So when Spiridon Loues, a tiny Greek shepherd, jogged into the Panathenaic Stadium well in front of the other distance runners, the partisan crowd of nearly seventy thousand was ecstatic. Fifteen hundred years after the demise of the ancient games, the Greeks finally had another Olympic champion.

1900—Paris

The second chapter in the history of the modern Olympic games read like a zany comedy of errors. According to one authority, the American athletes in the world track and field championships weren't even aware they were competing in the Olympics until they received their gold, silver, and bronze Olympic medals. Their confusion was prompted by the fact that the games were part of the 1900 International Exposition in Paris. They were a sideshow in the larger circus of the exposition.

And circus isn't a bad word to describe the atmosphere in Paris. Baron de Coubertin, the father of the modern Olympics, wasn't given control over preparation for the games until the situation was so hopelessly snarled that even his genius and determination couldn't set things straight again. Until shortly before the games, the French hadn't laid out a track and field for the track and field events. Even with the efforts of the baron, the best they could muster was a make-shift, unlevel track at the Racing Club de France in the Bois de Boulogne.

But if the preparations in France fell far short of the Greek effort four years earlier, the Americans were ready for Paris. Fifty-five Americans, including many of the national track and field champions, attended the games. And this time the powerful New York Athletic Club was in on the action.

On their way to Paris, the Americans swept the English track and field championships and they were no less successful in France. Despite a dispute over the French decision to hold track and field events on Sunday, 15 July, which kept some of the American athletes out of the competition for religious reasons, the unofficial U.S. team won seventeen of the twenty-two track and field events.

It was in 1900 that Ray Ewry, perhaps the greatest jumper of all time, began the string of Olympic victories that would not end until he won his tenth gold medal in 1908. And Ewry's success also marked the beginning of the kind of touching and compelling Olympic story that transcends athletics. As a boy in Lafayette, Indiana, Ewry was stricken with polio, and his doctor suggested that he attempt to recondition his muscles through exercise. He was so successful that he later became the captain of the track team at Purdue University. At the age of twenty-six, Ewry attended his first Olympic games. He won gold medals in all the standing jumps: the high jump, the broad jump, and the hop, step, and jump. Since the standing jumps were eliminated from the Olympic program in 1912, we'll never know how long Ewry's records would have lasted. But they undoubtedly would have remained intact for many years. Just imagine jumping a bar 5'6" high from a flat-footed position.

Another record was set at the Paris games by Alvin Kraenzlein, of the University of Pennsylvania, who won four gold medals. He was the first Olympic athlete to achieve that feat.

1904 — St. Louis

The third Olympiad, like the second, was upstaged by another international event—the Louisiana Purchase Exposition. Although initial plans called for holding the games in Chicago, President Theodore Roosevelt, honorary leader of the newly formed U.S. Olympic Committee, insisted on linking the Olympic games and the exposition.

Despite their lack of independence, the 1904 games were certainly much better organized and drew much larger crowds than the Paris games. The cost of bringing athletes to America, however, cut down on the participation by European athletes. The English track and field team, the second-best in the world, did not attend the 1904 Olympics and neither did the French team. As a result, American domination of the games was even greater than in Paris and Athens. The U.S. team won twenty-one of the twenty-two track and field events and seventy-seven gold medals overall. Its closest competitor was Cuba, which won seven golds in the fencing competition.

With the dearth of foreign athletes, it's no wonder that four Americans won three gold medals apiece in St. Louis. Ray Ewry repeated his world domination of the standing jump with wins in all three events; Harry Hillman of the New York Athletic Club, who would later become track coach at Dartmouth, won golds in the 200-meter hurdles, the 400-meter hurdles, and the 400-meter run; Archie Hahn, a University of Michigan graduate, won the 60-meter, 100-meter, and 200-meter dashes; and Jim Lightbody of the Chicago Athletic Association won the 800-meter run, the 1500-meter run, and the 2500-meter steeplechase.

The real competition in St. Louis was between the New York Athletic Club and the Chicago Athletic Association. A. G. Spalding, the sporting goods manufacturer, had donated a trophy that would go to the team that accumulated the most points in the games. The New York group won by one point.

Although there was an impressive turnout of American athletes in the 1904 games and two of the races, the 400-meter and 800-meter runs, were said to have been among the greatest contests in the history of sport, the poor showing by foreign athletes was very disappointing to the Olympic organizers. Clearly, the games were losing their international character.

1906—Athens

The poor international turnout in St. Louis in 1904 convinced Baron de Coubertin, head of the International Olympic Committee, that a quick shot in the arm was necessary to keep the Olympic games alive. The first of the modern games in Athens in 1896 had been a great success, but disorganization in Paris and American dominance in St. Louis had marred the two subsequent games. In an effort to save his brainchild, Baron de Coubertin accepted the Greeks' standing offer to host the games. Only this time he didn't wait the customary four years.

The Athens games served their purpose well. The international representation was well balanced; the pageantry and showmanship of the Greeks restored the dignity and excitement of the Olympics; and huge crowds attended the games in the reconstructed Panathenaic Stadium, where the modern Olympic games had been initiated ten years earlier.

It was also a year of important firsts for the Americans. For the first time, there was an official U.S. Olympic team selected by the U.S. Olympic Committee. And it was the first Olympics in which team uniforms were worn by the American athletes.

The American hero of the 1906 Olympics was a twenty-one-year-old member of the New York Athletic Club—Paul Pilgrim. And, ironically, Pilgrim almost didn't make it to Athens at all.

American athletes for the Athens games were chosen on the basis of reputation rather than through a system of Olympic trials, as they are today. Consequently, the USOC chose Harry Hillman and Jim Lightbody Olympic champions in 1904, to compete, respectively in the 400- and 800-meter runs in Athens. Unfortunately, there seemed to be no need to take along the relatively unknown Pilgrim, who also was a specialist in those events.

But Pilgrim was the favorite of Matt Halpin, the NYAC official who was also manager of the U.S. team. At the last minute Halpin added Pilgrim to the U.S. team. The coach's controversial decision turned out to be a wise one.

In the first place, several American athletes, including Hillman, were injured when the ship they were travelling on, the *S.S. Barbarossa,* encountered a storm en route to Athens. Although Hillman, who had an injured knee, was well enough to enter the 400-meter run, he rapidly fell behind the pace, and it looked as if the Americans were going to run out of the money. Then Pilgrim, the obscure, unseeded stowaway, turned on a tremendous sprint to the finish and won by a meter.

The following day Pilgrim was entered in the 800-meter run, in which Lightbody, who hadn't been hurt in the storm, was the heavy favorite. Lightbody led the race until Pilgrim, with another furious sprint in the last 50 meters, passed him. To this day, no other athlete has won both the 400- and 800-meter runs in the Olympics.

1908—London

The 1908 Olympic games in London were among the most controversial on record. The British had prepared well for the games. They had constructed a huge stadium, with a seating capacity of almost 70,000, in London. But the intense competition between the Britons and the Americans produced a level of Olympic bickering that reached new heights.

The Irish Question, the political feud between England and Ireland that continues today, was partly responsible for the controversy. Many of the best athletes on the American squad were members of the Irish-American Athletic Club in New York. And that irritated the Britishers, who had forced athletes from Ireland to compete on the British team or not at all.

American Olympic officials were convinced that the British officials who ran the games were using their influence whenever possible to frustrate the American competitors. Likewise, the British public was highly suspicious of the Americans, not having quite forgiven them for achieving their independence.

The most exciting event in 1908 was the marathon, and it, too, was shrouded in controversy. The London marathon covered 26 miles, 385 yards, now the official distance for a marathon, and stretched from Windsor Castle, the home of the royal family, to the Olympic stadium. Near the end of the race, Dorando Pietri, a twenty-two-year-old Italian, broke into a substantial lead. As he entered the stadium, he seemed a certain victor. The he turned the wrong way on the stadium track, spun back around, and fell down.

As the excited crowd looked on in shock, British track officials tried to pull Pietri to his feet. Because the runner was unable to stand, the officials literally dragged him across the finish line. Less than a minute later, John Hayes of the Irish-American Athletic Club crossed the finish line.

Although it was obvious that Pietri should have been disqualified for not having finished the race under his own steam, the British ran the Italian flag up the flagpole and declared the little candymaker from Capri the winner. It was not until several hours later that the British gave in to their better judgment and awarded the victory to Hayes.

The controversy in London reached its peak when the American winner of the 400-meter run was disqualified by officials, allegedly for interferring with a British runner. Afterwards, the other two Americans in the race withdrew and the Englishman, the only contestant left, won by default.

Despite the apparent enmity of the British track officials, the American track and field team won handily in London. The U.S. athletes accumulated fifteen gold medals, more than all the other countries combined. An outstanding member of the U.S. team was Mel Sheppard, who set an Olympic record in the 1500-meter run and a world record in the 800-meter run. Ray Ewry won his ninth and tenth gold medals in London, and Martin Sheridan won two gold medals in the discus throw events.

Although they dominated the track and field events, the Americans had to settle for a second-place ranking in the overall Olympic tally. British did very well in such sports as tennis, boxing, and cycling and captured first place.

The controversy over the officiating in the London games convinced the International Olympic Committee that the practice of having the host country provide officials for the Olympics should be discontinued. Thereafter, the officials were chosen by an international group.

1912—Stockholm

After the acrimony of the London games, the harmony and organization of the 1912 Olympic games in Stockholm, Sweden, refreshed the Olympic spirit. From start to finish, the games were virtually flawless.

And so was the performance of Jim Thorpe, who took Stockholm by storm. Considered by some sports authorities to be the greatest athlete in history, Thorpe was a Sauk and Fox Indian who was born in Oklahoma and attended college at the Carlisle Indian School in Carlisle, Pennsylvania. Under the tutelage of Coach Glenn ("Pop") Warner, he became a spectacular competitor in football, basketball, baseball, and track.

Thorpe's best sport was football. In 1907, when Thorpe first began playing for Carlisle, the tiny college became a national football power. Thorpe was an All-American halfback in 1911 and 1912, and during the 1912 season he scored a total of twenty-five touchdowns and 198 points. He was clearly a superstar.

Thorpe's deeds in the 1912 Olympics were no less spectacular. He won gold medals in both the decathlon and the pentathlon. In those days, the pentathlon included the broad jump, the discus throw, the 200-meter dash, the 1500-meter run, and the javelin throw. Thorpe placed first in every event except the javelin, in which he fell to third. In the ten-event decathlon, Thorpe ran up a commanding lead by winning four events—the 1500-meter run, the high hurdles, the high jump, and the shot put. He was acclaimed "the best athlete in the world" and invited to meet with the Swedish king, Gustav V. Thorpe reportedly turned down the invitation.

Another star of 1912 was the Finnish runner Hannes Kolehmainen, who some believe was the first great distance runner. He won gold medals in the 5,000- and 10,000-meter runs and the cross-country. He started a tradition of Finnish dominance of the long runs that lasted for years.

The Stockholm games were considered the most successful Olympics since the tradition was revived in 1896, but something that occurred a year later tarnished the luster of the games somewhat. It was discovered that the Stockholm hero, Jim Thorpe, had played professional baseball prior to 1912 and Thorpe was stripped of his gold medals. His Olympic records were stricken from the record books.

After leaving Carlisle, Thorpe played professional baseball in the National League for six years. In 1919, he turned to professional football and became one of its early stars. He was the first president of the American Professional Football Association, which later became the National Football League.

After his retirement from sports in 1926, Thorpe had difficulty adjusting to employment off the athletic fields. He died in near-poverty in 1953.

Another U.S. competitor in the Stockholm games fared much better in later life. He was an army lieutenant who placed fifth in the military pentathlon. Later he was known as "Old Blood and Guts." He was George S. Patton, Jr.

1920—Antwerp

The Stockholm games had nourished enthusiasm for the Olympics, but the Olympic spirit was not powerful enough to transcend the horrible war that swept through Europe from 1914 to 1918. The 1916 games had been scheduled for Berlin, but they were, of course, canceled. Immediately following the end of hostilities, however, it was decided to hold the 1920 Olympics in war-torn Belgium, and despite the great problems of recovery it faced, that country did its best to make the games a success.

Although the Americans had become the world's greatest power since the 1912 Olympic games, they were to learn in Stockholm that they could no longer take for granted their usual dominance of track and field events. In 1920, they were thwarted by a strong Finnish team led by a remarkable distance runner known as the "Phantom Finn," Paavo Nurmi.

It was in that year that Nurmi began a string of Olympic victories that continued through the 1928 games and might have continued even further had he not finally been disqualified for professionalism. Although Nurmi would eventually break nearly every world record for footraces of a mile or more, he faced tough competition in Antwerp from a French war hero, Jacques Guillemot, who had been gassed by the Germans.

Their first meeting was in the 5,000-meter run, which the Frenchman won with a furious sprint. In the second contest, the 10,000-meter run, Nurmi turned the tables on the Frenchman and came from behind with a sprint of his own. In their third match, the Frenchman was leading the 10,000-meter cross-country run when he stumbled and injured himself; Nurmi was again the winner.

The Finnish team, including Hannes Kolehmainen, who won the marathon, was strong enough to tie the Americans in the track and field events. The two teams each won eight gold medals. There were twenty-seven track and field events.

Although the Americans failed to win any flat race over 200 meters, their celebrated sprinter Charley Paddock became the first Olympic athlete to be called "the world's fastest human," after his victory in the 100-meter dash.

In Belgium, for the first time since the beginning of the modern games, the Americans began to take an interest in some of the ancillary Olympic events. In 1920, they brought along teams in rugby, gymnastics, rowing, shooting, wrestling, boxing, and other events that they had almost ignored in previous games. As a result, the American athletes accumulated an overall total of forty-one gold medals. Their only other overall victory was in the farcical St. Louis games in 1904.

Yet the Americans were still somewhat shaken by the growing track and field prowess of Finland, England, and other countries. For years, top American athletes had been going abroad to teach American training techniques to foreign athletes. Now, their students were returning to haunt them.

1924 — Paris

The Olympic games held in Paris in 1900 had been a miracle of disorganization and squabbling, but in 1924 the

French cleaned up their act. The 1924 games were a superb combination of efficiency and pageantry.

The American athletes came to Paris determined to reinstate themselves as the undisputed masters of track and field. The group was referred to by one official as the greatest track and field team ever assembled.

But the Finns weren't going to give up without a fight. One reason was the return of Paavo Nurmi, whose superiority was so pronounced that he didn't bother with the competition. He wore a stopwatch on his wrist and competed against the clock. He normally defeated his nearest rival by at least a furlong.

Nurmi set Olympic records in the 1500- and 5,000-meter runs on the same day in Paris, and he also captured a gold medal in the 10,000-meter cross-country. His Finnish teammate, Ville Ritola, was usually the only runner who could come anywhere close to the remarkable Nurmi. Ritola captured two gold medals himself—in the 10,000-meter run and the 3,000-meter steeplechase.

In the final tally for the track and field events, the U.S. athletes won ten gold medals and the Finns, eight.

Overall, the U.S. athletes captured gold medals in nine of the seventeen sports. The American swimmers left Paris with thirteen first-place medals, seven brought back by the men, six by the women. And besides their expected victories in shooting, tennis (a sport no longer on the Olympic program), wrestling, rowing, boxing, and gymnastics, the Americans surprisingly won the rugby football title.

Johnny Weissmuller, a young swimmer whose film career as Tarzan the Ape Man would some day overshadow his Olympic performance, set Olympic records in the 100-meter and 400-meter free style races and won a third gold medal as part of the 800-meter relay team.

Weissmuller was a remarkable swimmer. He was a champion in both sprints and long-distance races—a rare combination of speed and endurance. He eventually set world records in sixty-seven different events. Weissmuller became a great swimmer by submitting himself at the age of fifteen to the iron-willed instruction of William Bachrach, who coached the swimming team of the Illinois Athletic Club in Chicago. And just as Tarzan the Ape Man never seemed flustered when attacked by lions, tigers, or nefarious white hunters, Weissmuller the swimmer was known for his ability to be utterly relaxed until the starter's gun was fired.

Weissmuller retired from competition after winning two more gold medals in the 1928 games, but he kindled great interest in the sport of swimming and it became a much more important part of the Olympics for Americans.

1928—Amsterdam

The big news in Amsterdam in 1928 was the collapse of the American track team. Except for two team relays, the Americans won only one race, the 400-meter run, and that came on the last day of track and field competition.

The Americans were shut out of their usual bailiwick—the dashes—by a nineteen-year-old high school student from Vancouver, Canada. Percy Williams was such an unknown that he was forced to hitchhike to the Canadian Olympic Trials, but he rapidly became a hero in Amsterdam with dramatic wins in the 100-meter and 200-meter dashes. His victories represent one of the biggest surprises in Olympic history.

Another embarrassment to the U.S. team was its loss of control over the 400-meter hurdles. American athletes had never lost the event in Olympic competition until a cheerful British aristocrat changed the course of history in Amsterdam. David George Cecil Brownlow, better known as Lord Burghley, or just Davy, took the prize away from the Americans and won the hearts of the huge crowds as well.

The Flying Finns, according to their custom in those days, ran off with everything over 800 meters, and as the track and field competition drew to a close, it appeared that the Americans would be left without a solo track championship. Then Ray Barbuti, a football star at Syracuse University, scored an upset victory in the last race—the 400-meter dash. Barbuti won the race with a desperate dive at the tape that left him face-down in the cinders. Prior to that victory, the Americans hadn't won even a silver or bronze medal in the footraces.

There was some evidence that the U.S. track team in Amsterdam had overtrained for the Olympics, and some writers even contended that the athletes had overeaten during their voyage across the Atlantic. But one thing was clear in Amsterdam: the international competition was getting stiffer. The American athletes won only eight gold medals in the track and field events.

A bright spot for the American track and field athletes in 1928 was that for the first time in the Olympics women were allowed to compete in track and field. Soon the American women would attain the kind of dominance in competition that the men had once had.

1932—Los Angeles

The Olympic games of 1932 were held at the height of the Great Depression, but that didn't prevent the people of Los Angeles from putting on a good show. In fact, the Olympic accommodations provided by that thriving western city were the most elaborate in the thirty-six-year history of the modern games.

The old Los Angeles Coliseum, refurbished and expanded to hold 105,000 spectators, was the biggest of the Olympic stadiums. A large Olympic auditorium and a swimming stadium were also provided for the games. The Angelenos also constructed the first Olympic Village, separate quarters where the Olympic athletes were billeted by nation and ate together in a great hall. It was the beginning of a new tradition in Olympic accommodations.

Perhaps the most significant of the many fine facilities for the Los Angeles games was a track constructed of crushed peat. It was the fastest track used thus far in the Olympic Games, and it produced record-breaking times in nearly every track event. The athletes compared the track to a springboard.

On its home turf for the first time in twenty-eight years,

the U.S. Olympic team reasserted its dominance of the prestigious men's track and field events by winning eleven gold medals. It racked up forty-one gold medals overall.

And it was in Los Angeles that American women began to show their prowess in track and field. They were led by the great Mildred ("Babe") Didrikson, the first female Olympic superstar.

Babe came to Los Angeles only two weeks after single-handedly winning the national women's track and field team championship. It was a remarkable feat, in which she outscored entire teams of women athletes with victories in the shot put, javelin throw, broad jump, baseball throw, 80-meter hurdles, and the high jump.

The eighteen-year-old Texan probably could have repeated the feat in the Olympics, but the Olympic rules of that period limited women to competition in only three separate events. In the Olympics, she decided to compete in the javelin throw, the hurdles, and the high jump. She set world records for the javelin throw and the hurdles and would have set another in the high jump if she hadn't been disqualified for improper jumping style.

Babe was the talk of the world during the Olympics, but her performance there was only the beginning of an incredibly successful career as an athlete. In 1934, she took up golf and became the best woman professional in the game. In 1946, she returned to amateur status and won a record seventeen straight golf championships. In 1950, the Associated Press sportswriters voted her the best female athlete of the first half of the twentieth century.

1936—Berlin

Some people believe that the 1936 Olympic games in Germany should never have taken place—or at least that the United States shouldn't have entered a team in the games. For the German games were intended from the very first to be a showcase for Nazi Germany and a test of the twisted ideas of the German Führer, Adolf Hitler.

But if you put politics aside, the Berlin games were perhaps the most spectacular on record. The Germans built a gigantic Olympic stadium with a seating capacity of 100,000. Other facilities for the games, including an elaborate Olympic Village, were equally impressive. It wasn't until a few years later that the world realized that Hitler believed he was making a long-term investment. He was certain that after his conquest of the world all future Olympic games would be held in the German capital.

The Nazis believed that the Olympics would prove Hitler's demonic theory of the supremacy of the Aryan race, and in the years prior to the games, Jews were systematically eliminated from German athletics. Although the Germans had to place a few Jews on their Olympic squad to appease world opinion, the Nazi Olympics were held in an atmosphere heavy with racism, in addition to the usual national rivalries.

Onto this stage walked an American Olympic team that included ten black men, all of whom were track and field stars of tremendous ability. The best athlete among them was a young man from Ohio State University—Jesse (James Cleveland) Owens.

It had not been easy for black athletes to break into the top ranks of the American sports world. Even in 1936, professional baseball, for instance, was still a segregated sport. But black track and field men had proven themselves in the 1932 games in Los Angeles, where Eddie Tolan had won both the 100-meter and 200-meter dashes. And in Berlin the black athletes from the U.S. would dominate the track and field events.

Owens was the son of an Alabama cotton picker and the grandson of a slave. He was a great, unschooled runner. He drew national attention while still in high school when he scored easy victories in the long jump and the 100- and 200-yard dashes in an interscholastic meet in Chicago. The following year he set a national record of 9.4 seconds in the 100-yard dash that lasted for more than twenty years.

A year later he was a student at Ohio State University, where his track performance was inconsistent but sometimes brilliant. In one day in 1935 he tied the world record for the 100-yard dash and set world records in the long jump, the 220-yard low hurdles, and the 220-yard dash. His long jump record stood for twenty-five years.

Despite Hitler's theories, Owens was the darling of the German crowd. Even the Nazi barrage of venomous racism could not overcome the traditional German respect for excellence. In Berlin, he set Olympic records in the long jump (or broad jump) and the 200-meter dash, and he won easily in the 100-meter dash. He won another gold as a member of the U.S. 400-meter relay team.

In all, the ten black athletes on the American track and field team won eight gold, three silver, and two bronze medals. Cornelius Johnson set an Olympic record in the high jump; Archie Williams took first in the 400-meter run; and John Woodruff of the University of Pittsburgh scored an American victory in the 800-meter run for the first time since the Finns began to dominate the long distance races in 1912.

The U.S. athletes won twelve of the twenty-three track and field events. German and Finnish athletes won three gold medals each.

The U.S. track and field athletes, however, were not the only Americans to score impressive victories in Berlin. Marjorie Gestring, a thirteen-year-old diver, won the springboard event and Dorothy Poynton-Hill captured her second straight gold in the platform diving. Jack Medica also swam to a gold in the 200-meter freestyle and a silver in the 1500 meters.

1948—London

After the Nazi Olympics of 1936, the world had to wait twelve years for another Olympic games. The 1940 games had been scheduled for Tokyo, but by that time the Japanese were engaged in a more deadly form of international competition. By 1944, of course, the rest of the world had followed suit.

It was a miracle that the English were able to put on the

Olympic games in 1948. But despite the devastation of the war, the nations of the world were eager to compete again in athletics, and the English provided adequate, if not elaborate, facilities for them.

The American star in the London games was a seventeen-year-old high school student from Tulare, California—Bob Mathias. This remarkably gifted schoolboy athlete was completely unknown in national sports circles only six months before the Olympics. As a matter of fact, he had never even competed in the decathlon. Yet within that six-month period, Mathias won the national decathlon championship and a position on the U.S. Olympic team.

In London, Mathias became the youngest decathlon champion in history. In the grueling ten-event contest that was crammed into two long days of agony, Mathias won the title of "world's greatest athlete."

Four years later, Mathias returned to the Olympics and again won the decathlon championship, racking up a record-setting number of points and overwhelming his rivals.

The London games also produced an outstanding female star, a woman who overshadowed even the phenomenal performance of Babe Didrikson in 1932. She was Fanny Blankers-Koen, a Dutch housewife, who had waited patiently through the long Olympic layoff for her chance at an Olympic title.

Her performance was well worth waiting for. She won gold medals in the 100-meter dash, the 200-meter dash, and the 80-meter hurdles. She won a fourth gold medal as part of the Dutch 400-meter relay team. In 1948, the women's rules still limited athletes to participation in only three individual events. If that rule hadn't been in effect, the housewife might have won even more championships.

The athletes from the United States did well in the London games despite a record turnout of athletes from all over the world. They won eleven gold medals in the track and field competition. Swedish athletes also scored surprisingly well with five gold medals.

The Russians were eligible to compete in the Olympics for

the first time in 1948, but they decided to wait and prepare for the 1952 games.

1952—Helsinki

Although the Russians did not send a team to the 1952 winter games in Oslo, they showed up in Helsinki prepared to show that the communist system produced superior athletes. Since the 1948 games, in which they had participated only as observers, the Russians had launched a massive national sports program aimed at scoring a victory in the Olympics. With their arrival in Helsinki, the story of the 1952 Olympics became one of the confrontation between the superpowers, the showdown between capitalist and communist—U.S. versus USSR.

Yet neither a Russian nor an American was the hero of Helsinki. The honor went to a wiry, balding, career military man from Czechoslovakia—Emil Zatopek. This great long distance runner was a celebrity at Helsinki because he was nearly as good an actor as he was an athlete. When he ran, he appeared to be undergoing some new form of torture. His face contorted into a guise of pain. He groaned and grunted and appeared to be near death or something worse.

Yet he had no problems with his legs. He ran like a machine from the waist down. He had a remarkable ability to regulate his pace, to run as fast or as slow as he pleased and still finish in front of the pack.

In Helsinki, he proved that he was one of the great runners of all time. Four years before, he had won a gold medal in the 10,000-meter and a silver medal at 5,000 meters. In 1952, he broke his own record in the 10,000 meters and set a new Olympic record in the 5,000 meters. Then he won another gold medal in the marathon, setting another Olympic record in that event despite the fact that he had never run a marathon before in his life.

But even the heroics of Zatopek could not overshadow the growing athletic battle between Russia and the U.S. Although the U.S. athletes won fourteen gold medals in track and field, their best effort in many years, the Russian athletes did extremely well in other areas of the Olympics.

The American boxing team put on a spectacular performance winning five gold medals on the last day of competition. One of the winners that day was young Floyd Patterson, a seventeen-year-old middleweight with a quick, lethal punch. He later, of course, became heavyweight champion of the world.

With all eyes focused on the U.S.-Russian competition, it began to appear that the Olympics might become another theater of the Cold War, an arena in which the two giants would gradually squeeze out the smaller countries as serious competitors and hence destroy the international spirit of the Olympic games.

1956—Melbourne

The summer Olympic games in Melbourne, Australia, took place in a troubled world. In Hungary the Russians were putting a brutal end to the October revolution, while in the Middle East, the Suez crisis had erupted into war. Several Arab countries and the Communist Chinese boycotted the games. You could cut the tension between the Hungarian and Russian Olympic teams with a knife. Yet, despite the political atmosphere, the athletes finally won out and the games were a success.

Participating in only its second summer Olympics, the Russian team made a small dent in the traditional United States dominance in the track and field events.

The Russian track and field star was Vladimir Kuts. In 1952, the Russians had failed to win a single championship in men's track and field, but in 1956 Kuts alone won two gold medals while setting Olympic records in the 5,000- and 10,000-meter runs. The Russians also won a gold medal in the 20,000-meter walk.

The American performance in men's track and field was its best in many years. Led by Bobby Morrow, who won gold medals in the 100- and 200-meter dashes and as a member of the 400-meter relay team, the U.S. athletes earned fifteen golds.

A touch of glamor and romance was provided by Harold Connolly, U.S. gold medal winner in the hammer throw, and Olga Fikotova, the Olympic discus champion from Czechoslovakia. Connolly was immediately attracted to the comely brunette, and the couple was the talk of the Olympic village in Melbourne. A year later the two were married, and the U.S. Olympic team picked up another top competitor.

1960—Rome

There have been many gregarious athletes in the history of the Olympic games—athletes who were known as much for their personalities as for their abilities on the athletic field. But perhaps none has been as outgoing as the young American boxer who won the light-heavyweight championship in Rome, Italy, in 1960.

Cassius Marcellus Clay, now known as Muhammad Ali, began in 1960 the combination of theater and athletics that has placed him in the American spotlight for the last twenty years. In Rome, the eighteen-year-old from Louisville, Kentucky, was a true student of the world. He was everywhere in the Olympic Village, talking, asking questions, and taking pictures. He must have learned a great deal about the peoples of the world; certainly, the world learned a great deal about him. By the time he returned to the United States as an Olympic champion, his name was virtually a household word. He would soon tell Americans matter-of-factly that he was "the greatest."

If the brash boxer from Louisville was the glamour boy of Rome, Wilma Rudolph was the glamour girl. But she caught the attention of the world not with her mouth but with her legs. The long-legged twenty-year-old from Tennessee State had, like so many great athletes, overcome great odds in becoming a champion. As a child she had suffered pneumonia and scarlet fever, and she couldn't even walk properly during much of her childhood. By the time she got to Rome, she had already proved herself a formidable competitor—and there was more to come.

The first American woman to win three gold medals in track and field, Wilma set Olympic records in the 100- and

200-meter dashes and led the 400-meter relay team to victory.

By a twist of fate, the best competitive matchup in Rome took place between two young men who, despite their different nationalities, were longtime friends. C. K. Yang and Rafer Johnson were both students at UCLA, but Yang was competing in the Olympics under the banner of Nationalist China. The two fought tooth and nail in the decathlon, and the championship was not decided until the last event. Johnson scored a narrow victory in total points, dashing the only hope of the Chinese for an Olympic gold medal.

Another small nation was more successful in bringing home its first championship. Abebe Bikila, a guard at the palace of Emperor Haile Selassie of Ethiopia, won the marathon in record time—and he did it barefoot. Four years later Bikila would win another gold medal.

In Rome, the Russians put on an outstanding performance for the second consecutive time. The American athletes were disappointed that their men's track and field total fell to nine gold medals, a drop of six from their performances in Melbourne.

1964—Tokyo

Since 1952, when the Russians entered their first Olympics, the intense competition between the two superpowers—Russia and America—had often overshadowed the performances of individual athletes. But it was proved beyond a shadow of a doubt in Tokyo, Japan, in 1964, that an individual athlete from a small country could capture the attention of sports fans around the world. The center of this attention was Peter Snell of New Zealand.

Having set an Olympic record in Rome in 1960, Snell came to the Olympics four years later as the widely acknowledged champion of middle distance runners. He was clearly the greatest runner in the world. He had set world records in the mile and half-mile events, and he had trained himself into peak condition for the Olympic equivalents of those events— the 800- and 1500-meter runs.

When he arrived in Tokyo, the main question on his mind

was whether he should attempt to win both events—a feat not accomplished for many years—or limit himself to the more prestigious 1500-meter run. Finally, he entered both events and committed himself to a series of races that would have worn down a lesser athlete. As it turned out, he won both races in record times, and he even won easily in the 1500-meter run.

The U.S. athletes in general did very well in Tokyo, and one athlete in particular emerged a hero that year—Don Schollander. The eighteen-year-old Californian became the first Olympian to win four swimming championships in one year. Showing incredible speed and stamina, Schollander set an Olympic record in the 100-meter free style and a world record in the 400-meter free style and swam on the world-record–setting 400- and 800-meter relay teams.

There were two other stars in Tokyo whom Americans would hear much about in the years to come. They were Bob Hayes, who set an Olympic record in the 100-meter dash and anchored the victorious 400-meter relay team, and Henry Carr, who ran a record-setting 200-meter dash. Both athletes would later climb to fame and fortune in the National Football League.

Bob Schull won the 5,000-meter run and Billy Mills took the 10,000-meter—two events no American had ever won before.

1968—Mexico City

Prior to the opening of the summer Olympic games in Mexico City in 1968, the sports world was somewhat uneasy. There was some concern about the ability of the Mexicans to stage a successful Olympics, but the major worry was the altitude. Mexico City is 7,350 feet above sea level. What effect would the thin air have on Olympic performances?

As it turned out, the concerns were unfounded. The Mexicans were splendid hosts. The facilities were magnificent; the ritual and pageantry, superb. Even the thin air proved to be no problem, as the athletes broke more records than ever before.

Although the Mexicans were the perfect hosts, the other countries of the world were less than ideal guests in some respects. There was a rhubarb before the games about the eligibility of South Africa. That country had been excluded from competition in 1968 because of its racial policies. When the International Olympic Committee decided to allow the South African team to compete in Mexico City, forty African nations threatened a boycott. The IOC later reversed its decision.

Another racial issue involved black athletes in the United States. There had been some effort to persuade black athletes to boycott the games as a protest against American racial prejudice, but the idea had failed to draw adequate support and had been cast aside. The black protest issue didn't re-surface until two American sprinters, Tommie Smith and John Carlos, gold and bronze medal winners in the 200-meter dash, were being awarded their medals. Then, to the aston-ishment of practically everyone, as the band played "The Star-Spangled Banner," the athletes raised black-gloved fists in a black power salute. The action was interpreted as a flagrant violation of Olympic etiquette, and the U.S. Olympic Committee suspended Carlos and Smith from the team.

From an apolitical perspective, the men's track and field competition in Mexico City was one of the most exciting in the history of the games. Aided by a track constructed of synthetic material, the runners and jumpers of the world had a field day.

The first to prove that thin air didn't necessarily produce winded athletes, at least in the short races, was Jim Hines of the U.S. Hines set an Olympic record in the 100-meter dash and tied the world mark.

Then Bob Seagren, a twenty-two-year-old California pole-vaulter, proved that the thin air didn't bother airborne ath-letes either. Seagren won the pole vaulting championship with a jump of 17 feet 8½ inches. In previous Olympics, no athlete had vaulted as high as 17 feet.

Another aerialist made an even more dramatic break-through—one that has been called one of the greatest sports milestones of all time. Bob Beamon of the University of Texas at El Paso was a lanky twenty-two-year-old long jumper. In Mexico City, he jumped 29 feet 2½ inches, breaking the world record by almost two feet. In fact, he almost jumped all the way across the pit.

A record for Olympic longevity was set by Al Oerter of the New York Athletic Club. Oerter had won his first gold medal for the discus throw in 1956. He won again in 1960 and in 1964, and he did it again in 1968. Each time Oerter was the underdog, and each time Oerter made the longest throw of his career. He always seemed to rise to the occasion.

1972—Munich

Like the Mexico City games, the summer Olympic games in Munich, Germany, were prefaced by an African contro-versy. This time the protagonist was Rhodesia.

The white-supremacist government of Rhodesia had de-clared its independence from Britain, but Rhodesia was to be allowed to compete in the 1972 games under the British flag. When the Rhodesian athletes arrived at Munich with uni-forms bearing the name of their country, apparently flouting the conditions laid down by the International Olympic Com-mittee and agreed to by the Rhodesian government, the Af-rican nations for the second time in four years threatened to boycott the Olympics. As it had in 1968, the IOC sided with the African majority. It withdrew its invitation for the Rho-desians to compete in Munich.

With the quadrennial racial controversy set aside for an-other four years, it appeared that the Munich games would be a success. And for the first ten days at least, they were.

The hero of those quiet days before the storm of Black Tuesday was Mark Spitz. The stoic American swimmer, whose specialty was the butterfly stroke, put on the greatest performance in the history of American swimming. It was an athletic tour de force that probably will not be matched for many years to come.

Spitz, who had won gold medals in two team events in Mexico City, was the favorite in Munich. But no one could have predicted the spectacular show he put on. In his first race, the 200-meter butterfly, Spitz was never seriously challenged. He led from the outset and broke a world's record. The same day he anchored the four-man, 400-meter free-style team to another world-record–breaking performance. The following day, Spitz set a third world record in the 200-meter free style. Several days later he won two more gold medals, one in the 100-meter butterfly and the other as anchor of the 800-meter free style team. World records were set in both events. He then became the first Olympian in history to win six gold medals in one year with a world-record–setting victory in the 100-meter free style. Still not satisfied, on the tenth day of Olympic competition he won a seventh gold medal as a member of the 400-meter medley team.

On the eleventh day of the 1972 Olympics, a group of Palestinian terrorists crept into the Olympic Village, killed two Israeli athletes, and held nine more hostage. As the world watched in disbelief, the terrorists demanded that the government of Israel relase two hundred imprisoned Arab guerrillas. They also wanted transportation out of the country.

The terrorists and their hostages were taken by helicopter to an airfield after a long day of negotiations with German officials. Because of a news blackout, the world believed the hostages had been released safely at the airport. They learned the truth the following day. All nine of the hostages had been killed, along with a German policeman and five of the terrorists.

There was much sentiment after the tragedy for canceling the remainder of the Olympics. But influential members of the International Olympic Committee believed that if the terrorists were allowed to force cancellation of the games, the Olympic movement would grind to a halt. And so, after a memorial service attended by eighty thousand people, the games continued. But the tragedy that took place in Munich on 5 September 1972 would forever overshadow the triumphs of the athletes.

1976—Montreal

The world breathed a sigh of relief when the 1976 summer Olympic games in Montreal ended without serious mishap. In preparing for the games, the Canadians were plagued by strikes and inflation, and this time the African nations carried out their threat to boycott the games. But once the competition began, the athletes outdistanced the political disputes that seemed to be occurring with increasing frequency.

The U.S. team brought another exceptional swimming star to the Olympics—a gregarious, 6-foot-6-inch tall Californian named John Naber. The backstroke specialist won four gold medals and a silver one. He set world records in the 100- and 200-meter backstroke events.

An East German swimmer dominated the women's events. Kornelia Ender, a seventeen-year-old blonde who had developed tremendous strength by lifting weights, became the first woman swimmer to win four gold medals. Her most remarkable feat was setting world records in the 100- and 200-meter freestyle races with only twenty-five minutes of rest between the two events.

In another coup for the communist nations, Cuba produced its first great running star in Montreal. Alberto Juantorena won the 400- and 800-meter runs. He also set a world record in the 800.

American boxers provided a pleasant surprise for U.S. partisans. They won five gold medals. Two of the champions were brothers—Leon and Mike Spinks. Leon, 23, won the light-heavyweight crown. He later would win the professional heavyweight championship from the former Olympic champion, Muhammad Ali, but would hold onto the title for only a short time. His brother, Mike, 20, was the middleweight champion in Montreal. The lightweight champion was Howard Davis, and the light-welterweight crown was won by a promising young boxer—Sugar Ray Leonard.

THE WINTER OLYMPICS

The very first time a winter sport appeared on an Olympic program was in 1908 in London. Men's and women's figure skating competitions were held in conjunction with the regular summer Olympic events. The skating events did not draw particularly large crowds or stimulate much interest and the winter sports were dropped for the Stockholm games.

World War I preempted the 1916 Olympics, but in Antwerp in 1920 figure skating was reintroduced, along with a new addition, ice hockey. After the 1920 games the proponents of skiing and bobsledding began hounding the International Olympic Committee about including their respective sports in the summer games. The IOC chose not to put them in the 1924 summer program, opting for a separate Olympics. Thus Chamonix became the site for the first official winter games.

There were sixteen events in the 1924 games, in five categories of sport—figure skating, speed skating, skiing, bobsledding, and ice hockey. The very first individual gold medal won in the games was earned by a speed skater named Charlie Jewtraw of Lake Placid, New York. Anders Haugen, a U.S. ski jumper, won what up until 1976 was the only Nordic medal ever captured by an American. Haugen had placed third in the ski jumping, but he had to wait fifty years before he received his bronze medal. The Chamonix judges had miscalculated and awarded third place to Thorlief Haug of Norway. A year later the mistake was discovered, but it wasn't until 1974 that Haugen received his just reward.

In 1928, the winter games moved to St. Moritz, then, in the bidding for the 1932 games, the IOC dealt the U.S. a pair— Los Angeles for the summer games and Lake Placid, New York, for the winter games.

Seventeen countries and 364 athletes competed in Lake Placid in 1932. The small village cut into the round-topped

Adirondacks comfortably accommodated the 20,000 spectators who attended the competitions each day. There were
only fourteen events—twelve for men, one for women and
one for skating pairs—in the third winter Olympiad. There
were no Alpine skiing events, and the entire cost of the
spectacle was $1.2 million. To help finance the games, the
local townspeople, all 2,900 of them, floated a $350,000 bond
issue. It took thirty years to pay off that tidy sum, and no
doubt the memory of the bond issue was still fresh in the
minds of the 580 Lake Placid villagers who voted against
holding the 1980 games in their hamlet. However, 726 people—perhaps with shorter memories about the cash and
fonder ones of the winter of '32—voted aye and the 1980
games were on.

The 1932 games were the first Olympics where the speed
skating was conducted under American rules. The Europeans
had been used to racing in pairs, but against the clock, so
that the time for the one race determined the winner. American rules stipulated head-to-head competition, with the winners of the trial heats advancing until only two were left to
skate it out. Under the American system the times were
basically unimportant, whereas pace and strategy became
critical factors. Prior to the races, the Europeans vigorously
protested, but to no avail. Two American speed skaters, Irving
Jaffe and Jack Shea, a hometown boy, copped four gold medals between them. Shea still lives in Lake Placid and has
been a vocal supporter of the 1980 games.

In the 1980 Lake Placid games there are also two U.S.
speed skaters—a brother and sister parlay, Eric and Beth
Heiden—who figure to leave the games with a few gold
medals around their necks. Shea and Jaffe were two of four
hundred athletes at the 1932 games. The Heidens will be
among twelve hundred winter sports gods and goddesses
from forty different countries. Somewhere around five thousand people witnessed the victory runs of Shea and Jaffe; the
feats of the Heidens will probably be seen by six million, all
but about eighty-five hundred of whom will watch on
television.

Amazingly, the Lake Placid of 1980 is still pretty much the sleepy town of three thousand people, 260 miles from the "Big Apple," it was forty-eight years ago. And a lot of those folks who watched the 1932 games are still around. In fact, a few of them had a great deal to do with Lake Placid's hosting the 1980 affair. Most of the members of the 1980 Lake Placid Olympic Organizing Committee, led by the Reverend Bernie Fell, a policeman turned Methodist minister, had been involved in previous efforts to bring the games back to the village that curves around Mirror Lake. Six times since 1932 Lake Placid had bid for the Winter Olympic games. In 1954 Lake Placid dropped a decision to Squaw Valley for the 1960 games. In 1962 Lake Placid's bid looked very strong; the Olympic Organizing Committee spent $150,000 on a sophisticated audio-visual exhibit, and they wined, dined, and cajoled the IOC members. Still, they came up short of the necessary votes; Grenoble hosted the 1968 Winter games.

In 1966 Lake Placid's bid didn't even make it out of the country. The USOC threw its support behind Salt Lake City as the U.S. entry. However, the predominantly Mormon city was never a serious threat to the spectacular offensive display put on by the Japanese. Sapporo took the '72 Games.

In 1968 the Lake Placid Committee again threw its hat in the ring, but again the USOC looked elsewhere. Denver received the USOC endorsement for the '76 games. Four years before the games were to take place, the ecology-minded citizens of Colorado voted down a referendum supporting the games, and the USOC was left holding the bag. Lake Placid earnestly offered to help out, but the USOC went back to the Salt Lake City contingent. This time the mayor of Salt Lake City and the governor of Utah stated publicly that they wanted no part of the games. One week before the IOC vote on the 1976 site, the undaunted Lake Placid Committee responded to the USOC's plea to mount at least a token bid, knowing full well that the odds against putting together a potentially winning bid on such short notice were insurmountable. The 1976 winter games went to Innsbruck.

It has been said that good things come to those who wait. That's assuming, of course, that winning the right to host a massive international spectacle like the Olympics in these complex, unpredictable times is a good thing. The 1980 Lake Placid bid was organized, to the point, and finally right on target for the mood of the IOC. The committee presented a concept of smallness, of a manageable Olympics that would make use of the many already existing facilities.

The committee proposed returning the games to the athletes and putting the emphasis back on competition. Grenoble had spent $400 million, Sapporo $700 million, and Innsbruck $250 million. The Lake Placid Committee estimated they could stage the 1980 games for $30 to $35 million; with $23 million going for new construction, and $6 million of that earmarked for the new Olympic Village.

Just let the French or Austrians try to steal this one away: Lake Placid was ready for all comers—1980 was their year. The funny thing is nobody tried. There were originally four other cities competing for the 1980 winter games, but by the time the IOC vote rolled around, Lake Placid was shadowboxing. Vancouver, the last of the other four cities, had dropped out a few months before.

Most of the excitement in Vienna on 23 October 1974 centered on two much larger cities—cities that had apartment complexes bigger than Lake Placid. The big question in Vienna was whether Moscow or Los Angeles would host the 1980 summer games. When Lord Killanin announced Moscow as the summer choice, the Russians whooped and hollered and hugged each other, then took the microphone and made gracious statements, grand promises, and overtures of peace offerings to the Red Chinese. Twenty minutes later, the Lake Placid representatives greeted a somewhat depleted press corps and expressed their delight and excitement. The lack of attention didn't matter to the Adirondack contingent. Forty-eight years after the third winter Olympiad had been staged, the winter games were coming back home. The victory was sweet—even if it had been by forfeit.

Two twisting roads, routes 73 and 86, snake into the village of Lake Placid, which is located in the town of North Elba in the Adirondack State Park. It is 260 miles from New York City, 40 miles from Vermont, and 100 miles south of Montreal.

The Adirondack Airport in Saranac Lake services the area.

Lake Placid is a place suited to the games of winter. The world's largest instructional school for figure skaters is located there, and many world championships have taken place within its boundaries, including the World University Winter Games in 1972, bobsled competitions in 1973, and, most recently, the pre-games Nordic competitions.

Many of the facilities needed to stage the winter games already existed in Lake Placid. Even before the 1980 construction began, there were biathlon and cross-country trails, the only bobsled run in North America, a 2,500-seat figure skating arena, a 70-meter ski jump, and the Whiteface Mountain ski area, which has the steepest vertical drop in the east (3,212).

The new construction plans originally called for a new 90-meter ski jump, a new 8,500-seat fieldhouse for hockey and figure skating, the Olympic Village, a speed-skating oval, several new ski lifts, snowmaking equipment, a new refrigeration system for the bobsled runs, and a stadium for the opening and closing ceremonies. In Vienna in 1974, the organizing committee had told the IOC that the total cost of the winter games would be $35 million. But even as early as a year and a half before the opening ceremonies, the dark clouds of inflation and miscalculation began to form over Lake Placid and the intention of its well-meaning citizens to return the games to the athletes. As of August 1979, the initial $35 million estimate had ballooned to a staggering $155 million.

What happened? Well, for instance, the existing 70-meter jump that was only supposed to be renovated was declared inadequate and a new 70-meter ski jump was deemed necessary. The construction costs for the fieldhouse, the renovation of the Town Hall to provide office space for the administrators, the village, and the speed-skating oval soared past $70 million. The improvements in the two-lane roads and the building of new parking lots and spectator areas cost an additional $32 million. Suddenly the modest games of 1980 were anything but.

The $155 million breaks down like this: $70 million in

federally financed construction; $30 million in state financed construction; and $50–55 million for administrative expenses (to be raised by private individuals and enterprises and ticket sales).

The $155 million price tag has created quite a controversy, but the biggest brouhaha of all has to do with the new Olympic Village. The original cost of the village was set at $6 million. At last glance the tab was $49 million. Even though the cost has risen to nine times the initial estimate, the real story lies in who is picking up the check. As it turns out, the big spender is the Federal Bureau of Prisons.

After the twelve hundred athletes have departed Lake Placid and the 102-odd medals have been distributed, the forty-eight-acre, fourteen-building facility will become a minimum security prison for first-time offenders. And therein lies the rub. What in the way of accommodations will apparently be just fine for the future inmates of the prison-to-be will not be just fine for the athletes of many European nations.

It's not that the fourteen sand-colored buildings are particularly unattractive, though they do have a certain utilitarian air. And no objections have been raised to the proposed discotheque, saunas, and cafeteria. What has the European sports federations hot under their turtleneck collars is that their prized athletic specimens will be expected to sleep in rooms—cells—that are barely large enough to turn around in.

And it all seemed like such a good idea. No more building Olympic facilities that have no function after the crowds and competitors depart. The 1980s require new thinking; function must triumph over aesthetics. This is the age of the recycling phenomenon.

The five dormitories (the organizing committee's press releases compare the village to a college campus) contain 937 sleeping rooms. When the new tenants take over in 1981, the plans call for one prisoner per each ten-by-ten-foot room. Yet the Olympic athletes will sleep two to a unit. Each room contains two steel bunk beds, one small table, two chairs, two wardrobe closets, and a small sink. Most of the rooms have a window, nine feet high by fifteen inches wide, that doesn't open. Some of the rooms, however, are without natural light. The doors, made of heavy steel, are equipped with the peepholes through which the "screws" will check on the inmates. The cost to each national sports federation for room and board is $27.50 per day per athlete.

The entire compound is surrounded by two concentric twelve-foot-high chain-link fences, with a twenty-foot "no man's land" in between them. The outer perimeter road will be patrolled by the New York State police. There are two entry checkpoints, one at each fence, and the guards checking credentials will be assisted by the usual mechanical army of electronic medal-testing devices. Though history has certainly proved that the precautions are necessary, one imagines that the favorite movie among the athletes will be *Escape from Alcatraz.*

Predictably, many of the foreign athletes are "escaping" the village even before they've checked in. The Swedish Olympic team has rented two Lake Placid houses in which to billet certain athletes for one or two days before their competitions. The Austrians have actually bought an old boardinghouse on Main Street for $125,000 to house some of their squad.

The tide of dissatisfaction does not stop with the Swedes and the Austrians. The Italians and the Japanese have complained about the monastic life-style; the Norwegians have spent $30,000 on rented villas; and the East and West Germans are also planning on living outside the facility.

The two hundred U.S. athletes will stay in the village. Bob Paul, communications director for the USOC, said, "We always stay in the facilities that are provided." The Lake Placid Organizing Committee has said that most of the countries will also remain in the village, although they do acknowledge that there has been something of a "renters' revolution."

The IOC has given very little support to Lake Placid during the controversy, choosing to avoid confrontations whenever possible. In March 1979, Monique Berlioux, an IOC director, made an unusual proclamation: "Although it is general policy that the countries must pay for Olympic housing even if they don't stay there, this time the accommodations are so poor that the delegations will not have to pay for them if they move somewhere else. However, security is another matter. Suitable security has been arranged for the Olympic Village, but teams living elsewhere will have to be responsible for their own security." From the looks of the mass exodus, the European delegations are more concerned with comfort than with safety.

It is worthwhile to note, however, that there has not been a winter games in the history of the Olympics in which at least one team, coach, or competitor did not criticize the facilities, officials, beds, or food. In St. Moritz in 1928 and in Lake Placid in 1932, the weather was so warm the skating rinks were reduced to goo and the bobsled runs were filled with mud. In St. Moritz in 1948, in Oslo in 1952, and in Innsbruck in 1964, there was an absence of a very essential ingredient—snow. It had to be trucked in and shoveled onto the mountain by soldiers. Problems and complaints obviously come with the Olympic territory.

Facts and Figures for the Lake Placid Games

There will be an estimated 51,000 spectators per day at the games, plus another 17,000 athletes, media personnel, and support staff. Since there are only 12,000 beds in Lake Placid and the four surrounding counties, most of the fans will have to find lodging in adjacent areas. Albany has 10,000 beds, Saratoga 3,000, Burlington, Vermont, 12,000, and Montreal 60,000. All of the cities are within a 2½-hour commute. The state of New York has set a maximum rate for motel and hotel rooms in the Olympic region. Innkeepers may charge summer rates plus 20 percent plus $19.50.

For two years the organizing committee has been working on a plan for moving the 68,000 people a day into and around the venues. Fortunately, all of the sites are within an 8½-mile area. As it stands now, the roads into the village will be blocked off and private cars banned. Parking lots six to twenty-five miles away are to be utilized, and a fleet of 400 buses will transport fans to and from the competitions.

On 31 January 1980 the first torch will be lighted in Greece. The flame will be flown to Yorktown, Virginia, and from there a succession of fifty-two runners will carry it the 1,000 miles to Lake Placid. At Albany the two relay teams will split and travel separate routes, arriving in the stadium simultaneously on Wednesday, 13 February, at 2:30 P.M.

Tickets to the opening ceremonies will sell for $35 to $45. For the closing ceremonies the cost will be $10 to $25. The rest of the ticket prices will range from a low of $10 to a high of $60. The individual breakdown by sport is as follows:

Figure Skating and Ice Hockey	$10–$60
90-meter Jump	$25–$45
70-meter Jump	$20–$35
Alpine Skiing	$15–$25
Speed Skating	$15–$20
Bobsled	$15–$20
Cross-Country and Biathlon	$10–$15

Most of the tickets are being sold in packages to ensure an even distribution of spectators at the events. In other words, if you wish to buy a ticket to the figure skating, you will also be obliged to purchase other tickets in the package for events such as the bobsled and cross-country.

The village will officially open for the athletes in January, but preliminary ice hockey training exhibitions will take place in December, and the actual ice hockey tournament will begin one day prior to the opening ceremonies.

The figure skating and hockey competitions will be staged in the fieldhouse. The hockey tournament is scheduled for February 12, 13, 14, 16, 18, 20, 22, and 24. Figure skating is scheduled for February 15, 17, 18, 19, 20, 21, and 23.

The ski jumping at Intervale is scheduled for February 17, 18, and 23. The cross-country, biathlon, bobsled, and luge competitions will take place at Mount Van Hoevenberg, six miles southeast of Lake Placid. Cross-country will be held on February 14, 15, 17, 18, 19, 20, 21, and 23; the biathlon on February 15, 16, 19, and 22; the bobsled on February 15, 16,

23, and 24; and the luge on February 13, 14, 15, 16, and 19.

The Alpine events are scheduled for Whiteface Mountain, eight miles northeast of Lake Placid, on February 14, 17, 18, 19, 20, 21, 22, and 23.

American Olympic Prospects

Before taking over in March 1979 as the U.S. Alpine Ski Director, Bill Marolt was the very successful coach of the University of Colorado ski team. In ten years his teams piled up seven national titles.

Heading up any Olympic squad is an arduous task. But Marolt's job has been made all the more difficult by the rash of injuries that have crippled both the men's and women's teams.

For starters, Phil Mahre, the top giant slalom and slalom prospect and the most consistent skier in U.S. history, is recovering from a broken ankle he received in a February fall on Whiteface Mountain. Let's hope that isn't a portent of trouble, since Whiteface is the site of the 1980 Alpine competitions. Mahre's ankle required seven screws, which were put into place during a three-hour operation. He was still on crutches when Marolt took over the reins.

Mahre is the only world class skier who has defeated the superb Swedish racer Ingemar Stenmark in both the slalom and giant slalom. Stenmark has said that Mahre is one of the skiers he fears most. Ingemar seems a sure bet to capture at least one gold medal, but he has every reason to worry about Phil Mahre, especially since the U.S. skier will be racing in front of home country crowds, where he always seems to do quite well. Also, along with the rest of the squad, Phil will be very familiar with Whiteface. It is likely he will win a medal, and a gold one is not out of his reach.

Then there's the other Mahre, Phil's twin brother, Steve, the number-two–ranked U.S. slalom skier. The Mahres are from White Pass, Washington, and in 1978 they both married hometown sweethearts. The Mahres have been the top U.S. slalom threats for the past several seasons. In a 1978 World Cup competition in Stratton, Vermont, Phil won the giant slalom and Steve took the slalom—it was the only time two American skiers had scored World Cup victories in the same season.

Marolt believes there are two other U.S. skiers with reasonable chances for medals in the slalom—Cary Adgate and Pete Patterson, twenty-one, who recently recovered from a broken femur. In the giant slalom, the second strongest event for the U.S. men, Patterson and Billy Doris join the Mahres as the top Olympic prospects.

The downhill has traditionally been the weakest of the three events for the men. The primary reasons are lack of training and the fact that our better racers have always gravitated to the slalom events. Right now the U.S. hopes in the downhill lie with twenty-six-year-old Andy Mill, Carl Anderson, and two young skiers, eighteen-year-old Doug Powell, who had knee surgery in 1978, and Mike Farny.

The women's team's casualty list is not much shorter than the men's. Twenty-one-year-old Abbi Fisher, one of the most talented skiers on the squad and a very strong competitor in the giant slalom, strained a knee in a downhill at Badgastum and twisted an ankle before the World Cup in Garmisch. As late as July 1979, Abbi was still on crutches.

The strongest medal hope among the U.S. women is Cindy Nelson, who at twenty-three is the team veteran, having competed on the World Cup circuit since 1973. Cindy captured the bronze in the downhill in Innsbruck in 1976 and is the only consistent world class threat among the U.S. women. Cindy is primarily a downhiller, but she has won a World Cup slalom.

Other potential downhill prospects are Holly Flanders, who took two tenth-places on the 78–79 World Cup circuit, and Jamie Kurlander.

In the slalom, seventeen-year-old Tamara McKinney from Squaw Valley has collected points in the World Cup (her brother Steve holds the world speed record at over 200 kph). Young Christin Cooper, nineteen, is a beautiful skier whose exceptional technique makes her a legitimate threat for a medal.

Vicki Fleckstein, twenty-four, has been a top racer in this

country since she was thirteen. In 1975 Vicki finished fifteenth in the first World Cup race she ever entered. In 1978 she gained three second-place finishes in World Cup events. Vicki bicycles and runs to help keep in shape and build up her stamina. She is a heady racer with the technical skills to place well under the right circumstances.

Other U.S. women who figure to be at Lake Placid are Becky Dorsey and Heidi Preuss.

In the Nordic events there are three U.S. athletes who have distinguished themselves above all others: Bill Koch, for his speed and stamina in the men's cross-country; Jim Denney, for his soaring ability; and Alison Owen-Spencer, for her speed and endurance in the women's cross-country.

In 1976 Koch, who was nineteen at the time, stunned the frosty Nordic world when he churned to a silver medal in the 30 km Olympic cross-country race. Now a seasoned twenty-two, Bill, who comes from Guilford, Vermont, should again be the top U.S. performer. Following Innsbruck, Koch was expected to continue to ski in the winter spotlight; instead his performances tapered off in 1977 and '78. But Koch is a competitor who obviously knows when and how to get himself into peak condition. In 1979 his performances began improving. In March he won two races, a 12 km and a 12.5 km in Sweden. And in the 1979 pre-games, against a solid international field, he finished a respectable eighth in the 30 km and seventh in the 15 km. Bill was not dissatisfied. "I've been working three years to peak at the Olympics," he said. "I'm happy with these results."

Other men's cross-country competitors are Stan Dunklee, who had a very fine outing in the 1978 Worlds, Tim Caldwell, and Doug Peterson.

Up until February 1979, the last time an American ski jumper had earned a medal in a world class competition was 1965. During the entire week of the World Nordic Pre-Games in Lake Placid this past winter, the temperature never rose above zero during the day and it chattered down to forty below at night. But Jim Denney, a twenty-one-year-old accounting major from the University of Minnesota at Duluth, sliced through the arctic air to place third in the 90-meter jump.

Denney, the oldest of three jumping brothers, knocked off the pre–Olympic games favorite, Joachen Danneberg of East Germany, and finished right behind Finland's Kokkonen and East Germany's Duschek. Chris McNeill of Polaris, Montana, finished a surprising ninth in the same event.

On 3 March 1979 Denney continued his successful jumping by winning the 70-meter event at the Finnish Ski Games in Laati. Denney has certainly established himself as a serious contender for a 1980 ski jumping medal.

Alison Owen-Spencer qualified for the 1966 Junior Nordic National Championships at the age of thirteen. She was the only girl entered in the competition. Twelve years later she won her first official cross-country World Cup race—a five-kilometer event. Alison, twenty-six, from Indian, Alaska, is the finest woman cross-country skier in the States. In the 1978–79 Women's Nordic World Cup standings she finished seventh.

In the Nordic pre-games in March against an exceptionally strong field, Alison placed twelfth in the 5 km, but dropped to twentieth in the 10 km, primarily because of equipment problems. Alison will have to come up with the finest performance of her life to win a medal in Lake Placid, and realistically speaking, even that might not be enough.

Leslie Bancroft and Beth Paxson are other Olympic hopefuls in the women's cross-country.

The U.S. chances for a medal in the biathlon are very slim. In an effort to help the U.S. athletes improve their performances, arrangements were made for the American team to train with the pre-games favorite, Alexander Tichinov of the USSR. If nothing else came of it, it was surely a demonstration of the Olympic ideal in action.

The top biathlon competitors in the U.S. come from opposite ends of the country. Don Nielson, twenty-eight, is from South Strafford, Vermont. Lyle Nelson, thirty-two, is from McCall, Idaho. Nielson finished second in the U.S.-Canada Dannon Yogurt Relays in Steamboat Springs. It is unlikely that either Nielson or Nelson will win a medal in 1980. The East Germans, Soviets, and Scandinavians are just too strong and experienced.

Other U.S. biathlon prospects are Glen Jobe and Martin Hagen.

Throughout the fifty-six year history of the winter Olympics, U.S. athletes have traditionally fared well in the skating competitions. In the initial program at Chamonix in 1924, Charlie Jewtraw of Lake Placid won the very first individual gold in the 500-meter speed skating, and Beatrix Loughran of the U.S. placed second in the women's figure skating.

In more recent Olympics four American figure skaters have captured the gold medal: Tenley Albright, Carol Heiss, Peggy Fleming, and Dorothy Hamill. Heiss, Fleming, and Hamill became instantly famous at the games, due to the extensive television coverage. After the Olympics they went on to parlay their Olympic victories into sparkling professional careers, following the pattern established early on by Sonja Henie.

In this year's winter games another American woman is favored to capture the gold, and with it will surely come the adoration of millions and not a small amount of riches. Linda Fratianne of Northridge, California, is the current World Champion and the pre-Olympic favorite in the women's figure skating competition. The nineteen-year-old first competed in the Olympics in 1976, where she placed a commendable eighth. She was all but lost, though, in the reflection of Dorothy Hamill's smile and the shadow of her haircut.

The next year Fratianne, who was sixteen at the time, began her ascension to the throne. She won the prestigious Skate Canada, the U.S. Ladies Championship, and the 1977 World Championship. The issue was settled; Linda Fratianne was the next queen of women's figure skating.

In 1978 Linda unexpectedly lost her world title to Anett Poetzsch of East Germany. But in 1979 Fratianne rebounded from defeat to take back the crown. Although theoretically the World Championship indicates the same thing as the Olympics, it is the Olympic gold which insures fame, wealth, and a measure of immortality. As Fratianne's longtime coach, Frank Carroll, said after the 1979 World Championships, "It's important that Linda remember she has a job to do. She can't get caught up in all the attention because there's one year left—1980, that's the goal."

Linda began her skating career at the age of nine and competed in her first tournament a year later. Since then she has practiced five hours a day for eleven months a year as part of her quest for the gold. She has also had her hair fashioned by Vidal Sassoon, commissioned sexy, splashy costumes, and undergone cosmetic surgery. Linda Fratianne has seemingly covered every conceivable contingency. Now, if she can just skate the compulsories and the four-minute freestyle with the skill everyone knows she has, the Olympic gold should be hers.

Other potential medal winners in women's figure skating include two Californians, Lisa-Marie Allen of Garden Grove and Carrie Reigh of El Segundo.

Until a few years ago, Allen, nineteen, was considering devoting her time to equestrian competitions instead of ice skating. The former Miss Teenage California finalist finished sixth in the 1979 World Championships. Reigh placed eleventh.

In the men's figure skating, Charlie Tickner of Littleton, Colorado, is a cofavorite for the gold medal with Vladimir Kovalev of the USSR. Tickner, the 1978 world champion, lost to Kovalev in the 1979 World Championship in March. Tickner, twenty-six, began skating competitively in 1965, finishing fourth in the Pacific Coast Championships that year. Since then he's worked long and hard, but has often been inconsistent in the big meets. He has the ability to take the 1980 gold; it is simply a matter of skating to his potential. Scott Cramer of Colorado Springs, who was fifth in the 1979 championships, and David Santee of Parkridge, Illinois, are other likely U.S. competitors.

No American twosome has ever won the Olympic pairs figure skating. But history may be made in Lake Placid in February. Tai Babilonia, twenty-one, and Randy Gardner, nineteen, are the current World Pairs Champions, having won the title in Vienna in March 1979.

Gardner and Babilonia have held the National Championship since 1976. The 5'7" Gardner and 5'5" Babilonia grew up in different sections of Los Angeles, but came together eight years ago. In their first competition as a pair, they garnered a sixth-place finish. In training for the games, they figure they have logged about twelve thousand hours of practice on the ice together. Tai and Randy will enter the Olympics with a great deal of pressure on them. Their toughest competition will come from the sport's longest reigning titlists, husband and wife team Irina Rodnina and Alexsander Zaitsev, the 1976 gold medalists.

In the relatively new Olympic sport of ice dancing, the team of Stacey Smith and John Summers are potential medal winners. The National Ice Dancing champions have been together for four years. Stacey, twenty-four, and John, twenty-one, have practiced for the games by skating at a local Wilmington, Delaware, rink every night from 11:00 P.M. to 4:00 A.M. John works in the Wilmington Holiday Inn as a desk clerk. Stacey worked as a cook in a French restaurant until she began devoting all her time to prepping for the Olympics. Summers and Smith will get plenty of domestic competition from Carol Fox and Richard Dalley.

The U.S. speed skating squad has an excellent chance to win a sleighfull of gold medals at the 1980 games. There are three reasons for this—Heiden, Heiden, and Mueller. The two Heidens, Eric and Beth, come from the same family. Leah Poulos-Mueller is the world's fastest woman over 500 meters of ice.

Eric Heiden is a 6'2" premed student at the University of Wisconsin, which is conveniently located in the Heidens' hometown of Madison. Heiden at twenty-one has risen to the pinnacle of a sport that captures very few headlines in this country, but is highly popular in Europe. As befits an athlete of his international stature, he is treated in Europe and Scandinavia like a rock superstar, to the point of being hounded by fans and the press. There has even been a song written about him.

In the last three years Eric, under the guidance of his coach, former Olympic speed skater Dianne Holum, has won eight straight World Championships. The son of a Madison orthopedic surgeon, Eric has skated since he was two. As a youngster he naturally concentrated on ice hockey, but eventually quit to take up speed skating at fourteen. He raced in the 1500 and 5,000 meters in Innsbruck in 1976 and took seventh and nineteenth respectively. But now, older and more mature, and with better training, he has become the premier speed skater in the world—and certainly the finest in the history of the U.S.

Eric is strong in every event, beginning with the sprints and moving through the 10,000, and it is almost a certainty that he will enter every one of them. It does not seem probable that the thick-legged skater will win all five, but there is no doubt he has the ability to sweep.

Beth Heiden is younger than Eric by two years, and compared to the other women speed skaters in the world, she is very small at 5'1" and 100 pounds. Yet Beth Heiden has overcome her size disadvantage and now must be ranked as the finest all-around woman speed skater in the world.

Unlikely as it is that one family would produce two such outstanding athletes, it is just as improbable that they would come from the U.S. In the entire country there are only two speed-skating ovals (the Netherlands has eleven). Nevertheless, in terms of quality and international success, speed skating is the number-one winter sport in this country.

Leah Poulos-Mueller of Dousman, Wisconsin, is the best woman ice sprinter in the world. The 500 meters is her specialty. Mueller is married to another outstanding U.S. speed skater, Peter, who won the gold medal in the men's 1,000 in Innsbruck in 1976. Peter Mueller, along with Dan Immerfall of Madison and Mike Woods, should round out the U.S. men's team.

What kind of ice hockey team could beat a squad composed of NHL All-Stars Guy LaFleur, Larry Robinson, Dennis Potvin, Brian Trottier, Daryl Sittler, and Gerry Cheevers? The USSR's national hockey team, that's what kind. The same team the U.S. Olympic squad will have to get past in Lake

Placid to win the gold medal. The U.S. team is made up of the finest college players in the country—twenty- and twenty-one-year-old kids, rowdy and rough and used to playing against other twenty-year-old kids. A gold medal doesn't seem likely. The U.S. is capable of grabbing the silver, but that won't be easy either. The Swedes, Czechs, Canadians, and West Germans are also quite capable.

"The Russians are awesome," says U.S. coach Herb Brooks, who recently led his University of Minnesota team to its third NCAA championship in seven years. Brooks played on the 1964 and 1968 U.S. Olympic teams. He should have a strong squad, especially if the pros can be delayed from swooping down and picking over the tasty crop.

Expected to start in the goal for the U.S. is Jim Craig, a Boston University All-American. In 1978, with Craig in the nets, BU went 16–0. Craig also has a reputation as an intelligent floor leader. Challenging him for the right to fend off 140-mph slapshots will be Steve Janaszak of the University of Minnesota.

At the forward positions look for two-time All-American Mark Johnson, a brilliant center from Madison, Wisconsin, who played high school hockey with speed skater Eric Heiden, and Steve Christoff and Eric Strobel, who played last year for Brooks at the University of Minnesota. At center for the University of Wisconsin, Johnson scored a hefty forty-one goals and forty-nine assists in forty games. Christoff netted thirty-eight goals and Strobel slapped thirty past enemy goalies.

Expected to round out the rest of the U.S. squad are Joe Muller, an outstanding forward at Boston College; Ralph Cox of New Hampshire; Mark Palevich of Minnesota–Duluth; Dave Delich of Colorado College; and Dave Christian of North Dakota.

On defense, expect to see Jim Craig's teammate at BU Jack O'Callahan, a two-time All-American, and Bill Baker and Mike Ramsy of Brooks's NCAA champs. Baker plays well at both ends, as is demonstrated by his piling up thirty goals and eighty-eight assists despite sitting out part of the season with an injury. Two other excellent defensemen are

Jim Korn, the 6'4", 215-pound captain of Providence, and Ken Morrow of Bowling Green.

The last U.S. medal won in the bobsled was gold and the year was 1936. It does not appear likely that anything close to the results at Garmisch will be repeated at Lake Placid in 1980. The Germans, both East and West, are extremely strong and so are the Swiss. In the 1979 World Bobsledding Championships, the two-man U.S. team of Brent Rushlaw and Jeff Gadly took tenth place. The USA II, driven by Bob Hickey with Les Farrell, finished seventeenth.

In the four-man, the number-one U.S. team, driven by Wade Whitney with Jim Tyler, Farrell, and Gadly aboard, crashed in the final heat. Farrell and Tyler suffered abrasions. The USA II, driven by Paul Vincent and supported by Joe Tyler, Fred Whittican, and Jeff Jost, wound up eleventh.

The same men and teams appear slated for the Lake Placid games.

In the luge singles John Fees of Plattsburgh, New York, is the strongest U.S. competitor. Fees took a fourth in the 1979 AAUs and twenty-third in the pre-games at Lake Placid. Others include Frank Maisley of Newark, Delaware, and Jim Moriarty of St. Paul, Minnesota. Possible Olympic teams in the luge doubles are Moriarty and John Skeldon, who took thirteenth in the pre-games, and Terry Morgan and Jim Mossey, who finished fourteenth.

In the women's singles, Donna Burke, twenty-four, a waitress from Lake Placid, was the top U.S. finisher in the pregames. She took nineteenth, a long way behind the East Germans, who went 1–2–3 in the event. Burke was a surprise winner in the AAU championships the previous month. Debbie Genovese came in twenty-first in the Nordic pre-games and Patti Herfurth placed twenty-third.

Events and Forecasts
Skiing

For the most part skiing today is associated with long

weekends, pretty girls, and chic mountaintop resorts. The skis of the modern sportsman are made of space-age materials, as are the colorful outfits. But the very first skis, which archaeologists tell us were animal bones strapped to the feet with leather, were implements of survival, rather than sport, in the frozen mountainous regions of Scandinavia.

Skiing is first mentioned in records dating from the fifth century, although skis were unquestionably used for transportation by Scandinavians, Finns, and Lapps thousands of years earlier. There are skis in the Djugarden Museum in Stockholm that are estimated to be three to four thousand years old. The word "ski" is probably derived from the Icelandic *scidh,* meaning piece of wood.

Skis have played an important part in the history of winter warfare. During the Battle of Oslo in 1200 A.D., King Sverre of Sweden equipped his troops with skis and sent them out to spy on their Norwegian enemies. In 1939 the crack Finnish ski troops held off superior Russian forces because of their ability to remain mobile in the crippling deep snow.

The first modern competition for skiing as a sport was in 1860, when the king of Norway awarded a trophy to the winner of a ski jumping contest outside of Oslo. The tournament was a great success, and the king commissioned a group of enthusiasts to create an annual program which would include cross-country races as well.

The first American ski club was founded in New Hampshire in 1872. A decade later local ski jumping contests began cropping up all over the Northeast. The first Americans to gain a measure of fame as ski jumpers were two brothers from Red Wing, Minnesota—Mikkel and Torgus Hemmestvedt. In an 1887 tournament in Red Wing, Mikkel captured first place. The first national tournament took place in 1904 under the auspices of the newly formed National Ski Association.

Alpine skiing developed much later than cross-country and ski jumping. In fact, it was not until 1936 in Garmisch-Partenkirchen, Germany, that the first Olympic competition—a combination downhill-slalom event—was held. In St. Moritz in 1948, the program divided the two events, and Gretchen

Fraser, a young skier from Vancouver, Washington, won the Olympic women's slalom and finished second in the women's downhill. In 1952 in Oslo, the giant slalom was added to the schedule. The three alpine events—downhill, slalom, and grand slalom—are enormously popular with spectators, particularly so when the games are held in one of the countries—Austria, for example—which have traditionally dominated the competition.

Over the years, U.S. women have managed four golds in the Alpine events; the men, however, have been totally locked out by the representatives of the Alpine countries.

Both ski jumping and cross-country events were on the first winter program in Chamonix. The Norwegians captured all the gold that year in the two categories. Up until Innsbruck, the finest performance by an American in a cross-country race was an eleventh place by Dick Parsons in 1932 in Lake Placid. But in the grueling 30 km (18.6 mile) race in 1976, Bill Koch pulled off the biggest upset of the games when he glided exhaustedly across the finish in second place, one-half minute behind Saveljev of the USSR. Bill had spent one hour and thirty minutes in the frozen, solitary woods. When he emerged, he had a pained smile on his face and a silver medal for his effort.

Rules

There are three events in Olympic alpine skiing: the downhill, the giant slalom, and the slalom. The object is the same in all three—get from the top to the bottom as quickly as possible.

The downhill course has a vertical drop of approximately 3,000 feet and a length of 1½ to 3 miles. The race is run against the clock, and each skier may take the route of his choice within the general boundaries of the course (there are "control points" he must pass through). Both men and women compete in downhill events, and the winners are decided from the time of the single run.

The slalom requires racers to negotiate a zigzagging course approximately 500 meters in length and with a vertical drop of at least 400 to 650 feet. The skiers must pass through a series of "gates" (two flag-topped poles stuck in the snow a few meters apart) in a specific order. There are sixty-five to seventy-five gates on a course, and failure to ski between any one set of designated poles means automatic disqualification. The women's course is approximately 350 meters long with forty-five to fifty gates. Each skier makes two slalom runs. The lowest combined time takes the gold.

The giant slalom is something of a combination of the downhill and slalom. The course approximates that of the downhill in length. The thirty or so slalom gates are spaced farther apart than in the slalom, and the gates themselves are wider (5–8 meters). The men make two runs, the women one.

Nordic or cross-country skiing is conducted over natural terrain. One-third of the course is uphill, one-third is downhill, and one-third is flat. There are five events for men in Nordic cross-country skiing; 15 km, 30 km, 50 km, 40-km relay, and the 70-meter Nordic combined jump.

In the 40-km relay, four men race 10 km each. In the 70-meter combined, the men jump from the 70-meter ski jump one day and race 15 km cross-country the next. The skiers' points for their times in the 15 km are added to their point totals for the 70-meter jump.

The women participate in a 5-km cross-country race and a 20-km relay (four women race 5 km apiece).

There are two ski jumping events for men: the 70-meter jump and the 90-meter jump. The jumpers are scored by a panel of judges who take into consideration execution (runway form, takeoff, in-flight posture, the landing) and, of course, distance.

Viewing Tips

The downhill is the most sensational alpine event. With no gates to negotiate, the skier basically has two things in mind—to stay on the skis and to get to the bottom. Although any route (as long as the skier passes through the control points) is acceptable, you will notice that most of the skiers follow the same general path. For that reason, the skiers who race last often have a more difficult time since the course will develop ruts. The downhill is a hellbent-for-leather event and the skiers often reach speeds of 70 mph. The racers try to avoid becoming airborne, as time in the air is costly. Whenever possible the racers assume a crouching position to lower their wind resistance.

The slalom events put a premium on style, as well as on speed. The slalom skis are shorter and therefore more maneuverable than the downhill skis. The slalom skiers try to take the shortest route through the gates, which means cutting the turns as close to the poles as possible. You will notice that they often hit the poles, but as long as they travel through the gate, all is legal. Though it may not seem like it to the untrained viewer, the slalom is more controlled and less daredevil than the downhill.

Nordic skis are much different from alpine skis. They are thinner and lighter and the boots are bound to them primarily at the toes. The Nordic skier's heel must be able to come off the ski so that he may gain momentum. Cross-country skiing utilizes a walking and gliding motion, and the skiers use their poles to propel themselves. If the alpine racers could be compared to the sprinters in track and field, the Nordic skiers are the equivalent of the marathoners. The Nordic events are tortuous contests that require incredible stamina.

An interesting aspect of Nordic skiing is the special "waxing" that is required. Wax is applied to the bottom of the skis to provide traction on the snow, especially for the uphill portions of the course. Waxing is a critical element of cross-country skiing. The skiers mix the different types of wax with the care of an alchemist, and they guard their personal techniques like top-secret information.

Ski jumpers have to rate as some of the most courageous athletes in the world. It takes almost inconceivable nerve to launch oneself off of a man-made ramp thirty stories high. The jumpers routinely soar distances of 200 to 300 feet. Jumping skis are heavier than alpine or Nordic skis and have deep grooves cut in the bottoms for stability on the landing. After takeoff, in order to become aerodynamically stable, the skier leans as far forward as possible, until his body is almost parallel to the skis; the arms are pasted to the sides and the hands rest at the hips. During the flight the hands are used like the rudders of a plane.

Forecast: Lake Placid

Men's Alpine Events
1976 Slalom Champion: Piero Gros, Italy
1980 Favorites: Ingemar Stenmark, Sweden; Bojan Krizai, Yugoslavia; Peter Popangelov, Bulgaria; Peter Luescher, Switzerland; Phil Mahre, USA

1976 Giant Slalom Champion: Heini Hemmi, Switzerland
1980 Favorites: Stenmark, Sweden; Luescher, Switzerland; Krizai, Yugoslavia; Andreas Wenzel, Liechtenstein; Mahre, USA

1976 Downhill Champion: Franz Klammer, Austria
1980 Favorites: Peter Mueller, Switzerland; Peter Wirnsberger, Austria; Ken Read, Canada

Women's Alpine Events
1976 Slalom Champion: Rosie Mittermaier, West Germany
1980 Favorites: Regina Sackl, Austria; Hanni Wenzel, Liechtenstein; Claudia Giordani, Italy

1976 Giant Slalom Champion: Kathy Kreiner, Canada
1980 Favorites: Christa Kinshoffer, Irene Epple, West Germany; Wenzel,Liechtenstein; Giordani, Italy; Cindy Nelson, USA

Men's Nordic Events
1976 15 km Cross-country Champion: Nikolai Bashukov, USSR
1980 Favorites: Oddvar Braa, Norway; Lars Erik Ericksen, Norway; Thomas Wassburg, Sweden

1976 30 km Cross-country Champion: Sergei Saveljev, USSR
1980 Favorites: Braa, Norway; Evgeini Beljajev, USSR

1976 50 km Cross-country Champion: Ivar Formo, Norway
1980 Favorites: Braa, Norway; Beljajev, USSR; Ove Aunli,
Norway

1976 40-km Relay Champion: Finland
1980 Favorites: Sweden; Norway; USSR

1976 70-meter Combined Jump Champion: Ulrich Wehling,
East Germany
1980 Favorites: Wehling, East Germany; Kazimierz Dlugo-
polski, Poland

1976 70-meter Ski Jump Champion: Hans Aschenbach, East
Germany
1980 Favorites: Joachen Danneberg, East Germany; Peter
Leitner, West Germany

1976 90-meter Ski Jump Champion: Karl Schnabl, Austria
1980 Favorites: Pentti Kokkonen, Finland; Danneberg, Harald Duschek, East Germany

Women's Nordic Events
1976 5 km Cross-country Champion: Helena Takalo, Finland
1980 Favorites: Raisa Smetanina, USSR; Marit Myrmal,
Norway

1976 10 km Cross-country Champion: Raisa Smetanina,
USSR
1980 Favorites: Smetanina, Galina Kulakova, USSR; Myrmal, Norway

1976 20-km Relay Champion: USSR
1980 Favorites: USSR; Norway

Biathlon

The biathlon combines cross-country skiing and riflery. Like the other winter sports, it also has its origins in Scandinavia, where a man's survival depended upon his ability to ski and shoot well. The event, which is basically military in nature, is a national participatory sport in Sweden, Norway, Finland, and the USSR. There are perhaps 200 biathlon athletes in the United States. Finland alone claims 10,000, and the Soviet Union has 50,000 biathlon competitors.

The first U.S. biathlon competition was held at Camp Hale, Colorado, in 1957. The biathlon became part of the winter games in 1960 at Squaw Valley.

Rules

There are three biathlon events, the 10 km, the 20 km, and the 30-km relay. The competitors ski the cross-country circuits, stopping four times during the race to fire five shots from a small-bore .22-caliber rifle at a target 50 meters away. Poor shots translate into penalty minutes which are added to the racer's clock time for the race. The fastest time wins.

Forecast: Lake Placid

1976 20 km Biathlon Champion: Klaus Siebert, East Germany
1980 Favorites: Anatoli Aljabjev, USSR; Siebert, East Germany; Heikki Ikola, Finland; Alexsander Tichinov, USSR

1976 10 km Biathlon Champion: Frank Ulrich, East Germany
1980 Favorites: Odd Lirhus, Norway; Terje Krokstad, Norway; Vladimir Alikin, USSR

1976 30 km Biathlon Relay Champion: East Germany
1980 Favorites: East Germany; USSR; Norway

Skating

Just as skiing was at first a utilitarian endeavor, so, also, was ice skating. Eventually though, as skating became more widespread in Europe, it began to be practiced as a sport rather than as a mode of transportation. Scandinavian literature mentions a form of skating in the second century, but archaeologists believe it actually originated much earlier, in Denmark around 1000 B.C.

Until the fourteenth century, skate blades were made of animal bone. Around 1320 the bone blade was replaced by one made of heavily waxed wood. In 1572 the first iron skate blades were developed. Though the Scots are generally believed to have been the first to ice skate for sport, the word "skate" comes from the Dutch *schaats,* meaning stilts.

In 1642 Edinburgh boasted a skating club, and soon after that other clubs were organized in northern Europe and America.

In about 1770 the American artist, Benjamin West, made an ice skating championship the subject of one of his paintings. There is some dispute as to whether or not West himself won the championship he depicted. In 1850 B. W. Bushnell of Philadelphia developed the first pair of steel skates. With Bushnell's invention the sport experienced a new period of popularity. The lighter, sharper blades gave skaters a new freedom; they could move faster and turn more sharply. The way had been paved for figure skating.

At the outbreak of the American Civil war Jackson Haines was an impoverished ballet instructor. When the majority of his students quit their studies to don blue Union uniforms, he was forced to close the school. Aware of the popularity of ballet in Europe, he set sail in 1863 for Austria. During the winter of 1864, Haines found Vienna enthralled with ice skating. He also noticed that the skaters moved along aimlessly without regard to style or form. The American ballet instructor had an idea: he would combine ice skating with ballet and music. Shortly thereafter Haines began teaching ballet to skaters, incorporating delicate and acrobatic moves into their repertoires. The new ice skating movements of Jackson Haines became the talk of all Europe.

A Canadian student of Haines's, Louis Rubenstein, was the first to introduce the European figure skating techniques to North America. In 1878 he organized the Ice Skating

Association of Canada. In 1887 a national skating club was formed in the U.S.

Irving Brokaw organized the first American figure skating tournament in 1914. Theresa Weld won the women's competition and Norman Scott of Montreal won the men's crown. But it was Sonja Henie, with her daring routines and three Olympic gold medals, who launched figure skating into international prominence.

While figure skating had experienced its most exciting growth period after Jackson Haines's innovations, speed skating had always been a popular sport for both men and women. The U.S. held championships in 1891 and 1892 on outdoor rinks. By the 1920s several indoor rinks had been built and the popularity of the sport began to spread beyond the extreme northern states.

Figure skating competitions were a part of the Olympic program in 1908 in London and in 1920 in Antwerp—even before the separate winter games were initiated. Both figure skating and speed skating have been on the winter agenda since Chamonix in 1924.

Beginning with Dick Button, who, as an eighteen-year-old Harvard freshman, captured the first gold ever in figure skating for the U.S. at St. Moritz in 1948, Americans have fared well in figure skating. The success of such skaters as Button, Tenley Albright, Hayes and David Jenkins, Carol Heiss, Peggy Fleming, and Dorothy Hamill has helped to keep the sport extremely popular in this country.

In speed skating, the U.S. has recently begun to assert itself against such dominating powers as Russia and Norway.

Rules

In the figure skating competition, there are three events for men and women in the 1980 games: singles, pairs, and ice dancing.

In all three events the skaters execute a series of compulsory maneuvers, after which they perform a free skating routine. Once the compulsory section counted 60 percent of the scoring and the free skating, 40 percent. Now the compulsory is worth 30 percent and the free skating, 70 percent.

The compulsory section involves skating six of nine "school" figures. A list of sixty-nine acceptable school figures has been adopted for Olympic and world class competitions.

The free skating routines (five minutes for men and four minutes for the women) give the contestants the opportunity to perform to music and to execute the exciting and original moves they have perfected in their training.

The skaters' performances are scored subjectively by a panel of judges very similar to those used in diving and gymnastics. The judges look for the degree of difficulty of the moves, the manner of performance, changes in tempo, elements of surprise, elegance, and use of the arena.

The pair skaters also must complete compulsory and free skating programs. In the compulsory section the skaters execute a series of specific sequences. In the free skating the partners must give an overall impression of unison.

In the speed skating the winners are determined by time trials. The skaters race against the clock around a two-lane, 400-meter oval. The skaters switch lanes one time on each lap to make sure they travel the same distance—the outside man moves in and the inside man moves out. If the two skaters reach the crossover point at the exact same time, the skater on the outside has the right of way.

At Lake Placid there will be 500, 1,000, 1,500, 5,000 and 10,000 meter races for men.

The women will compete in the 500, 1000, 1,500, and 3,000 meters.

Viewing Tips

In the free skating section of the figure skating competition, watch the way the skater begins each different jump and spin. The success of a jump depends on timing and on the spring power at takeoff. Most jumps are executed in a counterclockwise rotation. Double and triple jumps have now become almost mandatory if a skater hopes to place.

The accent in pairs skating is on the lifts. Also note the "shadow skating" part of the program, in which the skaters perform the same movements while remaining separated.

In ice dancing, lifts are not permitted, nor are any other movements which rely on strength (to show off physical prowess). The British have consistently scored well in the ice dancing championships, as have the Soviets.

Speed skaters are the fastest self-propelled athletes in the world over flat ground. Speed skaters have been clocked at 30 mph for 500 meters. They can travel a mile in approximately three minutes, as compared to almost four minutes for the fastest runners.

Forecast: Lake Placid

Women's Figure Skating
1976 Champion: Dorothy Hamill, USA
1980 Favorites: Linda Fratianne, USA; Anett Poetzsch, East Germany; Emi Watanabe, Japan

Men's Figure Skating
1976 Champion: John Curry, Great Britain
1980 Favorites: Charlie Tickner, USA; Vladimir Kovalev, USSR; Robin Cousins, Great Britain; Jan Hoffman, East Germany

Pairs Skating
1976 Champions: Irina Rodnina and Alexsander Zaitsev, USSR
1980 Favorites: Randy Gardner and Tai Babilonia, USA; Romy Kerner and Rolf Osterreich, East Germany

Ice Dancing
1976 Champions: Ludmilla Pakhomova and Alexsander Gorshkov, USSR
1980 Favorites: Pakhomova and Gorshkov, Irina Moiseeva and Andrey Minakov, USSR

Men's Speed Skating
1976 500 meters Champion: Evgeny Kulikov, USSR

1980 Favorites: Eric Heiden, USA; Frodde Ronning, Jan Storholt, Norway; Gaten Boucher, Canada

1976 1,000 meters Champion: Peter Mueller, USA
1980 Favorites: Heiden, Mueller, USA; Kay Stenshjemmet, Norway

1976 1,500 meters Champion: Jan Storholt, Norway
1980 Favorites: Heiden, USA; Stenshjemmet, Storholt, Norway; Yong Ha Lee, South Korea

1976 5,000 meters Champion: Stan Stenson, Norway
1980 Favorites: Heiden, Mike Woods, USA; Victor Leskin, USSR; Amund Sjobrend, Stenshjemmet, Norway

1976 10,000 meters Champion: Piet Kleine, Netherlands
1980 Favorites: Heiden, USA; Stenson, Norway; Leskin, Sergei Matchuk, USSR

Women's Speed Skating
1976 500 meters Champion: Sheila Young, USA
1980 Favorites: Beth Heiden, Leah Poulos-Mueller, USA; Silvia Albrecht, East Germany

1976 1,000 meters Champion: Tatiana Averina, USSR
1980 Favorites: Heiden, USA; Sylvia Burke, Canada; Averina, USSR

1976 1,500 meters Champion: Galina Stepanskaya, USSR
1980 Favorites: Heiden, USA; Burke, Canada; Natalie Petruseva, USSR

1976 3,000 meters Champion: Tatiana Averina, USSR
1980 Favorites: Heiden, USA; Bjorg Eva Jensen, Norway; Ria Visser, Netherlands

Sledding

Sleds of one design or another were used as transportation

vehicles as far back as 3000 B.C. The first sleds were made of two bone runners with an animal skin stretched between them. The American Indians used sleds made of long poles, which they dragged behind their horses to carry heavy loads. Late in the nineteenth century, a few brave souls began riding wooden sleds down snow-covered hills for fun. The "toboggans" (an Indian term) they used were very light and difficult to control. Soon heavier sleds, called bobsleighs, were developed, and from the bobsleigh evolved the sophisticated bobsleds used today.

The first international toboggan race was held in 1883 in Switzerland. Peter Minch of Klosters captured first prize. In 1898 the first bobsleigh competition was held in St. Moritz. In 1904 an American, Stephen Whitney, developed the first modern bobsled. That same year an artificial bobsled run was built in St. Moritz because the Crest Run in the Alps was considered too dangerous.

In 1908 the first international championship was staged in Austria, and in 1928 bobsledding was included on the Olympic program.

Luge riding as a sport began in the Alps during World War I. The word *luge* is French for sled, and that is all a luge is — a slightly modified version of the sled that every kid has ridden at one time or another. However, the luge competition as operated in the Olympic games is a very dangerous sport. It has crippled and even killed its share of athletes. The first European luge championships were held in 1951. In 1964 the luge was added to the Innsbruck Olympic program. Lake Placid now has the only luge run in North America. It was built in 1978.

Rules

There are two bobsled events in 1980: the two-man and the four-man. Women do not compete in the bobsled.

The men will compete in two luge events, singles and doubles; the women will compete in the luge singles.

Both bobsleds and luges are equipped with double runners. Bobsleds are large precision machines of steel and aluminum, with sophisticated steering and braking mechanisms.

The Europeans prefer rope steering, while Americans have generally opted for wheels. The bobsled is operated from a sitting position. The athletes sit tucked in behind a streamlined cowling that reduces wind resistance.

The bobsled run is conducted over an artificial chute one mile in length. It is constructed of concrete covered with ice and snow. Two-man sled crews cannot weigh more than 460 pounds. Four-man crews may not surpass 880 pounds. Championship events consist of four runs.

The luge is also conducted over a man-made course, but for safety reasons many of the recent chutes have been covered with artificial ice. The luge run is shorter and steeper than the bobsled course. The luge is operated from a position flat on the back. Steering is done by shifting weight, dragging the feet (the boots have spikes on the bottom), and a rope.

Viewing Tips

The bobsled events are easy enough to understand. The object is the same as that of downhill skiing—get to the bottom as fast as possible. Since so much in bobsledding depends on finding the right route, an intimate knowledge of the run is essential. The team must also be completely synchronized in its movements, as an ill-timed weight shift can send a sled out of control. And an out-of-control bobsled is a suicide machine. The men start the race by running alongside the sled pushing it to speed, then jumping in at the optimum moment. The Olympic bobsleds have been clocked at 90 mph as they snake their way through the course.

Standard equipment includes goggles, helmets, and knee and elbow pads.

The luge could be considered something of a lunatic sport. Men and women lying flat on their backs, barely able to see, roar down a slick ice chute at 60 mph. The luge racers turn with three basic movements; pulling up the runner on the side they wish to turn to; placing weight on the outward runner to cause it to go faster; and digging in the runner on the opposite side. There are usually a dozen turns on a luge course.

Forecast: Lake Placid

Bobsledding
1976 Two-Man Champions: Nehmer and Germeshrausen, East Germany
1980 Favorites: Switzerland; East Germany

1976 Four-Man Champions: East Germany
1980 Favorites: East Germany; West Germany; Switzerland; USA

Men's Luge
1976 Singles Champion: Detlef Gunther, East Germany
1980 Favorites: Gunther, Bernhard Glass, East Germany; Vladimir Shitov, USSR

1976 Doubles Champions: Rinn and Hahn, East Germany
1980 Favorites: East Germany; USSR; West Germany

Women's Luge
1976 Singles Champion: Margit Schumann, East Germany
1980 Favorites: Melitta Sollmann, Iona Brandt, Stenzel Roswitha, East Germany

Ice Hockey

Ice hockey was first played in Canada around 1850, by children using frozen horse dung for a puck and sticks fashioned from tree branches. As the game became more popular, it eventually moved indoors to artificial ice rinks. In 1875 a Montreal newspaper referred to a game played in the Victoria Skating Rink as ice hockey.

During the 1880s various leagues were organized, and in 1893 the governor-general of Canada, Lord Stanley, purchased a trophy for fifty dollars to be awarded to the finest hockey team in the country. That trophy, which bears the governor's name, is now awarded annually to the best professional hockey team in the NHL.

Ice hockey was included in the program of the 1920 Summer games in Antwerp. As expected, the Canadians triumphed. From 1920 until 1936 the Canadian teams captured every gold medal. But in Garmisch in 1936, Great Britain wrested the crown from the surprised Canadians with the help of Jimmy Foster in the nets. Foster was a British-Canadian who had been suspended from playing in Canada but was allowed to play for England.

Canada reclaimed the gold medal when the games resumed in 1948, and again in 1952. In 1956 the USSR athletes made their first appearance in the games and in their initial try captured the ice hockey gold medal. Since then, with the exception of 1960 in Squaw Valley, the USSR hockey team has won every Olympic hockey tournament, including the 1976 version in Innsbruck.

In 1960 a young, raw U.S. squad composed of collegians, a fireman, two carpenters, and two insurance agents pulled off the biggest upset of the games when they defeated Czechoslovakia in the finals. The U.S. goalie, Jack McCartan, made thirty-nine saves in the semifinal game against the USSR.

Rules

Twelve teams will qualify for the 1980 Olympic games based upon their performances in the previous year. The twelve-team field is composed of all eight teams in Group A of the World Championships and the top four teams from Group B. In Lake Placid thirty-five games will be played over the thirteen-day period. Teams will be divided into two groups (Red and Blue) for round-robin play. After each group has completed its round-robin schedule, the top two teams will play for the gold and silver. The semifinalists will play for the bronze.

The standard hockey rink is 85 by 200 feet. Olympic hockey is played in three 20-minute periods with two 10-minute intermissions. There are six men per side—a goalie, three forwards (two wings and a center), and two defensemen.

The two most common playing violations are icing and offsides. Icing occurs when a defensive player shoots the puck from his team's half of the ice across the opponent's goal line. Icing is not called if the offending team has fewer men on the ice due to a penalty. Offsides occurs when an attacking player crosses the blue line into the opposing team's defensive zone ahead of the puck.

A power play occurs when a team sends all its players except the goalie into the opposing team's defensive zone in an effort to score while one or two men from the opposing team are in the penalty box.

Minor infractions—such as holding, tripping, hooking, and charging—send a man to the penalty box for two minutes. Major offenses, such as fighting, bring five minutes.

Forecast: Lake Placid

1976 Champion: USSR
1980 Favorites: USSR; Sweden; Czechoslovakia; Canada; West Germany; USA

The Winter Games—A Retrospective

1924—Chamonix

Since the beginning of the modern Olympic games in 1896, the competition had been largely dominated by the Western European countries and the United States. Those countries, with their large populations, had a much wider range of choice in selecting Olympic competitors than did the smaller countries. They also had strong track and field traditions.

Yet there were other sports, excelled in by the Alpine and Nordic nations, that could not be included in the regular Olympic schedule. It was, after all, somewhat difficult to hold a bobsledding race in the middle of a sweltering Paris summer.

So in 1924 a new Olympic tradition began. A second set of Olympic games was held that winter in Chamonix, France. Nearly 300 athletes from sixteen countries entered the competition, which included events in skiing, bobsledding, speed skating, figure skating, and hockey.

The winter games in Chamonix, as was the intention of the International Olympic Committee, were dominated by the cold-weather countries. The athletes of Norway, Finland, Sweden, and Switzerland scored many victories. The Canadians, of course, won the ice hockey championship in a final battle with the U.S. team.

1928—St. Moritz

The second winter games, held in St. Moritz, Switzerland, produced a hero, or heroine, rather, who put to shame even the summer stars. Her name was Sonja Henie.

The tiny daughter of an Oslo cyclist won ten consecutive world figure skating championships between 1927 and 1936 and three Olympic gold medals. She appeared in her first Olympics in 1924 at the age of eleven. She appeared in her fourth Olympics in 1936 at the age of twenty-three.

Sonja Henie virtually revolutionized figure skating. After doing miserably in the 1924 winter games, she returned to Norway and studied ballet. She was the first skater to combine sport and music in such a way that figure skating became the art form it is today. The petite blonde invented dozens of new turns and maneuvers, all of which she performed with incredible speed. She was the toast of the kings and queens of Europe.

When she turned professional in 1936, she toured the United States and did much to popularize figure skating in this country. Following in the footsteps of the great swimmer, Johnny Weissmuller, she became an American matinee idol. She wasn't much of an actress, but she sure could skate, and she was one of the top box office draws in the motion picture business of the 1930s.

1932—Lake Placid

The most surprising thing about the 1932 winter games in Lake Placid, New York, was that the U.S. athletes captured the most gold medals. Not known for their ability in the mountain sports, the Americans did surprisingly well.

American athletes won four gold medals in speed skating and two in bobsledding. Their success, however, was largely due to the low turnout from the Alpine and Scandinavian countries. The Americans enjoyed a great numerical advantage at Lake Placid, similar to the one in the 1904 summer games in St. Louis.

An indication of the rather light competition in the games was the participation of Edward Eagan in the four-man bobsledding race. Eagan had won an Olympic boxing championship in 1920, but until a few weeks before the competition at Lake Placid he had never even ridden on a bobsled. Nevertheless, he was a member of the four-man team that won a gold medal in the winter games. He is still the only Olympian to have won championships in both the summer and the winter Olympics.

1936—Garmisch-Partenkirchen

The German winter games were the largest yet. More than a thousand athletes from twenty-eight countries descended on the twin cities of Garmisch and Partenkirchen near Munich.

The facilities for the winter games were not quite as elaborate as those prepared for the summer games, which would be held later that year in Berlin. But lest the winter athletes feel slighted, the Germans did build a mountain for them. There were several good ski runs in the area, but the Germans wanted a hill that would end right in the middle of the winter stadium—and so they built one.

The huge crowds that drove up from Munich to attend the games seemed to be primarily interested in the figure skating events. Sonja Henie was appearing in her fourth and last Olympics. She was, by then, the princess of the skating world and one of the best-known athletes in history. Her performances at Garmisch were superb, and she easily won the heart of the German Führer—in retrospect, a dubious honor.

Figure skating fans were treated to a superb show by the German couple Ernst Baier and Maxie Herber, whose controlled, elegant ballet on ice perfectly combined music, dance, and athletics. Baier and Herber were nearly upset, however, by a more spontaneous brother and sister team from Austria,

Ilse and Erik Pausin, who were only fifteen and sixteen years old respectively.

In the most controversial event of the games, the British ice hockey team unseated the Canadians for the first time in Olympic history. The Canadians had protested because the British team consisted largely of English-born Canadians, including the best goalie in the world, Jimmy Foster, but their protest had been disallowed.

Norwegian athletes won gold medals in all of the speed skating events, as well as in ski jumping and women's figure skating.

1948—St. Moritz

A record number of cold-weather athletes attended the 1948 winter games at St. Moritz, Switzerland. The long layoff since the 1936 Olympics in Germany and the intervening years of war seemed to have whetted the world's appetite for peaceful competition.

The winter Olympics weren't without controversy. Two hockey teams showed up to represent the United States, and because no one could decide which was the legitimate U.S. entry, both were declared ineligible. But such disagreements were to be expected after the twelve-year hiatus.

A milestone of sorts was passed by the U.S. team at St. Moritz. It won its first figure skating championship. The American hero was Dick Button, an eighteen-year-old who trained himself ruthlessly for the Olympics. He would win a second Olympic figure skating championship in 1952 before accepting a professional offer to go on tour with the Ice Capades.

1952—Oslo

The Norwegians, perennial winter Olympic powers, were hosts for the first time in 1952.

The outstanding individual athlete at Oslo was Hjalmar Anderson of Norway, who won half of his country's six gold medals with victories in the 1500-, 5,000-, and 10,000-meter speed skating contests.

The U.S. star was Andrea Mead Lawrence, a nineteen-year-old from Vermont who had also competed in the 1948 games. She won gold medals in the giant slalom and the regular slalom.

The Russians would become an important factor in the summer Olympics later that year, but they did not enter the winter competition in Oslo.

1956—Cortina d'Ampezzo

The winter Olympic games in Cortina d'Ampezzo, Italy, produced the most talked about athlete of the year. He was a twenty-year-old skier from Kitzbühel, Austria, where skiing is a way of life.

Toni Sailer was a natural athlete. He seemed to move down the slopes by reflex—and his reflexes were very, very fast.

Snow conditions for the winter games in 1956 were extremely treacherous. In fact, the ski runs were virtually solid sheets of ice, a circumstance likely to provoke second thoughts in even the most hardened veterans.

But Toni Sailer wasn't a hardened veteran. He was just the best skier in the world. He earned that accolade by pulling off the first grand slam in Alpine skiing. He won all three Alpine events—the giant slalom, the special slalom, and the downhill race.

The Russian athletes competing in the winter games for the first time, racked up six gold medals, compared with four for the Austrians. The Russians excelled in speed skating and took the ice hockey championship away from the Canadians.

1960—Squaw Valley

The Russians continued their dominance of the winter Olympics in the 1960 games in Squaw Valley, California.

Speed skating was the Russians' forte at Squaw Valley. They won three gold medals in the women's speed skating events and three more in the men's events.

But the Americans could skate too. As they had in 1956, they won the men's and women's figure skating titles. The new champions were Carol Heiss and David Jenkins, whose older brother, Hayes Alan Jenkins, had won the men's figure skating four years earlier.

And the skating prowess of the U.S. team wasn't limited to the artistry and grace of figure skating. The U.S. hockey team astounded the world by winning its first Olympic gold medal.

1964—Innsbruck

Although the new Russian preeminence in Olympic competition would be shaken later that year, the Russians were still very successful in the 1964 winter games in Innsbruck, Austria. While the Russian athletes won a record eleven gold medals, the U.S. participants were limited to only one championship.

The heroine of Innsbruck was a twenty-four-year-old Russian schoolteacher, Lidija Skoblikova, who won four gold medals in speed skating events. She became the first athlete to win that many championships in a winter Olympics.

The single American victory was captured by Terry McDermott, who broke the Russian hold on the 500-meter speed skating event.

Another American star was Billy Kidd. The young skier, who placed second in the men's slalom event, did better than any American ever had in an event traditionally dominated by the Alpine and Scandinavian countries.

1968—Grenoble

Unlike most sites for the winter Olympics, Grenoble, France, is no Alpine village. It is a thriving city, and the French government spent more than $200 million getting it ready for the Olympics.

It was appropriate, then, that the hero of Grenoble should be a dashing twenty-four-year-old Frenchman—Jean-Claude Killy. The darling of all France, Killy was known as "le superman," and in the 1968 winter Olympics, he lived up to his nickname.

With his daring and sometimes reckless style, Killy narrowly defeated another Frenchman in the downhill race, the first of the prestigious Alpine skiing events. The second contest, the giant slalom, he won easily. But his last victory, in the special slalom, was controversial. The men's slalom took place in a dense fog that made it difficult for the skiers, the judges, and the spectators to see what was actually going on. Killy won the event and became the first skier since 1956 to win the Alpine grand slam, but his victory is still disputed in Austria. For it was Karl Schranz, the Austrian star, who actually completed the two slalom runs in a better time than Killy's. Unfortunately for the Austrians, however, Schranz was disqualified for allegedly missing a gate in the fog.

If Killy was the male heartthrob at Grenoble, nineteen-year-old Peggy Fleming of Colorado was the female star. An immensely graceful ballerina on ice, Fleming easily captured the women's figure skating championship.

1972—Sapporo

The great Austrian skier Karl Schranz was a somewhat unlucky Olympian. After having lost a controversial decision to Jean-Claude Killy in the 1968 winter games, he was banned from competition altogether in the 1972 games in Sapporo, Japan.

Schranz was the victim of a dispute between Avery Brundage, then president of the International Olympic Committee, and the Fedération Internationale de Ski, which governs the world's skiers. Brundage had been critical in 1968 of the manner in which amateur skiers were supported financially by the manufacturers of ski equipment. In Sapporo, Brundage threatened to disqualify several top skiers. When the international federation then threatened to boycott the games, Brundage singled out Schranz for suspension. The skiing organization acquiesced in the decision, and Schranz was eliminated.

The Austrian people were infuriated by the ousting of their hero, and as the games proceeded they were given even more reason to be angry. With Schranz out of the games, the Austrians pinned their hopes on their female star, Annemarie Proell, who had won several European championships. Those hopes were dashed by young Marie-Therese Nadig of Switzerland, who upset the Austrian skier in both the women's downhill and the giant slalom.

The hero of Sapporo was Ard Schenk of the Netherlands. Known as the "Flying Dutchman," the 194-pound mastiff captured gold medals in the 5,000-, 1500-, and 10,000-meter speed skating events. He was the first athlete to win a triple in men's speed skating since 1952.

1976—Innsbruck

After the tragedy of Munich, it was important to have an Olympic experience that was without controversy. The Austrians provided the peace and quiet in the low-key winter Olympic games of 1976 in Innsbruck.

Austria, a traditional power in alpine skiing, had suffered disappointments four years earlier with the disqualification of Karl Schranz and the defeat of the country's top woman skier, Annemarie Proell. The Austrians were hungry for an alpine victory.

Franz Klammer, a twenty-two-year-old world champion in the downhill race, gave them what they wanted in the very first event of the cold-weather contest. Screaming down the mountain at speeds approaching 70 mph, the young Austrian soared over the moguled hill, seemingly airborne for minutes, to win the gold medal in the downhill before 50,000 delirious home country fans.

The Austrians had gotten off to a good start, but they were unable to follow up. In fact, the Austrian alpine team didn't win another gold until the last day of the competition, when they were vindicated by first- and second-place finishes in the jumping competition.

Innsbruck produced two female American stars—Sheila Young and Dorothy Hamill. Young, a big, strong speed skater, became the first American to win three medals in speed skating. She set an Olympic record in the 500-meter event, placed third in the 1500-meter contest, and won a silver medal for her effort in the 3,000-meter race. Hamill, a graceful and inventive young skater who charmed the Olympic crowds, took the figure skating championship.

Metric Conversion Chart

ONE Meter .... 39.37 inches
100 Meters .... 109 yards, 1 foot, 1 inch
200 Meters ....121 yards, 10¾ inches
400 Meters ....437 yards, 1 foot, 4 inches
800 Meters ....874 yards, 2 feet, 8 inches
1,500 Meters .... 1640 yards, 1 foot, 3 inches
                  (119 yards, 2 feet, short of a mile)
1,600 Meters ....1749 yards, 2 feet, 6 inches
3,000 Meters ....one mile, 1520 yards, 2½ feet
5,000 Meters .... 3 miles, 178 yards, 2 inches
10,000 Meters .... 6 miles, 356 yards, 4 inches
Marathon ....26 miles, 385 yards

FEBRUARY — Winter Games / Lake Placid

Event	SUN 24	SAT 23	FRI 22	THUR 21	WED 20	TUE 19	MON 18	SUN 17	SAT 16	FRI 15	THUR 14	WED 13	TUE 12	MON	SUN	SAT
OPENING CEREMONY												●				
ALPINE SKIING		●	●	●	●	●					●					
BIATHLON			●			●			●	●						
BOBSLED	●	●							●	●						
CROSS-COUNTRY		●		●	●		●	●	●		●	●				
FIGURE SKATING		●		●	●	●		●	●	●						
ICE HOCKEY	●					●			●		●	●	●			
LUGE						●	●		●	●						
90-METER JUMP		●							●	●						
70-METER JUMP		●							●	●						
SPEED SKATING					●	●	●	●	●	●	●	●				

JULY – AUGUST — Summer Games / Moscow

Event	SUN 3	SAT 2	FRI 1	THUR 31	WED 30	TUE 29	MON 28	SUN 27	SAT 26	FRI 25	THUR 24	WED 23	TUE 22	MON 21	SUN 20	SAT 19
OPENING CEREMONY																●
ARCHERY		●	●	●	●											
BASKETBALL						●	●	●	●	●	●	●	●	●	●	
BOXING		●				●	●	●	●	●	●	●	●	●	●	
CANOEING			●	●	●	●										
CYCLING, ROAD								●								●
CYCLING, TRACK									●	●	●	●	●			
EQUESTRIAN	●				●	●	●		●	●	●	●				
FENCING					●	●	●	●	●	●	●	●	●			
FIELD HOCKEY			●		●	●	●	●	●	●	●	●	●	●	●	
FOOTBALL		●	●				●		●			●	●	●	●	
GYMNASTICS												●	●	●	●	
HANDBALL					●	●	●		●			●	●	●	●	
JUDO		●	●	●	●	●	●									
MODERN PENTATHLON											●	●	●	●	●	
ROWING									●	●	●	●	●	●	●	
SAILING						●	●	●			●	●	●	●	●	
SHOOTING									●	●	●	●	●	●	●	
SWIMMING, DIVING, WATER POLO							●	●	●	●	●	●	●	●	●	
TRACK and FIELD				●	●	●	●	●	●	●	●					
VOLLEYBALL			●	●	●	●	●	●	●	●	●	●	●	●	●	
WEIGHTLIFTING					●	●	●	●	●			●	●	●	●	
WRESTLING, FREESTYLE				●	●	●	●	●								
WRESTLING, GRECO-ROMAN											●	●	●	●	●	
CLOSING CEREMONY	●															

OLYMPIC GAMES SUMMARIES

SUMMER GAMES

MEN'S TRACK AND FIELD WINNERS

100-METER		Sec.
1896	Tom Burke, United States	12.0
1900	Frank Jarvis, United States	10.8
1904	Archie Hahn, United States	11.0
1908	Reg Walker, South Africa	10.8
1912	Ralph Craig, United States	10.8
1920	Charlie Paddock, United States	10.8
1924	H. M. Abrahams, Great Britain	10.6
1928	Percy Williams, Canada	10.8
1932	Eddie Tolan, United States	10.3
1936	Jesse Owens, United States	10.3
1948	Harrison Dillard, United States	10.3
1952	Lindy Remigino, United States	10.4
1956	Bobby Morrow, United States	10.5
1960	Armin Hary, Germany	10.2
1964	Bob Hayes, United States	10.0
1968	Jim Hines, United States	9.9
1972	Valery Borzov, USSR	10.1
1976	Hasely Crawford, Trinidad-Tobago	10.06

200-METER		Sec.
1900	J. W. Tewksbury, United States	22.2
1904	Archie Hahn, United States	21.6
1908	Bob Kerr, Canada	22.6
1912	Ralph Craig, United States	21.7
1920	Allan Woodring, United States	22.0
1924	Jackson Scholz, United States	21.6
1928	Percy Williams, Canada	21.8
1932	Eddie Tolan, United States	21.2
1936	Jesse Owens, United States	20.7
1948	Mel Patton, United States	21.1
1952	Andy Stanfield, United States	20.7
1956	Bobby Morrow, United States	20.6
1960	Livio Berutti, Italy	20.5
1964	Henry Carr, United States	20.3
1968	Tommie Smith, United States	19.8
1972	Valery Borzov, USSR	20.0
1976	Donald Quarrie Jamaica	20.23

400-METER		Sec.
1896	Thomas Burke, United States	54.2
1900	Maxey Long, United States	49.4
1904	Harry Hillman, United States	49.2
1908	Wyndham Halswelle, Great Britain	50.0
1912	Charles Reidpath, United States	48.2
1920	Bevil Rudd, South Africa	49.6

1924	Eric Liddell,		
	Great Britain	47.6
1928	Ray Barbuti,	
	United States	47.8
1932	William Carr,	
	United States	46.2
1936	Archie Williams,	
	United States	46.5
1948	Arthur Wint, Jamaica	46.2
1952	George Rhoden,	
	Jamaica	45.9
1956	Charles Jenkins,	
	United States	46.7
1960	Otis Davis,	
	United States	44.9
1964	Mike Larrabee,	
	United States	45.1
1968	Lee Evans,	
	United States	43.8
1972	Vince Matthews,	
	United States	44.1
1976	Alberto Juantorena,	
	Cuba	44.26

800-METER — *Min./Sec.*

1896	Edwin Flack,	
	Great Gritain	2:11.0
1900	Alfred Tysoe,	
	Great Britain	2:10.4
1904	James Lightbody,	
	United States	1:56.0
1908	Melvin Sheppard,	
	United States	1:52.8
1912	James Meredith,	
	United States	1:51.9
1920	Albert Hill,	
	Great Britain	1:53.4
1924	Douglas Lowe,	
	Great Britain	1:52.4
1928	Douglas Lowe,	
	Great Britain	1:51.8
1932	Thompson Hampson,	
	Great Britain	1:49.8
1936	John Woodruff,	
	United States	1:52.9
1948	Mal Whitfield,	
	United States	1:49.2
1952	Mal Whitfield,	
	United States	1:49.2
1956	Thomas Courtney,	
	United States	1:47.7
1960	Peter Snell,	
	New Zealand	1:46.3

1964	Peter Snell,	
	New Zealand	1:45.1
1968	Ralph Doubell,	
	Australia	1:44.3
1972	Dave Wottle,	
	United States	1:45.9
1976	Alberto Juantorena,	
	Cuba	1:43.50

1,500-METER — *Min./Sec.*

1896	Edwin Flack,	
	Great Britain	4:33.2
1900	Charles Bennett,	
	Great Britain	4:06.2
1904	James Lightbody,	
	United States	4:05.4
1908	Melvin Sheppard,	
	United States	4:03.4
1912	Arnold Jackson,	
	Great Britain	3:56.8
1920	Albert Hill,	
	Great Britain	4:01.8
1924	Paavo Nurmi,	
	Finland	3:53.6
1928	Harry Larva,	
	Finland	3:53.2
1932	Luigi Beccali, Italy	3:51.2
1948	Henry Ericksson,	
	Sweden	3:49.8
1952	Joseph Barthel,	
	Luxembourg	3:45.2
1956	Ron Delany, Ireland	3:41.2
1960	Herb Elliott,	
	Australia	3:35.6
1964	Peter Snell,	
	New Zealand	3:38.1
1968	Kip Keino, Kenya	3:34.9
1972	Pekka Vasala,	
	Finland	3:36.3
1976	John Walker,	
	New Zealand	3:39.17

5,000-METER — *Min./Sec.*

1912	Hannes Kolehmainen,	
	Finland	14:36.6
1920	Joseph Guillemot,	
	France	14:55.6
1924	Paavo Nurmi,	
	Finland	14:31.2
1928	Willie Ritola,	
	Finland	14:38.0
1932	Lauri Lehtinen,	
	Finland	14:30.0

1936	Gunnar Hockert, Finland	14:22.2
1948	Gaston Reiff, Belgium	14:17.6
1952	Emil Zatopek, Czechoslovakia	14:06.6
1956	Vladimir Kuts, USSR	13:39.6
1960	Murray Halberg, New Zealand	13:43.4
1964	Bob Schul, United States	13:48.8
1968	Mohamed Gammoudi, Tunisia	14:00.0
1972	Lasse Viren, Finland	13:26.4
1976	Lasse Viren, Finland	13:24.76

10,000-METER *Min./Sec.*

1912	Hannes Kolehmainen, Finland	31:20.8
1920	Paavo Nurmi, Finland	31:45.8
1924	Willie Ritola, Finland	30:23.2
1928	Paavo Nurmi, Finland	30:18.8
1932	Janusz Kusocinski, Poland	30:11.4
1948	Emil Zatopek, Czechoslovakia	29:59.6
1952	Emil Zatopek, Czechoslovakia	29:17.0
1956	Vladimir Kuts, USSR	28:45.6
1960	Petr Bolotnikov, USSR	28:32.2
1964	Billy Mills, United States	28:24.4
1968	Naftali Temu, Kenya	29:27.4
1972	Lasse Viren, Finland	27:38.4
1976	Lasse Viren, Finland	27:40.38

MARATHON *Hr./Min./Sec.*

1896	Spiros Loues, Greece	2:55:20.0
1900	Michael Teato, France	2:59:00.0
1904	Tom Hicks, United States	3:28:53.0
1908	John Hayes, United States	2:55:18.4
1912	Ken MacArthur, South Africa	2:36:54.8
1920	Hannes Kolehmainen, Finland	2:32:35.8
1924	Albin Stenroos, Finland	2:41:22.6
1928	El Quafi, France	2:32:57.0
1932	Juan Zabala, Argentina	2:31:36.0
1936	Kitei Son, Japan	2:29:19.2
1948	Dolf Cabrera, Argentina	2:34:51.6
1952	Emil Zatopek, Czechoslovakia	2:23:03.2
1956	Alain Mimoun, France	2:25:00.0
1960	Abebe Bikila, Ethiopia	2:15:15.2
1964	Abebe Bikila, Ethiopia	2:12:11.2
1968	Mamo Wolde, Ethiopia	2:20:26.4
1972	Frank Shorter, United States	2:12:19.8
1976	Waldemar Gerpinski, East Germany	2:09:55

110-METER HURDLES *Sec.*

1896	Thomas Curtis, United States	17.6
1900	Alvin Kraenzlein, United States	15.4
1904	Frederick Schule, United States	16.0
1908	Forrest Smithson, United States	15.0
1912	Frederick Kelley, United States	15.1
1920	Earl Thomson, Canada	14.8
1924	Daniel Kinsey, United States	15.0
1928	Sydney Atkinson, South Africa	14.8
1932	George Saling, United States	14.6
1936	Forrest Towns, United States	14.2

1948	William Porter,		1924	Willie Ritola,	
	United States	13.9		Finland	9:33.6
1952	Harrison Dillard,		1928	Toiva Loukola,	
	United States	13.7		Finland	9:21.8
1956	Lee Calhoun,		1932	Volmari Iso-Hollo,	
	United States	13.5		Finland	10:33.4
1960	Lee Calhoun,			(3,460-meters—extra	
	United States	13.8		lap run by error)	
1964	Hayes Jones,		1936	Volmari Iso-Hollo,	
	United States	13.6		Finland	9:03.8
1968	Willie Davenport,		1948	Thore Sjostrand,	
	United States	13.3		Sweden	9:04.6
1972	Rod Milburn,		1952	Horace Ashenfelter,	
	United States	13.2		United States	8:45.4
1976	Guy Drut, France	13.30	1956	Chris Brasher,	
				Great Britain	8:41.2

400-METER HURDLES		Sec.	1960	Zdzislaw Krzyszkowiak,	
1900	John Tewksbury,			Poland	8:34.2
	United States	57.6	1964	Gaston Roelants,	
1904	Harry Hillman,			Belgium	8:30.8
	United States	53.0	1968	Amos Biwott, Kenya	8:51.0
1908	Charles Bacon,		1972	Kip Keino, Kenya	8:23.6
	United States	55.0	1976	Anders Garderud,	
1920	Frank Loomis,			Sweden	8:08.02
	United States	54.0			
1924	F. Morgan Taylor,		20,000-METER		
	United States	52.6	WALK		Hr./Min./Sec.
1928	Lord David Burghley,		1956	Leonid Spirine,	
	Great Britain	53.4		USSR	1:31:27.0
1932	Robert Tisdall,		1960	Vladimir Golubnichy,	
	Ireland	51.8		USSR	1:34:07.2
1936	Glenn Hardin,		1964	Ken Matthews,	
	United States	52.4		Great Britain	1:29:34.0
1948	Roy Cochran,		1968	Vladimir Golubnichy,	
	United States	51.1		USSR	1:33:58.4
1952	Charles Moore,		1972	Peter Frenkel,	
	United States	50.8		East Germany	1:26:42.4
1956	Glenn Davis,		1976	Daniel Bautista,	
	United States	50.1		Mexico	1:24:40.6
1960	Glenn Davis,				
	United States	49.3	50,000-METER		
1964	Rex Cawley,		WALK		Hr./Min./Sec.
	United States	49.6	1932	Thomas Green,	
1968	Dave Hemery,			Great Britain	4:50:10.0
	Great Britain	48.1	1936	Harold Whitlock,	
1972	John Akii-Bua,			Great Britain	4:30:41.4
	Uganda	47.8	1948	John Ljunggren,	
1976	Edwin Moses,			Sweden	4:41:52.0
	United States	47.64	1952	Guiseppe Dordoni,	
				Italy	4:28:07.8
3,000-METER			1956	Norman Read,	
STEEPLECHASE		Min./Sec.		New Zealand	4:30:42.8
1920	Percy Hodge,		1960	Donald Thompson,	
	Great Britain	10:00.4		Great Britain	4:25:30.0

1964	Abdon Pamich, Italy	4:11:12.4
1968	Chris Hohne, East Germany	4:20:13.6
1972	Bernd Kannenberg, West Germany	3:56:11.0

400-METER RELAY

Year	Country	Sec.
1912	Great Britain	42.4
1920	United States	42.2
1924	United States	41.0
1928	United States	41.0
1932	United States	40.0
1936	United States	39.8
1948	United States	40.3
1952	United States	40.1
1956	United States	39.5
1964	United States	39.0
1968	United States	38.2
1972	United States	38.2
1976	United States	38.33

1,600-METER RELAY

Year	Country	Min./Sec.
1912	United States	3:16.6
1920	Great Britain	3:22.2
1924	United States	3:16.0
1928	United States	3:14.2
1932	United States	3:08.2
1936	Great Britain	3:09.0
1948	United States	3:10.4
1952	Jamaica	3:03.9
1956	United States	3:04.8
1960	United States	3:02.2
1964	United States	3:00.7
1968	United States	2:56.1
1972	Kenya	2:59.8
1976	United States	2:58.65

POLE VAULT

Year	Athlete	Height
1896	William Hoyt, United States	10'9¾"
1900	Irving Baxter, United States	10'9⁹⁄₁₀"
1904	Charles Dvorak, United States	11'6"
1908	Albert Gilbert, United States	12'2"
	Edward Cook, Jr., United States	12'2"
1912	Harry Babcock, United States	12'11½"
1920	Frank Foss, United States	12'5⁹⁄₁₆"

1924	Lee Barnes, United States	12'11½"
1928	Sabin Carr, United States	13'9⅜"
1932	William Miller, United States	14'1⅞"
1936	Earle Meadows, United States	14'3¼"
1948	O. Qinn Smith, United States	14'1¼"
1952	Robert Richards, United States	14'11¼"
1956	Robert Richards, United States	14'11½"
1960	Don Bragg, United States	15'5⅛"
1964	Fred Hansen, United States	16'9"
1968	Bob Seagren, United States	17'8½"
1972	Wolgang Nordwig, East Germany	18'0½"
1976	Tadeusz Slusarski, Poland	18'0½"

HIGH JUMP

Year	Athlete	Height
1896	Ellery Clark, United States	5'11¼"
1900	Irving Baxter, United States	6'2⅘"
1904	Samuel Jones, United States	5'11"
1908	Harry Porter, United States	6'3"
1912	Alma Richards, United States	6'4"
1920	Richard Landon, United States	6'4¼"
1924	Harold Osborn, United States	6'5¹⁵⁄₁₆"
1928	Robert King, United States	6'4⅜"
1932	Duncan McNaughton, Canada	6'5⅝"
1936	Cornelius Johnson, United States	6'7¹⁵⁄₁₆"
1948	John Winter, Australia	6'6"
1952	Walter Davis, United States	6'8¼"
1956	Charles Dumas, United States	6'11¼"
1960	Robert Shavlakadze, USSR	7'1"

1964	Valery Brumel, USSR	7'1¾"
1968	Dick Fosbury, United States	7'4¼"
1972	Yuri Tarmak, USSR	7'3¾"
1976	Jacek Wszola, Poland	7'4½"

LONG JUMP — *Distance*

1896	Ellery Clark, United States	20'10"
1900	Alvin Kraenzlein, United States	23'6⅞"
1904	Myer Prinstein, United States	24'1"
1908	Frank Irons, United States	24'6½"
1912	Albert Gutterson, United States	24'11¼"
1920	William Patterson, Sweden	23'5½"
1924	DeHart Hubbard, United States	24'5⅛"
1928	Edward Hamm, United States	25'4¾"
1932	Edward Gordon, United States	25'0¾"
1936	Jesse Owens, United States	26'5⅜"
1948	Willie Steele, United States	25'8"
1952	Jerome Biffle, United States	24'10"
1956	Gregory Bell, United States	25'8¼"
1960	Ralph Boston, United States	26'7¾"
1964	Lynn Davies, Great Britain	26'5½"
1968	Bob Beamon, United States	29'2½"
1972	Randy Williams, United States	27'0½"
1976	Arnie Robinson, United States	27'4¾"

TRIPLE JUMP (Hop-Step-Jump) — *Distance*

1896	James Connolly, United States	45'0"
1900	Myer Prinstein, United States	47'4¼"
1904	Myer Prinstein, United States	47'0"
1908	Timothy Ahearne, Great Britain	48'11¼"
1912	Gustof Lindblom, Sweden	48'5⅛"
1920	Vilho Tuulos, Finland	47'6⅞"
1924	Archibald Winter, Australia	50'11⅛"
1928	Mikio Oda, Japan	49'10¹³⁄₁₆"
1932	Chuhei Nambu, Japan	51'7"
1936	Naoto Tajima, Japan	52'5⅞"
1948	Arne Ahman, Sweden	50'6¼"
1952	Adhemar da Silva, Brazil	53'2½"
1956	Adhemar da Silva, Brazil	53'7½"
1960	Jozef Schmidt, Poland	55'1¾"
1964	Jozef Schmidt, Poland	55'3¼"
1968	Viktor Saneyev, USSR	57'0¾"
1972	Viktor Saneyev, USSR	56'11"
1976	Viktor Saneyev, USSR	56'8¾"

16-POUND SHOT PUT — *Distance*

1896	Robert Garrett, United States	36'9¾"
1900	Richard Sheldon, United States	46'3⅛"
1904	Ralph Rose, United States	48'7"
1908	Ralph Rose, United States	46'7½"
1912	Patrick McDonald, United States	50'4"
1920	Ville Porhola, Finland	48'7⅛"
1924	Clarence Houser, United States	49'2½"
1928	John Kuck, United States	52'0¹¹⁄₁₆"
1932	Leo Sexton, United States	52'6³⁄₁₆"

1936	Hans Woellke, Germany	53'1¾"
1948	Wilbur Thompson, United States	56'2"
1952	Parry O'Brien, United States	57'1½"
1956	Parry O'Brien, United States	60'11"
1960	Bill Nieder, United States	64'6¾"
1964	Dallas Long, United States	66'8½"
1968	Randy Matson, United States	67'4¾"
1972	Wladyslaw Komar, USSR	69'6"
1976	Udo Beyer, East Germany	69'0¾"

DISCUS THROW — Distance

1896	Robert Garrett, United States	95'7½"
1900	Rudolf Bauer, Hungary	118'2⁹/₁₀"
1904	Martin Sheridan, United States	128'10½"
1908	Martin Sheridan, United States	134'2"
1912	Armas Taiple, Finland	145'0⁹/₁₆"
1920	Elmer Ninklander, Finland	146'7"
1924	Clarence Houser, United States	151'5¼"
1928	Clarence Houser, United States	155'2⅘"
1932	John Anderson, United States	162'4⅞"
1936	Kenneth Carpenter, United States	165'7½"
1948	Adolfo Consolini, Italy	173'2"
1952	Sim Iness, United States	180'6½"
1956	Al Oerter, United States	184'10½"
1960	Al Oerter, United States	194'2"
1964	Al Oerter, United States	200'1½"
1968	Al Oerter, United States	212'6½"

1972	Ludvik Danek, Czechoslovakia	211'3½"
1976	Mac Wilkins, United States	221'5"

16-POUND HAMMER THROW — Distance

1900	John Flanagan, United States	167'4"
1904	John Flanagan, United States	168'1"
1908	John Flanagan, United States	170'4¼"
1912	Matthew McGrath, United States	179'7⅛"
1920	Patrick Ryan, United States	173'5⅝"
1924	Frederick Tootell, United States	174'10¼"
1928	Patrick O'Callaghan, Ireland	168'7½"
1932	Patrick O'Callaghan, Ireland	176'11⅛"
1936	Karl Hein, Germany	185'4¼"
1948	Imre Nemeth, Hungary	183'11½"
1952	Jozsef Csermak, Hungary	197'11¾"
1956	Harold Connolly, United States	207'3½"
1960	Vasiliy Rudenkov, USSR	220'1⅝"
1964	Romuald Klim, USSR	228'10½"
1968	Gyula Zsivotzky, Hungary	240'8"
1972	Anatoliy Bondarchuk, USSR	247'8½"
1976	Yuri Syedekh, USSR	254'3.9"

JAVELIN THROW — Distance

1908	Erik Lemming, Sweden	179'10½"
1912	Erik Lemming, Sweden	198'11¼"
1920	Jonni Myra, Finland	215'9¾"
1924	Jonni Myra, Finland	206'6¾"
1928	Erik Lundquist, Sweden	218'6⅛"

1932	Matti Jarvinen, Finland	238'7"
1936	Gerhard Stock, Germany	235'8⁵⁄₁₆"
1948	Tapio Rautavaara, Finland	228'10½"
1952	Cy Young, United States	242'0¾"
1956	Egil Danielson, Norway	281'2¼"
1960	Viktor Cybulenko, USSR	277'8⅜"
1964	Pauli Nevala, Finland	271'2¼"
1968	Janis Lusis, USSR	295'7¼"
1972	Klaus Wolfermann, West Germany	296'10"
1976	Miklos Nemeth, Hungary	310'4"

DECATHLON

		Points
1912	Hugo Weislander, Sweden	7724.49
1920	Helge Lovland, Norway	6804.35
1924	Harold Osborn, United States	7710.77
1928	Paavo Yrjola, Finland	8053.29
1932	James Bausch, United States	8462.23
1936	Glenn Morris, United States (New Point System)	7900.00
1948	Bob Mathias, United States	7193.00
1952	Bob Mathias, United States	7887.00
1956	Milt Campbell, United States	7937.00
1960	Rafer Johnson, United States	8392.00
1964	Willi Holdorf, Germany (New Point System)	7887.00
1968	Bill Toomey, United States	8193.00
1972	Nikolay Avilov, USSR	8454.00
1976	Bruce Jenner, United States	8618.00

WOMEN'S TRACK AND FIELD WINNERS

100-METER DASH

		Sec.
1928	Elizabeth Robinson, United States	12.2
1932	Stella Walsh, Walasiewiz, Poland	11.9
1936	Helen Stephens, United States	11.5
1948	Fanny Blankers-Koen, Netherlands	11.9
1952	Marjorie Jackson, Australia	11.5
1956	Betty Cuthbert, Australia	11.5
1960	Wilma Rudolph, United States	11.0
1964	Wyomia Tyus, United States	11.4
1968	Wyomia Tyus, United States	11.0
1972	Renata Stecher, East Germany	11.1
1976	Annegret Richter, West Germany	11.01

200-METER DASH

		Sec.
1948	Fanny Flankers-Koen, Netherlands	24.4
1952	Marjorie Jackson, Australia	23.7
1956	Betty Cuthbert, Australia	23.4
1960	Wilma Rudolph, United States	24.0
1964	Edith McGuire, United States	23.0
1968	Irene Szewinska, Poland	22.5
1972	Renata Stecher, East Germany	22.4
1976	Baerbel Eckert, East Germany	22.37

400-METER DASH

		Sec.
1964	Betty Cuthbert, Australia	52.0
1968	Colette Besson, France	52.0
1972	Monika Zehrt, East Germany	51.1

1976 Irina Szewinska,
    Poland   49.29

800-METER RUN   *Min./Sec.*
1928 Linda Radke,
    Germany   2:16.8
1960 Ludmila Shevtsova,
    USSR   2:04.4
1964 Ann Packer,
    Great Britain   2:01.1
1968 Madeline Manning,
    United States   2:00.9
1972 Hildegard Falck,
    West Germany   1:58.6
1976 Tatyana Kazankina,
    USSR   1:54.94

1,500-METER RUN   *Min./Sec.*
1972 Lyudmila Bragina,
    USSR   4:01.4
1976 Tatyana Kazankina,
    USSR   4:05.48

400-METER RELAY   *Sec.*
1928 Canada   48.4
1932 United States   47.0
1936 United States   46.9
1948 Netherlands   47.5
1952 United States   45.9
1956 Australia   44.5
1960 United States   44.5
1964 Poland   43.6
1968 United States   42.8
1972 West Germany   42.8
1976 East Germany   42.55

1,600-METER RELAY *Min./Sec.*
1972 East Germany   3:23.0
1976 East Germany   3:19.23

80-METER HURDLES   *Sec.*
1932 Mildred Didrikson,
    United States   11.7
1936 Trebisonda Villa, Italy 11.7
1948 Fanny Blankers-Koen,
    Netherlands   11.2
1952 Shirley Strickland de la
    Hunty, Australia 10.9
1956 Shirley Strickland de la
    Hunty, Australia 10.7
1960 Irina Press, USSR 10.8
1964 Karin Balzer, Germany 10.5

1968 Maureen Caird,
    Australia   10.3

100-METER HURDLES   *Sec.*
1972 Annelie Ehrhardt,
    East Germany   12.6
1976 Johanna Schaller,
    East Germany   12.77

HIGH JUMP   *Height*
1928 Ethel Catherwood,
    Canada   5'3"
1932 Jean Shiley,
    United States   5'5¼"
1936 Ibolya Csak,
    Hungary   5'3"
1948 Alice Coachman,
    United States   5'6⅛"
1952 Esther Brand,
    South Africa   5'5¾"
1956 Mildred McDaniel,
    United States   5'9¼"
1960 Ioland Balas,
    Roumania   6'0¾"
1964 Ioland Balas,
    Roumania   6'2¾"
1968 Miloslava Rezkova,
    Czechoslovakia 5'11¾"
1972 Ulrike Meyfarth,
    West Germany 6'3⅝"
1976 Rosemarie Ackerman,
    East Germany 6'3%0"

LONG JUMP   *Distance*
1948 Olga Gyarmati,
    Hungary   18'8¼"
1952 Yvette Williams,
    New Zealand 20'5¾"
1956 Elzbieta Krzeskinka,
    Poland   20'10"
1960 Vyera Krepina,
    USSR   20'10⅞"
1964 Mary Rand,
    Great Britain 22'2¼"
1968 Viorica Viscopoleanu,
    Roumania   22'4½"
1972 Heide Rosendahl,
    West Germany 22'3"
1976 Angela Voigt,
    East Germany 22'0½"

8-LB./13⅘ oz. SHOT PUT *Distance*
1948	Micheline Ostermeyer, France	45'1½"
1952	Galina Zybina, USSR	50'1½"
1956	Tamara Tishkyvich, USSR	54'5"
1960	Tamara Press, USSR	56'9⅞"
1964	Tamara Press, USSR	59'6¼"
1968	Margitta Gummel, East Germany	64'4"
1972	Nadezhda Chizhova, USSR	69'0"
1976	Ivanka Khristova, Bulgaria	69'7"

DISCUS THROW *Distance*
1928	Helena Konopacka, Poland	129'11⅞"
1932	Lilian Copeland, United States	133'2"
1936	Gisela Mauermayer, Germany	156'0³⁄₁₆"
1948	Micheline Ostermeyer, France	137'6½"
1952	Nina Romaschkova, USSR	168'8½"
1956	Olga Fikotova, Czechoslovakia	176'1½"
1960	Nina Ponomaryeva, USSR	180'8¼"
1964	Tamara Press, USSR	187'10¾"
1968	Lia Manoliu, Roumania	191'2½"
1972	Faina Melnik, USSR	218'7"
1976	Evelyn Schlaak, East Germany	226'4½"

JAVELIN THROW *Distance*
1932	Mildred Didrikson, United states	143'4"
1936	Tilly Fleischer, Germany	148'2¾"
1948	Hermine Bauma, Austria	149'6"
1952	Dana Zatopek, Czechoslovakia	165'7"
1956	Inese Janzeme, USSR	176'8"

1960	Elvira Ozolina, USSR	183'8"
1964	Mihaela Penes, Roumania	198'7½"
1968	Angela Nemeth, Hungary	198'0½"
1972	Ruth Fuchs, East Germany	209'7"
1976	Ruth Fuchs, East Germany	216'4"

PENTATHLON *Points*
1964	Irina Press, USSR	5246
1968	Ingrid Becker, West Germany	5098
1972	Mary Peters, Great Britain	4801
1976	Sigrun Siegl, East Germany	4745

MEN'S SWIMMING AND DIVING WINNERS

100-METER FREESTYLE *Min./Sec.*
1896	Alfred Hajos, Hungary (100 yards)	1:22.2
1904	Zoltan de Halmay, Hungary	1:02.8
1908	Charles Daniels, United States	1:05.6
1912	Duke Kahanamoku, United States	1:03.4
1920	Duke Kahanamoku, United States	1:01.4
1924	John Weissmuller, United States	59.0
1928	John Weissmuller, United States	58.2
1932	Yasuji Miyazaki, Japan	58.6
1936	Ferenec Csik, Hungary	57.6
1948	Walter Ris, United States	57.3
1952	Clarke Scholes, United States	57.4
1956	Jon Henricks, Australia	55.4
1960	John Devitt, Australia	55.2
1964	Don Schollander, United States	53.4

1968	Mike Wenden, Australia	52.2
1972	Mark Spitz, United States	51.2
1976	Jim Montgomery, United States	49.99

200-METER FREESTYLE — Min./Sec.

1900	Fred Lane, Australia	2:25.2
1968	Mike Wenden, Australia	1:55.2
1972	Mark Spitz, United States	1:52.7
1976	Bruce Furniss, United States	1:50.29

400-METER FREESTYLE — Min./Sec.

1896	Paul Neumann, Austria (500 meters)	8:12.6
1904	Charles Daniels, United States (440 yards)	6:16.2
1908	Henry Taylor, Great Britain	5:36.8
1912	George Hodgson, Canada	5:24.4
1920	Norman Ross, United States	5:26.8
1924	John Weissmuller, United States	5:04.2
1928	Albert Zorilla, Argentina	5:01.6
1932	Clarence Crabbe, United States	4:48.4
1936	Jack Medica, United States	4:44.5
1948	William Smith, United States	4:41.0
1952	Jean Boiteaux, France	4:30.7
1956	Murray Rose, Australia	4:27.3
1960	Murray Rose, Australia	4:18.3
1964	Don Schollander, United States	4:12.2
1968	Mike Burton, United States	4:09.0

| 1972 | Brad Cooper, Australia | 4:00.2 |
| 1976 | Brian Goodell, United States | 3:51.93 |

1,500-METER FREESTYLE — Min./Sec.

1896	Alfred Hajos, Hungary (1,200 meters)	18:22.2
1900	John Jarvis, Great Britain (1,000 meters)	13:40.2
1904	Emil Rausch, Germany (1,609 meters)	27:18.2
1908	Henry Taylor, Great Britain	22:48.4
1912	George Hodgson, Canada	22:00.0
1920	Norman Ross, United States	22:23.2
1924	Andrew Charlton, Australia	20:06.6
1928	Arne Borg, Sweden	19:51.8
1932	Kusuo Kitamura, Japan	19:12.4
1936	Noboru Terada, Japan	19:13.7
1948	James McLane, United States	19:18.5
1952	Ford Konno, United States	18:30.0
1956	Murray Rose, Australia	17:58.9
1960	Jon Konrads, Australia	17:19.6
1964	Robert Windle, Australia	17:01.7
1968	Mike Burton, United States	16:38.9
1972	Mike Burton, United States	15:52.5
1976	Brian Goodell, United States	15:02.4

100-METER BACKSTROKE — Min./Sec.

| 1900 | Ernest Hoppenberg, Germany (200 meters) | 2:47.0 |
| 1904 | Walter Brack, Germany (100 yards) | 1:16.8 |

1908	Arno Bieberstein, Germany	1:24.6
1912	Harry Hebner, United States	1:21.2
1920	Warren Kealoha, United States	1:15.2
1924	Warren Kealoha, United States	1:13.2
1928	George Kojac, United States	1:08.2
1932	Masaji Kiyokawa, Japan	1:08.6
1936	Adolph Kiefer, United States	1:05.9
1948	Allen Stack, United States	1:06.4
1952	Yoshinobu Oyakawa, United States	1:05.4
1956	David Thiele, Australia	1:02.2
1960	David Thiele, Australia	1:01.9
1964	Not held	
1968	Roland Matthes, East Germany	58.7
1972	Roland Matthes, East Germany	56.5
1976	John Naber, United States	55.49

200-METER BACKSTROKE   *Min./Sec.*

1900	Ernest Hoppenberg, Germany	2:47.0
1964	Jed Graef, United States	2:10.3
1968	Roland Matthes, East Germany	2:09.6
1972	Roland Matthes, East Germany	2:02.8
1976	John Naber, United States	1:59.19

100-METER BREASTSTROKE   *Min./Sec.*

1968	Don McKenzie, United States	1:07.7
1972	Nobutaka Tagushi, Japan	1:04.9
1976	John Hencken, United States	1:03.11

200-METER BREASTSTROKE   *Min./Sec.*

1908	Frederick Holman, Great Britain	3:09.2
1912	Walter Bathe, Germany	3:01.8
1920	Haken Malmroth, Sweden	3:04.4
1924	Robert Skelton, United States	3:56.6
1928	Yoshiyuki Tsuruta, Japan	2:48.8
1932	Yoshiyuki Tsuruta, Japan	2:45.4
1936	Tetsuo Hamuro, Japan	2:41.5
1948	Joseph Verdeur, United States	2:39.3
1952	John Davies, Australia	2:34.4
1956	Masura Furukawa, Japan	2:34.7
1960	William Mulliken, United States	2:37.4
1964	Ian O'Brien, Australia	2:27.8
1968	Felipe Munoz, Mexico	2:28.7
1972	John Hencken, United States	2:21.5
1976	David Wilkie, Great Britain	2:15.11

100-METER BUTTERFLY   *Sec.*

1968	Doug Russell, United States	55.9
1972	Mark Spitz, United States	54.2
1976	Matt Vogel, United States	54.35

200-METER BUTTERFLY   *Min./Sec.*

1956	William Yorzyk, United States	2:19.3
1960	Michael Troy, United States	2:12.8
1964	Kevin Berry, Australia	2:06.6
1968	Carl Robie, United States	2:08.7

1972	Mark Spitz,	
	United States	2:00.7
1976	Mike Bruner,	
	United States	1:59.23

200-METER MEDLEY Min./Sec.

1968	Charles Hickcox,	
	United States	2:12.0
1972	Gunnar Larsson,	
	Sweden	2:07.1

400-METER MEDLEY Min./Sec.

1964	Richard Roth,	
	United States	4:45.4
1968	Charles Hickcox,	
	United States	4:48.4
1972	Gunnar Larsson,	
	Sweden	4:31.9
1976	Rod Strachan,	
	United States	4:23.68

400-METER FREESTYLE RELAY Min./Sec.

1964	United States	3:33.2
1968	United States	3:31.7
1972	United States	3:26.4

800-METER FREESTYLE RELAY Min./Sec.

1908	Great Britain	10:55.6
1912	Australia	10:11.2
1920	United States	10:04.4
1924	United States	9:53.4
1928	United States	9:36.2
1932	Japan	8:58.4
1936	Japan	8:51.5
1948	United States	8:46.0
1952	United States	8:31.1
1956	Australia	8:23.6
1960	United States	8:10.2
1964	United States	7:52.1
1968	United States	7:52.3
1972	United States	7:35.7
1976	United States	7:23.22

400-METER MEDLEY RELAY Min./Sec.

1960	United States	4:05.4
1964	United States	3:58.4
1968	United States	3:54.9
1972	United States	3:48.1

1976	United States	3:42.22

SPRINGBOARD DIVING

1908	Albert Zurner, Germany
1912	Paul Guenther, Germany
1920	Louis Kuehn, United States
1924	Albert White, United States
1928	Pete Desjardins, United States
1932	Michael Galitzen, United States
1936	Richard Degener, United States
1948	Bruce Harlan, United States
1952	David Browning, United States
1956	Robert Clotworthy, United States
1960	Gary Tobian, United States
1964	Ken Sitzberger, United States
1968	Bernie Wrightson, United States
1972	Vladimir Vassin, USSR
1976	Phil Boggs, United States

PLATFORM (HIGH) DIVING

1904	Dr. G. E. Sheldon, United States
1908	Hjalmar Johannson, Sweden
1912	Erik Adlerz, Sweden
1920	Clarence Pinkston, United States
1924	Albert White, United States
1928	Pete Desjardins, United States
1932	Harold Smith, United States
1936	Marshall Wayne, United States
1948	Dr. Samuel Lee, United States
1952	Dr. Samuel Lee, United States
1956	Joaquin Capilla, Mexico
1960	Robert Webster, United States
1964	Robert Webster, United States
1968	Klaus Dibiase, Italy
1972	Klaus Dibiase, Italy
1976	Klaus Dibiase, Italy

WOMEN'S SWIMMING AND DIVING WINNERS

100-METER FREESTYLE

		Min./Sec.
1912	Fanny Durack, Australia	1:22.2
1920	Ethelda Bleibtrey, United States	1:13.6
1924	Ethel Lackie, United States	1:12.4
1928	Albina Osipowich, United States	1:11.0
1932	Helene Madison, United States	1:06.8
1936	Hendrika Mastenbroek, Holland	1:06.8
1948	Greta Anderson, Denmark	1:06.3
1952	Katalin Szoke, Hungary	1:06.8
1956	Dawn Fraser, Australia	1:02.0
1960	Dawn Fraser, Australia	1:01.2
1964	Dawn Fraser, Australia	59.5
1968	Jan Henne, United States	1:00.0
1972	Sandra Neilson, United States	58.5
1976	Kornelia Ender, East Germany	55.65

200-METER FREESTYLE

		Min./Sec.
1968	Debbie Meyer, United States	2:10.5
1972	Shane Gould, Australia	2:03.5
1976	Kornelia Ender, East Germany	1:59.26

400-METER FREESTYLE

		Min./Sec.
1920	Ethelda Bleibtrey, United States (300 meters)	4:34.0
1924	Martha Norelius, United States	6:02.2
1928	Martha Norelius, United States	5:26.4
1932	Helene Madison, United States	5:28.5
1936	Hendrika Mastenbroek, Holland	5:26.4
1948	Ann Curtis, United States	5:17.8
1952	Valeria Gyenge, Hungary	5:12.1
1956	Lauraine Crapp, Australia	4:54.6
1960	Chris Von Saltza, United States	4:50.6
1964	Virginia Duenkel, United States	4:43.3
1968	Debbie Meyer, United States	4:31.8
1972	Shane Gould, Australia	4:19.0
1976	Petra Thumer, East Germany	4:09.89

800-METER FREESTYLE

		Min./Sec.
1968	Debbie Meyer, United States	9:24.0
1972	Keena Rothhammer, United States	8:53.6
1976	Petra Thumer, East Germany	8:37.14

100-METER BACKSTROKE

1924	Sybil Bauer, United States	1:23.2
1928	Marie Braun, Holland	1:22.0
1932	Eleanor Holm, United States	1:19.4
1936	Dina Senff, Holland	1:18.9
1948	Karen Harup, Denmark	1:14.4
1952	Joan Harrison, South Africa	1:14.3
1956	J. Grinham, Great Britain	1:12.9
1960	Lynn Burke, United States	1:09.3
1964	Cathy Ferguson, United States	1:07.7
1968	Kaye Hall, United States	1:06.2
1972	Melissa Belote, United States	1:05.7

1976	Ulrike Richter, East Germany	1:01.83

200-METER BACKSTROKE *Min./Sec.*

1968	Pokey Watson, United States	2:24.8
1972	Melissa Belote, United States	2:19.1
1976	Ulrike Richter, East Germany	2:13.43

100-METER BREASTSTROKE *Min./Sec.*

1968	Djurdjica Bedov, Yugoslavia	1:15.8
1972	Cathy Carr, United States	1:13.5
1976	Hannelore Anke, East Germany	1:11.16

200-METER BREASTSTROKE *Min./Sec.*

1924	Lucy Morton, Great Britain	3:33.2
1928	Hilde Schrader, Germany	3:12.6
1932	Clare Dennis, Australia	3:06.3
1936	Hideko Maehata, Japan	3:03.6
1948	Nel Van Vliet, Netherlands	2:57.2
1952	Eva Szekely, Hungary	2:51.7
1956	U. Happe, Germany	2:53.1
1960	Anita Lonsbrough, Great Britain	2:49.5
1964	Galina Prozumenshirova, USSR	2:46.4
1968	Sharon Wichman, United States	2:44.4
1972	Bev Whitfield, Australia	2:41.7
1976	Marina Koshevaia, USSR	2:33.35

100-METER BUTTERFLY *Min./Sec.*

1956	Shelly Mann, United States	1:11.0
1960	Carolyn Schuler, United States	1:09.5
1964	Sharon Stouder, United States	1:04.7
1968	Lyn McClements, Australia	1:05.5
1972	Mayumi Aoki, Japan	1:03.3
1976	Kornelia Ender, East Germany	1:03.13

200-METER BUTTERFLY *Min./Sec.*

1968	Aaoje Kok, Netherlands	2:24.7
1972	Karen Moe, United States	2:15.5
1976	Andrea Pollack, East Germany	2:11.41

400-METER FREESTYLE RELAY *Min./Sec.*

1912	Great Britain	5:52.8
1920	United States	5:11.6
1924	United States	4:58.8
1928	United States	4:47.6
1932	United States	4:38.0
1936	Netherlands	4:36.0
1948	United States	4:29.2
1952	Hungary	4:24.4
1956	Australia	4:17.1
1960	United States	4:08.9
1964	United States	4:03.8
1968	United States	4:02.5
1972	United States	3:55.1
1976	United States	3:44.82

400-METER MEDLEY RELAY *Min./Sec.*

1960	United States	4:41.1
1964	United States	4:33.9
1968	United States	4:28.3
1972	United States	4:20.7
1976	East Germany	4:07.95

SPRINGBOARD DIVING

1920	Aileen Riggin, United States
1924	Elizabeth Becker, United States
1928	Helen Meany, United States
1932	Georgia Coleman, United States
1936	Marjorie Gestring, United States
1948	Victoria Draves, United States

1952 Pat McCormick,
         United States
1956 Pat McCormick,
         United States
1960 Ingrid Kramer, Germany
1964 Ingrid Engel, Germany
1968 Sue Gossick, United States
1972 Micki King, United States
1976 Jenni Chandler,
         United States

PLATFORM (HIGH) DIVING
1912 Greta Johansson, Sweden
1920 Stefani Fryland-Clausen,
         Denmark
1924 Caroline Smith,
         United States

1928 Elizabeth Pinkston,
         United States
1932 Dorothy Poynton,
         United States
1936 Dorothy Poynton,
         United States
1948 Victoria Draves,
         United States
1952 Pat McCormick,
         United States
1956 Pat McCormick,
         United States
1960 Ingrid Kramer, Germany
1964 Lesley Bush, United States
1968 Milena Duchkova,
         Czechoslovakia
1972 Ulrika Knape, Sweden
1976 Elena Vaytshekhovskaia,
         USSR

WINTER GAMES

ALPINE SKIING (MEN)

DOWNHILL RACE
1948 Henri Oreiller, France
1952 Zeno Colo, Italy
1956 Toni Sailer, Austria
1960 Jean Vuarnet, France
1964 Egon Zimmerman, Austria
1968 Jean-Claude Killy, France
1972 Bernhard Russi, Switzerland
1976 Franz Klammer, Austria

GIANT SLALOM
1952 Stein Eriksen, Norway
1956 Toni Sailer, Austria
1960 Roger Staub, Switzerland
1964 Francois Bonlieu, France
1968 Jean-Claude Killy, France
1972 Gustavo Thoeni, Italy
1976 Heini Hemmi, Switzerland

SLALOM
1948 Edi Reinalter, Switzerland
1952 Othmar Schneider, Austria
1956 Toni Sailer, Austria
1960 Ernst Hinterseer, Austria
1964 Pepi Stiegler, Austria
1968 Jean-Claude Killy, France
1972 Francisco Fernandez-Ochoa,
         Spain
1976 Piero Gros, Italy

ALPINE SKIING (WOMEN)

DOWNHILL RACE
1948 Hedi Schlunegger,
         Switzerland
1952 Trudi Jochum-Beiser,
         Austria
1956 Madeleine Berthod,
         Switzerland
1960 Heidi Beibl, Germany
1964 Christi Haas, Austria
1968 Olga Pall, Austria
1972 Marie-Therese Nadig,
         Switzerland
1976 Rosi Mittermaier,
         West Germany

SLALOM
1948 Gretchen Fraser,
         United States
1952 Andrea Mead Lawrence,
         United States
1956 Renee Colliard, Switzerland
1960 Anne Heggtveit, Canada
1964 Christine Goitschel, France
1968 Marielle Goitschel, France
1972 Barbara Cochran,
         United States
1976 Rosi Mittermaier,
         West Germany

GIANT SLALOM
1952 Andrea Mead Lawrence,
     United States
1956 Ossi Reichert, Germany
1960 Yvonne Ruegg, Switzerland
1964 Marielle Goitschel, France
1968 Nancy Greene, Canada
1972 Marie-Therese Nadig,
     Switzerland
1976 Kathy Kreiner, Canada

SKI JUMP

ONE-HILL JUMP
1924 Jacob Thams, Norway
1928 Alfred Andersen, Norway
1932 Birger Ruud, Norway
1936 Birger Ruud, Norway
1948 Peter Hugsted, Norway
1952 Arnfinn Bergman, Norway
1956 Antti Hyvarinen, Finland
1960 Helmut Recknagel,
     Germany

90-METER JUMP
1964 Toralf Engan, Norway
1968 Vladamir Beloussov, USSR
1972 Wojciech Fortuna, Poland
1976 Karl Schnabl, Austria

70-METER JUMP
1964 V. Kankkonen, Finland
1968 J. Raska, Czechoslovakia
1972 Yoko Kasaya, Japan
1976 Hans-Georg Aschenbach,
     East Germany

SPEED SKATING (MEN)

500 METERS	Sec.
1924 Charles Jewtraw,	
United States	44.0
1928 Clas Thunberg, Finland	
and Bernt Evensen,	
Norway	43.4
1932 John A. Shea,	
United States	43.4
1936 Ivar Ballangrud,	
Norway	43.4

1948	Finn Helgesen, Norway	43.1
1952	Ken Henry,	
	United States	43.2
1956	Evgenij Grishin,	
	USSR	40.2
1960	Evgenij Grishin,	
	USSR	40.2
1964	Terry McDermott,	
	United States	40.1
1968	Erhard Keller,	
	West Germany	40.3
1972	Erhard Keller,	
	West Germany	39.4
1976	Yevgeni Kulikov	
	USSR	39.17

1,500 METERS		Min./Sec.
1924	Clas Thunberg,	
	Finland	2:20.8
1928	Clas Thunberg,	
	Finland	2:21.1
1932	John Shea,	
	United States	2:57.5
1936	Charles Mathisen,	
	Norway	2:19.2
1948	Sverre Farstad,	
	Norway	2:17.6
1952	H. Andersen,	
	Norway	2:20.4
1956	Evgenij Grishin,	
	USSR	2:08.6
1960	Evgenij Grishin,	
	USSR	
	Roald Aas	2:11.5
1964	Ants Antson, USSR	2:10.3
1968	Kees Verkerk,	
	Netherlands	2:03.4
1972	Ard Schenk,	
	Netherlands	2:02.9
1976	Jan Egil Storholt,	
	Norway	1:59.38

5,000 METERS		Min./Sec.
1924	Clas Thunberg,	
	Finland	8:39
1928	Ivar Ballangrud,	
	Norway	8:50.5
1932	Irving Jaffee,	
	United States	9:40.8
1936	Ivar Ballangrud,	
	Norway	8:19.6
1948	Reidar Liaklev,	
	Norway	8:29.4

1952	H. Andersen, Norway	8:10.6
1956	Boris Shilkov, USSR	7:48.7
1960	Viktor Kosichkin, USSR	7:51.3
1964	Knut Johannesen, Norway	7:38.4
1968	Fred Anton Maier, Norway	7:22.4
1972	Ard Schenk, Netherlands	7:23.6
1976	Sten Stensen, Norway	7:24.48

10,000 METERS		Min./Sec.
1924	Julien Skutnabb, Finland	18:04.8
1928	Irving Jaffee, United States	18:36.5
1932	Irving Jaffee, United States	19:13.6
1936	Ivar Ballangrud, Norway	17:24.3
1948	Ake Seyffarth, Sweden	17:26.3
1952	H. Andersen, Norway	16:45.8
1956	Sigvard Ericsson, Sweden	16:35.9
1960	Knut Johannesen, Norway	15:46.6
1964	Johnny Nilson, Sweden	15:50.1
1968	Johnny Hoeglin, Sweden	15:23.6
1972	Ard Schenk, Netherlands	15:01.3
1976	Piet Kleine, Netherlands	14:50.59

SPEED SKATING (WOMEN)

500 METERS		Sec.
1960	Helga Haase, Germany	45.9
1964	Lydia Skoblikova, USSR	45.0
1968	Ludmilla Titova, USSR	46.1
1972	Anne Henning, United States	43.3
1976	Sheila Young, United States	42.76

1,000 METERS		Min./Sec.
1960	Klara Guseva, USSR	1:34.1
1964	Lydia Skoblikova, USSR	1:33.2
1968	Carolina Geijssen, Netherlands	1:32.6
1972	Monika Pflug, West Germany	1:31.4
1976	Tatyana Averina, USSR	1:28.43

1,500 METERS		Min./Sec.
1960	Lydia Skoblikova, USSR	2:25.2
1964	Lydia Skoblikova, USSR	2:22.6
1968	Kaija Mustonen, Finland	2:22.4
1972	Dianne Holum, United States	2:20.8
1976	Galina Stepenskaya, USSR	2:16.58

3,000 METERS		Min./Sec.
1960	Lydia Skoblikova, USSR	5:14.3
1964	Lydia Skoblikova, USSR	5:14.9
1968	Johanna Schut, Netherlands	4:56.2
1972	Stien Baas-Kaiser, Netherlands	4:52.1
1976	Tatyana Averina, USSR	4:45.19

ICE HOCKEY

1920	Canada
1924	Canada
1928	Canada
1932	Canada
1936	Great Britain
1948	Canada
1952	Canada
1956	USSR
1960	United States
1964	USSR
1968	USSR
1972	USSR
1976	USSR

FIGURE SKATING (MEN'S)

1908 Salchow, Sweden
1920 Gillis Grafstrom, Sweden
1924 Gillis Grafstrom, Sweden
1928 Gillis Grafstrom, Sweden
1932 Karl Schaefer, Austria
1936 Karl Schaefer, Austria
1948 Dick Button, United States
1952 Dick Button, United States
1956 Hayes Alan Jenkins,
         United States
1960 David Jenkins,
         United States
1964 Manfred Schnelldorfer,
         Germany
1968 Wolfgang Schwarz, Austria
1972 Ondrej Nepela,
         Czechoslovakia
1976 John Curry, Great Britain

FIGURE SKATING (WOMEN'S)

1908 Syers, Great Britain
1920 Julin, Sweden
1924 Heima Szabo-Planck,
         Austria
1928 Sonja Henie, Norway
1932 Sonja Henie, Norway
1936 Sonja Henie, Norway
1948 Barbara Ann Scott, Canada
1952 Jeanette Altwegg,
         Great Britain
1956 Tenley E. Albright,
         United States
1960 Carol Heiss, United States
1964 Sjoukje Dijkstra,
         Netherlands
1968 Peggy Fleming,
         United States
1972 Beatrix Schuba, Austria
1976 Dorothy Hamill,
         United States

FIGURE SKATING (PAIRS)

1908 Anna Hubler and Heinrich
         Burger, Germany
1920 Ludovika and Walter
         Jacobsson, Finland

1924 Helene Engelmann and
         Alfred Berger, Austria
1928 Andree Joly and
         Pierre Brunet, France
1932 Andree and Pierre Brunet,
         France
1936 Maxie Herber and
         Ernst Baier, Germany
1948 Micheline Lannoy and
         Pierre Baugniet, Belgium
1952 Ria and Paul Falk, Germany
1956 Elizabeth Schwarz and
         Kurt Oppelt, Austria
1960 Barbara Wagner and
         Robert Paul, Canada
1964 Ludmilla Beloussova and
         Oleg Protopopov, USSR
1968 Ludmilla Beloussova and
         Oleg Protopopov, USSR
1972 Irina Rodnina and
         Aleksei Vlanov, USSR
1976 Irina Rodnina and
         Alexander Zaitsev, USSR

BOBSLED

4-MAN BOB
1924 Switzerland
1928 United States
1932 United States
1936 Switzerland
1948 United States
1952 Germany
1956 Switzerland
1960 Not held
1964 Canada
1968 Italy
1972 Switzerland
1976 East Germany

2-MAN BOB
1932 United States
1936 United States
1948 Switzerland
1952 Germany
1956 Italy
1960 Not held
1964 Great Britain
1968 Italy
1972 West Germany
1976 East Germany

LUGE (SMALL SLED)

MEN'S SINGLES
1964 Thomas Koehler, Germany
1968 Manfred Schmid, Austria
1972 Wolfgang Scheidel,
    East Germany
1976 Detlev Guerther,
    East Germany

MEN'S DOUBLES
1964 Pfiestmantl and Stengl,
    Austria
1968 Bonsack and Koehler,
    East Germany
1972 Hildgartner and Plaikner,
    Italy
1976 Hornlein and Bredow,
    East Germany

WOMEN'S SINGLES
1964 Ortrun Enderlein, Germany
1968 Erica Lechner, Italy
1972 Anne Marie Muller,
    East Germany
1976 Margitt Schumann
    East Germany

OTHER AMERICAN AND
SELECTED WINTER WINNERS

MEN'S NORDIC SKIING
1928 J. Grottumsbraaten, Norway
    combined race-jump
1932 J. Grottumsbraaten, Norway
    combined race-jump
1952 Hallgeir Brenden, Norway
    15 km. cross-country
1956 Hallgeir Brenden, Norway
    15 km. cross-country
    Sexten Jernberg, Sweden
    50 km. cross-country
    Veikko Hakulinen, Finland
    30 km. cross-country
1960 Veikko Hakulinen, Finland
    50 km. cross-country

    Sexten Jernberg, Sweden
    30 km. cross-country
1964 Sexten Jernberg, Sweden
    50 km. cross-country
    Eero Meantyranta, Finland
    15 km. cross-country
    Eero Meantyranta, Finland
    30 km. cross-country
1968 Magnar Solberg, Norway
    biathlon
1972 Sven-Ake Lundback, Sweden
    15 km. cross-country
    Vyacheslav Vedenin, USSR
    30 km. cross-country
    Paal Tyldum, Norway
    50 km. cross-country
    Ulrich Wehling,
    East Germany
    combined race-jump
    Magnar Solberg,
    Norway   biathlon
    USSR   team relay
1976 Nikolai Bayukov, USSR
    15 km. cross-country
    Sergei Saveilev, USSR
    30 km. cross-country
    Iver Formo, Norway
    50 km. cross-country
    Ulrich Wehling,
    East Germany
    combined race-jump
    Nikolai Kruglov, USSR
    biathlon
    USSR   team relay

WOMEN'S NORDIC SKIING
1964 Claudia Boyarskich, USSR
    5 and 10 km. cross-country
1968 Toini Gustafsson, Sweden
    5 and 10 km. cross-country
1972 Galina Koulacova, USSR
    5 and 10 km. cross-country
1976 Helena Tukkalo, Finland
    5 km. cross-country
    Raisa Smetanina, USSR
    10 km. cross-country

INDEX

Beyer, Udo, 63, 117
biathlon, 274
Bikila, Abebe, 108, 243
Bivens, Elee, 214
Blackaller, Tom, 97
Blagoev, Boris, 200
Blankers-Koen, Fanny, 64, 239
Blazejowski, Carol, 82
Bocca, Geoffrey, 37
Bock, Lothar, 15, 16-17, 20, 21, 22-23
Bogdanova, Julia, 191
Boggs, Phil, 75, 186, 192
Bohling, Ivan, 201
Boldt, Harry, 144
Bollersten, Julie, 93
Bonk, Gerd, 200
Booth, Jill Kinmont, 215
Boozer, Bob, 122
Bora, Salih, 205
Borchelt, Fred, 90-91
Borchelt, Mark, 90-91
Borzov, Valery, 104
Bottom, Joe, 72, 190
Boucher, Gaten, 279
Bowers, Gordy, 97
Bowers, Mark, 97
boxing, 82-84, 125-31
Bozek, Edward, 87
Braa, Oddvar, 272, 273
Bradley, Thomas 11, 12
Bradshaw, JoJo Starbuck, 215
Brady, Rhonda, 67
Brandt, Iona, 282
Brassy, Laurel, 93
Braun, Gregor, 139
Brehmer, Christine, 119
Brezhnev, Leonid, ix
Brigham, Craig, 63-64
Briley, Melissa, 193
Britt, Clay, 71, 190
Brokaw, Irving, 276
Brooks, Herb, 266
Brown, Carol, 90
Brown, Doug, 52
Browning, David, 186
Brownlow, David George Cecil, 234
Brundage, Avery, 3, 6, 7-8, 290-91
Bruner, Mike, 190
Brunetti, Luciano, 179
Bryant, Rosalyn, 66, 119
Buchan, Carl, 96, 97

Buchan, Willie, 97
Buerkle, Dick, 50
Bugar, Imrich, 118
Bumphus, John, 83
Burghley, Lord. *See* Brownlow,
    David George Cecil
Burke, Sylvia, 279
Burke, Tom, 183
Burleson, Tom, 123
Burley, Michael, 90
Burzev, Mikail, 148
Bushnell, B. W., 275
Buttner, Harold, 205
Button, Dick, 14, 276, 287
Butts, James, 60, 117
Bykov, Anatoly, 206

Caesar, Julius, 184
Cagnotto, Giorgio, 192
Cahoy, Phil, 78
Caldwell, Tim, 260
Calhoun, Bob, 59
Calhoun, Brenda, 67
Cameron, Mark, 94-95
Cameron, Steve, 95
canoeing, 84, 131-35
Carlisle, Dan, 91
Carlisle, Kim, 74, 192
Carlos, John, 245
Carlton, Guy, 95
Carnes, Jimmy, 44-47, 49-69
    passim
Carr, Henry, 244
Carrega, Michel, 179
Carroll, Frank, 263
Cartier, Jacques, 132
Casanas, Alejandro, 56, 116
Catherwood, Ethel, 110
Caulkins, Tracy, 43, 70, 72, 73-75,
    184, 191, 192
Chamberlain, Wilt, 215
Chandler, Jennifer, 76, 186, 193
Chapa, Rudy, 53
Charles, Fran, 97
Cheeseborough, Chandra, 65, 66
Cheeseman, Gwen, 88
Cheevers, Gerry, 265
Chillemi, Toni Marie, 215
Chochoshvili, Shota, 161
Christian, Dave, 266
Christoff, Steve, 266
Christov, Valentin, 200

Melges, Buddy, 97
Mennea, Pietro, 115
Meredith, Don, 215
Merrick, Sam, 96
Merrill, Jan, 66, 119
Meyer, Debbie, 184
Meyers, Ann, 82
Meyers, Dave, 82
Mezzani, Giovanni, 179
Michinaga, 101
Mikhilov, Alexander, 130
Mikita, Stan, 215
Mill, Andy, 259
Miller, Anita, 88
Miller, Karinne, 74
Miller, Len, 52
Mills, Billy, 244
Milo of Croton, 220
Milser, Rolf, 200
Minakov, Andrey, 278
Minch, Peter, 280
Minder, Mauritz, 178
Mitkov, Yordan, 200
Mittermaier, Rosie, 272
modern pentathlon, 89-90, 164-68
Moerken, Gerald, 71, 190
Moiseeva, Irina, 278
Monahan, Katie, 86, 87
Montgomery, Jim, 70, 189
Morehead, Brenda, 65, 66
Morett, Charlen, 88
Morgan, Terry, 267
Morgan, William, 193
Moriarty, Jim, 267
Morris, Michael. *See* Killanin, Lord
Morrison, Angus, 84
Morrow, Bobby, 241
Morrow, Ken, 267
Morton, Tommy, 89
Moses, Edwin, 43, 55-56, 109, 117
Moseyev, Leonid, 116
Mossey, Jim, 267
Mount, George, 85
Mueller, Peter, 265, 272, 279
Mukhina, Elena, 78, 158
Muller, Joe, 266
Mullins, Billy, 49, 115
Munkelt, Thomas, 116
Murdoch, Margaret, 91, 175-76, 178
Murphy, Dennis, 87
Mushoki, Stephen, 130
Mushta, Nadezhda, 119
Mustafin, Farhad, 206

Myricks, Larry, 59
Myrmal, Marit, 273

Naber, John, 190, 248
Nadig, Marie-Therese, 290
Naismith, James, 120-21
Nakasone, Keith, 89
Nalbandyan, Suren, 206
Neff, Stewart, 97
Nehemiah, Renaldo, 55, 56-57, 116
Nehmer, 282
Neipert, Une, 205
Nelson, Cindy, 259, 272
Nelson, Lyle, 261-62
Nemeth, Imre, 84
Nemeth, Miklos, 63, 84, 118
Nero, 221
Nevid, Nick, 71, 190
Nevzorov, Vladimir, 162
Nielson, Don, 261-62
Nieman, Bob, 89, 90
Nikanorova, 120
Ninomiya, Kazuhiro, 163
Nitz, Leonard, 86
Nonna, John, 87
Notary, Keith, 97
Nourikian, Norair, 199
Novikov, Ignati, 15, 17, 19, 20, 21, 24
Novikov, Sergei, 163
Nowicki, 136
Nurmi, Paavo, 231-32, 233
Nyambui, 51
Nygrynova, Jarmila, 119
Nyquist, Dwight, 80

O'Brien, Kurt, 76
O'Callahan, Jack, 266
Oerter, Al, 61-62, 246
O'Koren, Mike, 81
Olah, Belah, 199
Oliveira, Joao, 117
Olson, Billy, 59
Olson, Gail, 60
Onischenko, Boris, 166
Oravetz, Steve, 59
Ortis, Venanzio, 116
Oshoff, Otto, 197
Osterreich, Rolf, 278
Ovett, Steve, 115
Owens, Jesse, 237-38
Owen-Spencer, Alison, 260, 261

Pace, Darrell, 79, 100, 101
Paddock, Charley, 232
Paige, Don, 49, 50-51
Pakhomova, Judmilla, 278
Palevich, Mark, 266
Paley, William, 15, 17, 20
Palles, Lee, 64
Palusalu, Kristjan, 201
Panacek, Josef, 179
Parker, Adrian, 167
Parsons, Dick, 269
Patterson, Floyd, 126, 241
Patterson, Pete, 259
Patton, George S., Jr., 231
Paul, Bob, 255
Paul, Melvin, 83
Paumier, Tami, 74
Pausin, Erik, 287
Pausin, Ilse, 287
Paxson, Beth, 261
Pelé, 215
Penfield, David, 97
Pennington, Joan, 74, 192
Permunovic, Miodrag, 130
Pesthy, Paul, 87
Peterson, Ben, 95, 201-02, 205
Peterson, Doug, 260
Peterson, John, 95, 96, 201-02, 205
Petkov, Gheorghiu, 206
Petkovic, Momir, 206
Petruseva, Natalie, 279
Pheidippides, 223-24
Pietri, Dorando, 228-29
Pietrizykowski, 126
Pignatelli, Giovanni, 140
Pilgrim, Paul, 227-28
Pinigin, Pavel, 205
Pinkston, Clarence, 186
Pinot, Elie, 179
Pipenhagen, Gus, 86
Piskulin, Anatoly, 117
Pisoni, Athos, 179
Placak, Bob, 72
Place, Terry, 93
Plumb, Mike, 86-87, 141
Pochenchuk, Pyotr, 116
Poetzsch, Anett, 262, 278
Polit, Kornelia, 192
Pollack, Andrea, 72, 192
Popangelov, Peter, 272
Porter, John, 97
Potteck, Uwe, 178
Potter, Cynthia, 193

Potvin, Denis, 265
Poulos-Mueller, Leah, 264, 265, 279
Powell, Doug, 259
Poynton-Hill, Dorothy, 238
Prefontaine, Steve, 53
Preuss, Heidi, 260
Pringle, Mark, 86
Prinstein, Myer, 60
Pritchard, David, 97
Proell, Annemarie, 290, 291
Promyslov, Vladimir, ix, 2, 11-12
Providokhina, Tatyana, 119
Pullard, Bob, 59
Puscasu, Vasile, 205
Pusch, Alexander, 148
Pushkin, Alexander, 26
Pyciak-Peclak, Janusz, 165, 168
Pyfer, Leslie, 78
Pyke, Neal, 55
Pyttel, Roger, 190

Quarrie, Don, 115

Rabsztyn, Grazyna, 119
Rachkov, 130
Radaelli, Giuseppe, 145
Raker, Lee, 81
Ramsy, Mike, 266
Randolph, Leo, 128, 130
Rankin, Jill, 82
Ranniko, 179
Read, Ken, 272
Reczi, Laszlo, 206
Reigh, Carrie, 263
Reilly, Phillip, 88
Rethmeir, Helmut, 143
Reynolds, Mark, 97
Rezantsev, Valery, 206
Rheingans, Brad, 95
Riboud, Philippe, 148
Richter, Annegret, 118
Richter, Ulrike, 192
Rickey, Branch, 65
Riddick, Steve, 46, 47, 49
Riehm, Karl-Hans, 113, 118
Rigby, Cathy, 78, 215
Rigert, David, 200
Rinn, 282
Ripley, Dan, 58
Riskiev, 127
Ritola, Ville, 233
Roberti, Fiermo, 179
Roberts, Dave, 58

Shorter, Frank, 55
Shriver, Eunice Kennedy, 211, 212, 213, 218
Shumakov, Alex, 205
Sidorova, V., 148
Siebert, Klaus, 274
Siebold, 175
Siegl, Sigrun, 120
Silliman, Mike, 123
Silva, Carlos, 179
Simeoni, Sara, 110, 119
Simon, Mircea, 128
Sittler, Daryl, 265
Sitzberger, Ken, 186
Sizemore, Jeff, 91
Sjobrend, Amund, 279
Skanaker, Ragnar, 178
skating, 274-79
Skeldon, John, 267
skiing, 267-73
Skiod, Lars-Erik, 206
Skoblikova, Lidija, 289
sledding, 279-82
Slupianek, Ilona, 120
Slusarski, Tad, 117
Smetanina, Raisa, 273
Smieszek, Karl, 178
Smith, Adrian, 122
Smith, Dean, 81, 122, 124
Smith, Graham, 190
Smith, Harold, 48
Smith, Karin, 68
Smith, Mary, 67
Smith, Stacey, 264
Smith, Tommie, 245
Smith, Willie, 49, 115
Smythe, Randy, 97
Snell, Peter, 51, 243-44
Snoddy, William, 49
soccer, 92, 179-83
Soldatyenko, Venyamin, 116
Sollmann, Melitta, 282
Sonoda, Isamu, 163
Soria the Cuban, 127
Spees, Patty, 74
Spencer, Pam, 67
Spigarell, Sante, 101
Spinks, Leon, 126, 127, 131, 248
Spinks, Michael, 126, 127, 131, 248
Spitz, Mark, 69, 246-47
Srednicki, Henry, 130
Stadel, Ken, 62

Stahlberg, Reiji, 118
Stardomskaya, Svetlana, 18
Staver, Julie, 88
Steeples, Lemuel, 130
Stekic, Nenad, 117
Stenerud, Jan, 215
Stenmark, Ingemar, 258, 272
Stenshjemmet, Kay, 279
Stenson, Stan, 279
Stepanskaya, Galina, 279
Sterkel, Jill, 73, 74, 191, 192
Stetina, Dale, 86
Stetina, Wayne, 85
Steuk, Roland, 118
Stevenson, Teofilo, 83, 128, 131
Stille, Antie, 192
Stock, Tom, 95
Stone, Greg, 90
Stones, Dwight, 60, 68
Storholt, Jan, 279
Storrs, Nancy, 90
Stoudemire, Jeff, 131
Strachan, Rod, 190
Streckelberger, Christine, 144
Strobel, Eric, 266
Sulinski, Cathy, 68
Summers, John, 264
Sunderland, Paul, 92
Sverre, King, 268
swimming and diving, 69-76, 183-93
Syedekh, Yurity, 118
Szewinska, Irena, 118

Takalo, Helena, 273
Takata, Yuji, 204
Talavera, Tracie, 79
Tauber, Ulrike, 192
Taylor, Arthur, 16, 17
Taylor, Bernard, 130
Taylor, Chris, 201
Taylor, Steve, 97
Tediashvily, Levan, 205
Thomas, Kurt, 43, 76-77, 157, 215
Thomas, Randy, 55
Thompson, Daley, 63, 64, 118
Thorpe, Jim, 230-31
Thumer, Petra, 191
Thynel, Stephen, 178
Tichinov, Alexsander, 274
Tickner, Charlie, 263, 278
Tkac, Anton, 139

Tkachenko, Nad., 120
Todoroy, Valentin, 199
Tolan, Eddie, 237
Tomita, Yoichi, 158
Toomey, Bill, 114, 212
Toro, Andy, 84
track and field, 43-69, 101-20
Trevelyan, Ed, 97
Tripsa, Ian, 178
Trofimyenko, Vlad, 117
Trottier, Brian, 265
Tsukahara, Mitsuo, 157
Tubbs, Tony, 83
Tully, Mike, 58-59, 117
Tuokko, Markku, 118
Tuokonen, Ismo, 116
Turbyne, Ann, 68
Turnbow, Donna, 78
Turner, Ann, 84
Turner, Brent, 84
Turner, Howard, 84
Tuttle, Susan, 90
Tyler, Jim, 267
Tyler, Joe, 267

Uemura, Haruki, 163
Ukkola, Pertti, 206
Ullman, David, 97
Ulrich, Frank, 274

Vaino, Martti, 116
Valentine, Darnell, 81
Van Briggam, Millie, 87
Van Haute, Danny, 86
Van Pedro, Rita Stalman, 68
Vardanyan, Yuri, 200
Vassallo, Jesse, 71, 72, 190
Vaytsehovskaia, Elena, 193
Vincent, Paul, 267
Viren, Lasse, 107, 116
Virgil, 168
Virgin, Craig, 53, 55
Visser, Ria, 279
Vitelli, Camillo, 174
Vogel, Matt, 190
Voigt, Angela, 119
volleyball, 92-93, 193-95
Vollmar, Harald, 178
von Sauerbronn, Baron Drais, 135
Voronin, Alexander, 199

Walker, James, 117

Walker, John, 44, 45, 51, 106, 115
Walker, Patsy, 69
Waples, Debbie, 88
Warkenton, John, 64
Warner, Anne, 90
Warner, Glenn, 230
Wassburg, Thomas, 272
Watanabe, Emi, 278
water polo, 93-94, 195-97
Watson, Bryan, 215
Watson, John, 143
Watson, Martha, 67
Weaver, Andy, 86
Webster, Bob, 186
Weekly, Linda, 67
Wehling, Ulrich, 273
Weigand, Andy, 84
weightlifting, 94-95, 197-200
Weinstein, Barb, 193
Weiss, Anita, 119
Weissmuller, Johnny, 233-34, 285
Weld, Theresa, 276
Wells, Jeff, 55, 116
Wells, Wayne, 201
Wenzel, Andreas, 272
Wenzel, Hanni, 272
Wenzel, Peter, 200
Wessing, Michael, 118
Wessinghage, Thomas, 116
West, Benjamin, 275
West, Jerry, 122
Westbrook, Peter, 87
Whitaker, Tom, 91
White, Albert, 186
White, JoJo, 123
White, Leo, 89
White, Nancy, 88
White, Reg, 208
White, Terry, 84
Whitney, Stephen, 280
Whitney, Wade, 267
Whittican, Fred, 267
Whyte, Skip, 97
Wickham, Tracey, 73, 191
Wieser, Roland, 116
Wigger, Lones, 91, 178
Wilbur, Doreen, 100
Wilkie, David, 190
Wilkins, Mac, 62, 112, 118
Wilkinson, Celeste, 68
Williams, Archie, 238
Williams, Carl, 59

Williams, John, 100, 101
Williams, Percy, 234
Williams, Randy, 59
Williams, Steve, 43, 46, 49, 115
Williams, Ted, 77
Wiltgang, Gerd, 144
Winbigler, Lynne, 68
Wirnsberger, Peter, 272
Wood, Al, 81
Wood, Christopher, 90
Wood, Steve, 86
Woodard, Lynette, 82
Woodhead, Cynthia, 70, 72-73, 184, 191
Woodruff, John, 238
Woods, Mike, 265, 279
Woodson, Mike, 81
Woodstra, Sue, 93
wrestling, 95-96, 200-06
Wrightson, Bernard, 186
Writer, John, 175
Wszola, Jacek, 117

Wussler, Robert, 14, 15, 16, 17, 19, 20, 21

yachting, 96-97, 207-10
Yagla, Chuck, 96
Yang, C.K., 114, 243
Yang, Jung-Mo, 204
Yarygin, Ivan, 205
Yaschenko, Vladimir, 43, 60, 117
Yorty, Sam, 1
Young, Candy, 66
Young, Darius, 92
Young, Roger, 86
Young, Sheila, 279, 292
Yumin, Vladimir, 204

Zaichik, Boris, 118
Zaitsev, Alexsander, 264, 278
Zaitsev, Yurily, 200
Zakharova, Steila, 158
Zatopek, Emil, 240
Zeisner, Christoph, 179
Zirzow, Carola, 135